TRUE CANADIAN HEROES IN THE AIR

TRUE CANADIAN HEROES IN THE AIR

ARTHUR BISHOP

Foreword by Lieutenant-General F.R. Sutherland
Former Vice Chief of the Defence Staff

PROSPERO
B·O·O·K·S

Library and Archives Canada Cataloguing in Publication

Bishop, William Arthur, 1923–
   True Canadian heroes in the air / Arthur Bishop.

Includes index.
Originally published as courage in the air, v. 1 of the author's Canada's military heritage.
ISBN 1-55267-867-9

   1. Canada. Royal Canadian Air Force—Biography. 2. Air pilots,
Military—Canada—Biography. 3. Canada—History, Military—20th century. I. Bishop,
William Arthur, 1923– . Canada's military heritage. II. Title.

UG626.B57 2004   358.4'0092'271   C2004-904633-0

This collection produced for Prospero Books.

Key Porter Books Limited
Six Adelaide Street East, Tenth Floor
Toronto, Ontario
Canada M5C 1H6

www.keyporter.com

Printed and bound in Canada

08 09 10 5 4 3 2

"Courage is rightly esteemed the first of human qualities because it is the quality which guarantees all others."

Winston Churchill

CONTENTS

FOREWORD

Canadians can take deserved pride in their reputation as the great peacekeepers of the twentieth century, and Canada's commitment to that noble pursuit remains second to none. But no nation which considers itself a keeper of the peace can command respect from other members of the world community without a demonstrable and commensurate will to bear arms to make or regain the peace if no other alternative exists. Several times in this century, as a last resort, Canada has reluctantly but resolvedly gone to war in the name of freedom and humanity. In each instance, most recently in the Persian Gulf, Canadians have served with distinction and have contributed significantly to the successful resolution of aggression.

This book is a compilation of the exploits and biographies of a number of our country's aviation heroes. Arthur Bishop, with meticulous research and a unique insight, has done a masterful job of bringing the stories of these brave airmen together for the first time. It was an immensely difficult task, complicated by the simple fact that Canadians are, by nature, modest — perhaps too modest. His selection of subjects may be controversial, as no doubt some worthy individuals have been omitted, but such are the perils facing biographers.

Nevertheless, this book is representative of the hundreds of thousands of Air Force personnel who have served Canada gallantly in war and in peace. In particular, it is a lasting tribute to the many whose sacrifices can never be repaid and will never be forgotten. Those of us who wear the light blue today are fiercely and justifiably proud of our heritage. The reader is invited to share this pride as our history and our heroes are presented on the following pages.

Fred Sutherland

F.R. Sutherland, CMM, CD
Lieutenant-General
Former Vice Chief of the Defence Staff

ix

ACKNOWLEDGEMENTS

I would like to acknowledge all the people who helped me put this book together. Thank you.

Senator Hartland Molson

For your generous support and assistance without which this project would never have gotten off the ground.

The Air Force Heritage Fund

For your enthusiastic active participation in this venture, helping to make its accomplishment possible.

Lieutenant-General F.R. Sutherland
Vice Chief of the Defence Staff

For your kindness in writing the Foreword to this volume.

Captain Don Pearsons

For your assistance and guidance in numerous ways, including the vetting of the manuscript.

The Canadian War Museum
Hugh Halliday, Dick Malott

For your help and support in countless ways and areas.

General Paul Manson, former Chief of Defence Staff &
Commodore Gary Garnett of the Department of National Defence

For making arrangements and providing introductions.

The Royal Canadian Military Institute

For the use of your library and other facilities.

Anne Melvin, RCMI Librarian

For your helpfulness at all times in providing sources of information and ideas. (The Canadian War Heroes title concept originated with Anne.)

Directorate of History
Dr. W.A.B. Douglas, Director

For making arrangements and introductions.

Dr. Carl Christie

For your untiring efforts and cooperation in providing access to the biographical files as well as your assistance in other ways.

Diane Martineau of The National Archives of Canada

For your efforts, over and beyond the call of duty, in finding pictures unavailable from other sources.

Fellow Air-Warriors
Gib Coons, Bob Hayward, Dave McIntosh, Don Morrison, Rod Smith

For your assistance, guidance, suggestions and help in numerous ways.

My Publisher Don Loney
Who gave birth to the idea of this work in the first place — for your guidance, patience, understanding and eager support.

My Editor Margaret Henderson
For your unstinting help in close editing, correcting and attending to detail.

Stewart Taylor, Historical Expert on WW1 Aviation
For imparting your detailed knowledge of the WW1 fliers, their characteristics and other minutiae, and for checking that part of the manuscript.

Captain John Grodzinski, Historical Researcher
For your help and suggestions with the WW2 section of the manuscript.

Ken Molson, Canadian Aviation Historian
No book on Canadian aviation should be prepared without your advice.

Larry Milberry, Author
Your help and references were of inestimable value.

My Selection Committee
Who shall be nameless at their own request. A difficult chore — no Who's Who can ever be completely definitive for a number of reasons: restrictions on access to personnel files, permission of next of kin, information not available, to name only a few. And no matter how stringent the guidelines, there is always a matter of personal opinion. In addition several people whom we felt qualified asked not to be included for reasons best known to themselves. Selection was therefore no easy task, and there was certain disagreement even among ourselves. But thanks ladies and gentlemen for a job well done. For the final choice of participants I take full and sole responsibility.

My wife Cilla
Who suffered through countless discussions and debates in the execution of this work. Her expert editorial opinion and attention to detail kept this work on an even keel.

AND to countless others who helped in many ways — *Merci Beaucoup!*

During World War I 22,811 Canadians served with the British air service and one Canadian served with the French air service; 1,563 of them gave their lives.

In that conflict the top four Canadian air aces accounted for a total of 230 enemy planes shot down, more than any similar group among the Allied nations. By the end of that war, one third of those in uniform with the Royal Air Force (an amalgamation of the Royal Flying Corps and the Royal Naval Air Service) were Canadians.

ALEXANDER William Melville

"The Black Prince"

O ne of the original members of the famous "Black Flight," Mel Alexander shot down twelve planes and an observation balloon before reaching his twentieth birthday. Born and raised in Toronto, Ont., he enlisted in the RNAS in 1915 after taking his aviation training — at his own expense at the rate of a dollar an hour — at the Stinson Flying School in San Antonio, Tex., before qualifying as a pilot.

Shipped overseas in 1916, Alexander was posted to No 3 Naval Wing in France, the world's first strategical bombing force. In April 1917, when the wing was disbanded, he transferred to No 10 Squadron and was assigned to Raymond Collishaw's flight of Sopwith triplanes, which had their cowlings painted black. By the time his tour ended in May 1918 he had amassed a total of 557 hours, most of them in combat in his "Black Prince," with which he destroyed eight enemy planes (see below). On returning to civilian life, he entered the family lithography business.

DSC Capt Born Nov 8 1897 Died Oct 4 1988
RefScs: DHist bf OMAP(1) 68 P 27–29 30–31 37–39

The idea of painting the planes black, Alexander told me, was to scare the Germans. "I don't know if it worked," he chuckled, "but it seemed like fun."

No. *19*

Dated *Nov 7ᵗʰ* 19 *'7*

THIS IS TO CERTIFY that Mr. *William Melville Alexander*

has served as *Flight Commander (Act)* on board H.M.S. *Nᵒ 10 Naval Squadron*

under my command, from the *29ᵗʰ* day of *Sept.* 19 *17*

to the *14ᵗʰ* day of *Oct.* 19 *17*, during which period

he has conducted himself *
With sobriety & to my entire satisfaction. An exceptionally good flight leader a most capable & reliable officer

J.H. Redpath
Flt Colo   { Captain
              { H.M.S. *10 Naval Squadron*

* Here the Captain is to insert in his own handwriting the conduct of the Officer.

London : Printed for H.M. Stationery Office, by CLEMENTS, NEWLING & Co., Ltd.

RE 19264-1

RE 19243

APPLEBY Percival Ewart

"Star Marksman Observer"

As a rifleman with the British Army before transferring to the RFC as an observer Percy Appleby had already established himself as an expert shot. This talent was to serve him well on the twenty-five daylight bombing raids he made into Germany.

Born in Port-la-Tour, N.S., Appleby joined the CEF in 1914 and served in both France and the Near East. In 1918 he transferred to the RFC, trained as an observer and was posted to 104 Squadron, which became part of the Independent Force RAF, the British strategic bomber command. On July 1 he destroyed an enemy plane, the first of six with which he was credited by war's end and for which he was awarded the DFC.

During WW2 he served as a recruiting officer with the RCAF. He died in Middleton, N.S., in 1968 at the age of 73.

DFC Lt Born June 27 1894 Died May 20 1968
RefScs: ST(1) 6 TBYW app

ARNOLD Harwood James

"First Canadian Decorated for Service in the Air"

James Arnold became one of the earliest Canadians to enlist in the RNAS. Born in Vancouver, B.C., he trained in England in 1915 as a wireless operator. Upon graduation he was sent to South East Africa as part of a flight of biplanes based at Mafia Island. The squadron's mission was to direct shellfire for the British warships against a threat of the German cruiser *Konigsberg* lurking in the Rufiji Delta.

Shortly after noon on July 11, 1915, as the observer of a Henri Farman, Arnold directed the Royal Navy's fire even though the aircraft had been so badly damaged by shrapnel from the *Konigsberg* that the engine packed up. As the pilot glided the plane down onto the river Arnold was able to continue transmissions that were so accurate that Allied shellfire soon sank the German vessel. But when Arnold's aircraft landed it rolled over and trapped the pilot inside. Arnold, who had been thrown clear, swam back and rescued him from the wreckage. For this action he was awarded the DSO. Later, in 1918, he was one of the organizers of the shortlived RCNAS. On March 20 that year he accidentally drowned.

DSO F/S/L Born Jan 31 1890 KA Mar 20 1918
RefScs: CA 77 CA&FWW 139 CCMA 3 DHist bf

ATKEY Alfred Clayburn

"Two-Seater Pilot Downed Two in One Battle"

Alfred Atkey was credited with being the only Canadian two-seater pilot to have shot down a pair of German planes in a single combat. Born in Nunebar, Sask., Atkey joined the RFC, trained as a pilot and served with 18 and 22 Squadrons, flying both Bristol and DH 4 two-seater fighters. On February 4, 1918, he and his observer were returning from a photographing and bombing mission when ten German fighters attacked them. In the ensuing battle Atkey managed to destroy two of the enemy machines, forcing the remainder of their assailants to break off the engagement. Despite heavy damage to the DH 4 Atkey managed to fly back to base and land safely. By war's end he had been given credit for seventeen aircraft destroyed and, jointly with his observer, for shooting down another two.

MC & Bar Capt
RefScs: OMAP(1) 68   TBYW 274 290

BARKER William George

"Victor Over Sixty-to-One Odds"

Billy Barker, who ran up a score of fifty-three victories on the Italian and Western fronts, fought the most spectacular aerial dogfight of all time, an action that earned him the VC. In his last combat he single-handedly took on an entire German *Jagdgeschwader* and, though seriously wounded, destroyed six of the enemy.

Born in Dauphin, Man., a cavalryman-cum-foot-soldier, Barker transferred to the RFC shortly after his arrival in France in 1915, first as an observer and then as a scout (fighter) pilot. By September 1918, as one of the most experienced and successful combat Allied squadron commanders, he received orders to leave France to supervise an air-fighting school.

Taking off for England on the morning of October 27, Barker climbed his Sopwith Snipe (OdCWM) to 15,000 feet over the German lines for "one last look at the war," and promptly added to his score by destroying a Rumpler two-seater. But in the process a Fokker triplane snuck up behind him and shattered his right leg with an explosive shell. Fainting from pain Barker temporarily lost control and spun down, pursued by the enemy pilot. After plunging 2,000 feet he regained consciousness and turned to meet his attacker, whom he demolished with a short, close burst of fire. Then, as he headed for his own lines, twenty Fokkers pounced on the Snipe from above. Fighting nausea, Barker wheeled into the attack, his only good leg guiding the rudder bar. Incredibly, he shot three Fokkers down in quick succession. But in the exchange a bullet struck his left

AH-517

leg and Barker passed out again; and again his Snipe barrelled down rudderless. Revived by a rush of air, however, he levelled out to find himself in the middle of a gaggle of sixty more enemy fighters. Pulling into a tight turn Barker fired at everything that crossed his sights and another triplane fell to his guns. Then a bullet struck him in the left elbow and his arm went limp. He passed out again and lost another 5,000 feet before coming to. Bullets whizzed all around him. Feeling he had nothing to lose, Barker decided to take one enemy plane with him. Barker aimed his machine at the nearest Fokker and tried to ram it as he fired when, to his surprise, it disintegrated and allowed him to fly right through the debris.

Meanwhile incendiaries ripped into the Snipe's gas tank, which miraculously failed to catch fire. Semi-conscious, Barker piled up his stricken machine just inside the British lines where Scottish troops pulled him from the wreckage.

After the war, in partnership with Billy Bishop VC, Barker organized a flying boat service from Toronto, Ont. Later he re-enlisted in the air force and became the RCAF's first Director. In March 1930 he was killed in a flying accident at Ottawa, Ont.

VC DSO & Bar MC & 2 Bars CdeG(Fr) MV(It) Col W/C(RCAF)
Born Nov 3 1894 KFA March 12 1930
RefScs: CFA 105–81 CFP 11–48 DHist bf

Besides his other duties Barker also dropped spies by parachute behind the lines at night. To overcome any agent's last-minute reluctance to jump, Barker had a trap-door built into the floor of the observer's cockpit that sprang open when he pulled a lever. So, like it or not, the espionage agent dropped from the plane.

OdCWM: Remnants of Barker's Snipe is on display at the Canadian War Museum, Ottawa, Ont.

BARRON John Augustus

"First Canadian Naval Airship Pilot Acted as Air Advisor"

At age 14 John Barron became the first youngster appointed as a cadet in the Canadian Marine Service. A native of Stratford, Ont., at war's outbreak the RN accepted him as a midshipman. By March 1915, with the rank of sub-lieutenant, he took his airship pilot training at Kingsnorth RNAS station. On graduation in mid-May, Barron was assigned to anti-submarine patrols from Barrow-in-Furness on the Lancashire coast. On September 19, 1916, in an action for which he was mentioned in dispatches, he forced a German submarine, which had been attacking French shipping, to submerge.

In 1917 Barron, then a flight lieutenant, was posted to No 6 Wing RNAS in the Mediterranean to fly anti-submarine patrols from Taranto and Malta; he was twice decorated by the Italian government for these patrols.

In February 1918 he was posted to the U.S. to assist the navy in establishing anti-submarine patrols off the east coast; in June he arrived in Ottawa, Ont., to help plan and develop the RCNAS.

At war's end, as a captain in the RAF, Barron became a member of the Inter-Allied Aeronautical Control Mission in Berlin and from 1920 to 1922 served on the Canadian Air Board. After retiring from the service in 1925 he enlisted in the RCAF during WW2, serving as chief ground instructor at a flying training school.

MID COSMSL(It) Capt Born Mar 28 1894 Died 1956
RefScs: CA&FWW 526 DHist bf TBYW app

BELL-IRVING Alan Duncan

"First Canadian Ace Shot Down Four Times, Invented Gosport Intercom System"

D uncan Bell-Irving, who distinguished himself as a WW1 fighter pilot by becoming the first Canadian Ace, invented the nonelectrical aircraft intercom system that became standard equipment in training planes in WW2.

Born in Vancouver, B.C., Bell-Irving transferred from the CEF to the RFC in 1915; he served with 7 Squadron as an observer until he was wounded on December 14. After recuperating he trained as a pilot and in April 1916 joined 60 Squadron, flying the inadequate Morane scouts from Vert Galand in France.

On August 28, 1916, his twenty-first birthday, Bell-Irving learned just how unequal the Morane scouts were: an encounter with three German Roland fighters almost ended with them shooting him down. However he managed to score his first victory by destroying one of them near Bapaume.

By September the squadron was re-equipped with Nieuport 17s. On September 22 Bell-Irving attacked a Roland, but the German machine proved too fast even for his new French fighter. Next day, however, by sneaking up behind another Roland to within twenty yards and firing a short burst, he was successful in sending it diving into the ground. At the beginning of October he destroyed an observation balloon, for which he was awarded the MC. On October 15 he accounted for two German planes, his sixth and seventh victories. On the twenty-first, while escorting bombers, Bell-Irving himself was brought down. But he managed to crash-land among the British trenches. On November 9 he was shot down again — for the fourth time — in a melee with a swarm of Halberstadt scouts, one of the Germans' two new types of fighters. This time he was so severely wounded in the legs that he was taken out of combat. Later, in 1918, he became CFI of the Gosport Flying School, where he developed his intercom system.

Between wars Bell-Irving, who went into the insurance business, was active with the RCAF Auxiliary, commanding 100 Wing in Vancouver. He was also a member of the Honorary Air Advisory Committee, which was made up of WW1 air aces, and a founder of the Air Cadet League.

During WW2 he became CO of Jarvis Flying School, then Trenton Air Station, Ont., the hub of the BCATP. During that tenure Bell-Irving established a Canadian altitude record of 34,900 feet in a Hawker Hurricane.

Alan D. Bell-Irving (r.) RE 19428

He retired after the war with the rank of Air Commodore and went into the real estate business in Vancouver, where he died at age 70.

OBE MC & Bar CdeG(Fr) Capt A/C(RCAF) Born Aug 28 1894
Died April 25 1965
RefScs: DHist bf RS&A 100 220 ST 2 TBYW app TCNAF 388–89
200 TR50Y

Bell-Irving had a slight stutter which became more pronounced when he got angry or excited. Once, on returning from a sortie with his Morane badly shot up, he couldn't quite make the field and crashed into a tree. On climbing down he was confronted by an officer, who, he later learned, was a fairly senior official from HQ. The officer asked him if he had had some sort of trouble. "N-n-o you s-s-s-stupid b-b-b-bastard," Bell-Irving replied. "I a-a-a-always l-l-l-land th-th-that w-w-w-way!"

BELL-IRVING Malcolm McBean

"First Canadian Aerial Victory"

The first native-born Canadian to join the RFC, Mickey Bell-Irving of Vancouver, B.C., enlisted in the British air service in England in 1914. In December he joined No 1 Squadron at Netheravon, Eng.; the squadron's role was visual and photographic reconnaissance. Arriving at St Omer in France on March 7, 1915, Bell-Irving made his first operational flight two days later. Then on May 7, over Gheluvet, he engaged in his initial combat: an inconclusive encounter with a German AGO biplane, the first recorded Canadian aerial battle.

On December 19, 1915, while flying a Morane scout between Lille and Ypres, Bell-Irving was attacked by three German aircraft; he shot one down in flames and drove off the others. He then evaded three more attackers and was about to open fire when he was wounded by anti-aircraft shrapnel. His actions, however, earned him the DSO — the first decoration awarded a Canadian in the RFC — and also the service's first victory by a Canadian.

In June 1916 Bell-Irving returned to Canada to serve as liaison officer with the RFC, responsible for all matters affecting Canadians who had been seconded from the CEF to the RFC, a post he held until the end of WW1.

DSO MC MID(2) Maj Born Apr 9 1898 Died 1942
RefScs: CCMA 4 DHist bf OMAP(1) 5 ST(1) 2 TBYW 26–28 app

In the earliest stages of air fighting, when airmen were armed only with rifles and pistols, Bell-Irving is said to have once snuck up beside an adversary and, when his revolver failed to fire, threw it in frustration at the German pilot. It hit the enemy pilot on the side of the head.

BELWAY Frank

"Forced German Pilot to Land Behind Allied Enemy Lines"

Frank Belway held the rare distinction of forcing an enemy pilot to land behind his own lines. What made this feat all the more outstanding is the fact that he accomplished it not as a scout pilot but with a two-seater RE8 observation plane.

Belway, who hailed from Winchester, Ont., went overseas with the CEF then transferred to the RFC. Following his flying training he joined 13 Squadron and spent eleven months at the front registering artillery fire from the air and photographing German positions.

It was in December of 1917 that, after a brief skirmish, he forced down a German scout pilot inside the British lines. Belway was awarded the DFC for an action in September 1918 in which, at low level in the face of intense ground fire and shelling, he obtained reports of German troop locations and dropped them to his own forces.

After the war Belway resigned from the service. But when WW2 broke out he enlisted in the RCAF and held several command posts, including that of CO of Aylmer Gunnery School, Ont. He died in 1947 of a heart attack.

DFC Capt Born Mar 15 1892 Died May 11 1947
RefScs: ST 11 TBYW app

BIRKS Gerald Alfred

"Shot Wings off Enemy Scout to Bring It Down"

On May 8, 1918, not far from his base at Cara Pizza, Italy, Sopwith Camel pilot Gerald Birks became embroiled in a bitter fight with an Austrian-piloted Albatros, which he finally brought down by blasting its wings off. Three days later he enjoyed a similar satisfaction by destroying another enemy fighter in flames.

A native of Montreal, P.Q., Birks served in the Black Watch Regiment from 1914 until 1916, when he transferred to the RFC. He was one of several Canadian airmen sent south to the Austrian Front in 1917 to bolster the Italian Army after its defeat at Caparetto. During his tour the Montrealer also flew bombing missions against enemy airfields and bridges.

By the time the war ended Birks had been credited with twelve enemy aircraft shot down and had been awarded the MC twice.

MC & Bar   Lt   Born 1895   Died May 26 1991
RefScs: OMAP(1) 69   TBYW 81–83 app

BISHOP William Avery

"The Lone Hawk"

On the drizzly morning of June 19, 1918, Billy Bishop climbed into the cockpit of his SE5A fighter at St Omer airfield in France to take off alone on his last and most successful combat. With orders to return to England in his pocket, Bishop crossed the front lines at Ypres and flew over Ploegstreet Wood. To his left he suddenly spotted three German Pfalz scouts. Sweeping in behind them he opened fire. But the enemy fighters turned to meet his attack head-on and, potting Bishop's plane with tracers, they slid by underneath him. Then two more Pfalz dived out of the clouds behind him. Bishop gained height, which placed him in a perfect position to aim at the first three. A quick burst struck the rearmost fighter and sent it into a vertical dive out of control. The other pair then began to climb. But just as they reached the cloud base they slammed into each other, scattering bodies and debris earthward. The remaining two Pfalz scouts also tried to take refuge in the clouds, but one was too slow. From 50 yards Bishop spattered it with machine gun fire. Keeling over, it spun into the ground.

Bishop now headed for home. But just as he neared the lines a two-seater Aviatik suddenly appeared, its observer and pilot apparently unaware of his presence. With a short burst Bishop sent it diving down. Crashing into a hillock the airplane burst into flames.

Five in one sortie — his highest single score — brought Bishop's total number of enemy planes shot down to seventy-two, higher than any other British Empire pilot (see page 17).

Bishop was the supreme aerial duellist of WW1. Gifted with extraordinary eyesight he was a crack shot who constantly practised his markmanship. He was also endowed with a lion's share of luck; time and again he returned to his airfield after a dogfight with his machine riddled by bullets. And in all of his 200 combats, most of which he fought alone, he never so much as suffered a scratch.

Bishop, who was born in Owen Sound, Ont., attended RMC; at war's outbreak he joined the Canadian Cavalry with which he sailed overseas in June 1915. In Britain he transferred to the RFC as an observer and was sent to France with 21 Squadron to fly RE7 reconnaissance two-seaters on mapping, artillery-spotting and photographing sorties. In 1916, after completing that tour, Bishop applied for pilot training and was initially posted to 11 Home Defence Squadron.

Then, on March 17, 1917, he joined 60 Squadron, flying Nieuport scouts in France from Filescamp Farm. Eight days later Bishop scored his first victory when he dived 7,000 feet to bring down an Albatros scout near St Leger. But in the process his engine seized, forcing him to land just inside the British lines. Bishop scored a second kill eight days later when he brought down another Albatros near Arras then destroyed a third on April 7 in the same vicinity. Next day, Easter Sunday in the month that became known as Bloody April because both sides posted the heaviest aerial losses of the war, Bishop became an ace by bringing down two Albatros scouts and a two-seater; he also experienced his closest brush with death in his entire fighting career. In the encounter one of the German scouts got on his tail, grazing his flying helmet with a bullet and putting a hole in his windscreen. (See OdCWM, page 17.) A short time later he was awarded his first decoration, the MC. Then on May 27, a little over a month since he had arrived at Filescamp, he was made a flight commander.

One of Bishop's most memorable combats took place on the last day of April when he and the Red Baron, Manfred von Richthofen, squared off at 15,000 feet over Vitry. Richthofen fired first, a perfect right-angle, full-deflection shot that pierced a fold in Bishop's flying coat and shattered his Nieuport's instrument panel. Bishop pulled straight up, kicked the rudder bar, banked over and lunged down at the Baron's bright red Albatros. From 60 yards he pressed the firing button of his Lewis gun. The German machine rolled over and dived toward the ground spewing smoke. For a moment Bishop thought Richthofen had fallen to his gun. But it was the Baron's old ruse of pretending to be hit then flattening out and, with a defiant waggle of his wings, heading for home.

May 2, 1917, was another banner day for Bishop. During four different patrols he not only shot down two German aircraft but also engaged a total of twenty-three. Later that month he received the DSO.

After a leave in London, Bishop returned to France to execute a solo raid on a German aerodrome. He had originally planned to make the sortie with Albert Ball, who had been the leading British ace. But Ball had been killed during Bishop's absence so he decided to undertake it alone. At dawn on June 2 he took off, flying at low level until he reached Estourmel where four Albatros fighters were trying to take off. Bishop destroyed three of them and scared off the fourth; but in the process Bishop's own machine was riddled by ground-fire. This exploit won him the VC (see page 17).

PL 21077

By this time Bishop learned that the Germans had put a price on his head, so to make his plane easy to spot he had the spinner of his Nieuport painted bright blue (see OdCWM, page 17). In mid-August Bishop, with forty-seven victories to his credit, was taken off operations and a Bar was added to his DSO.

After leave in Canada he served a stint with the British War Mission in Washington, D.C., assisting the American Staff in building their air force. In January 1918 he returned to England and in April took command of a new Squadron, 85 RAF (after the RFC and RNAS had been amalgamated on the first of the month), known as the Flying Foxes. After a period of training at Hounslow, near London, the unit flew to France during the last week of May. They first took up quarters at Petit Synthe. From there Bishop scored his first victory of his new tour on May 28, shooting down a two-seater 14,300 feet over Passchendale. On June 8, by which time his score had risen to fifty-nine (surpassing the new British record set by Jimmy McCudden while Bishop was in Canada), the squadron moved to St Omer. There was no flying until June 15 due to poor weather. But during the next five days Bishop brought his total tally of enemy aircraft destroyed to seventy-two. In twelve days of flying as CO of the Flying Foxes he had shot down twenty-five planes, a record never equalled and one for which Bishop received the DFC.

Bishop went back to England to help form the Canadian Air Force then returned to Canada where he went on a lecture tour.

After retiring from the RAF at the end of 1918 Bishop formed an airline in Toronto with Billy Barker VC. When that failed he sold scrap metal in England and finally went into the oil business in Montreal, P.Q.

When WW2 began he became head of recruiting for the RCAF as an Air Marshal. After that conflict ended he again returned to civilian life, retiring from the oil business in 1950. He died in Palm Beach, Fla., in 1956 at age 62.

VC CB DSO & Bar MC DFC MID CdeG(Fr) Ld'H Lt/Col
A/M(RCAF) Born Feb 8 1894 Died Sept 10 1956 Ind CAHF 1973
Author *Winged Warfare Winged Peace*
RefScs: CFA 13–56 CFP 66–75 109 123–24 DHist bf   TCOFTEM

Some sources state that Mick Mannock shot down seventy-three planes, making him the top British Empire ace. Not so. Official records fail to bear this out. The London Gazette of July 18, 1919, in recognizing Mannock's award of the VC, credits him with fifty "machines definitely accounted for." The whole issue has an interesting if somewhat rough-and-tumble background. It began with a fist fight in the officers mess between my father and Ira "Taffy" Jones, who in 1918 were stationed at Vert Galand with 74 Squadron. To get even Jones listed Mannock as having shot down one more plane than Bishop in his book, *Tiger Squadron*. My father could have cared less, but a lot of academicians, would-be historians and a few fanciful writers made something of it.

Confirmed by Spencer Horn, a member of Bishop's flight who, with two other pilots, flew over the field later in the morning and surveyed the damage.

> OdCWM: Both the windshield as well as the propeller and spinner from his Nieuport, along with my father's uniform and medals, are on display at the Canadian War Museum in Ottawa, Ont.

BREADNER Lloyd Samuel

"Held Highest RCAF Rank"

P opularly known as "Bread," Lloyd Breadner, whose energy and vision helped build Canada into a major military air power, became one of only two RCAF officers ever to attain the rank of Air Chief Marshal.

Born in Carleton Place, Ont., he enlisted in the RNAS, graduated

HQ 1970

from the Wright Flying School and went overseas at the end of 1915. Known in battle as a "fire-eater," he commanded two different naval squadrons as a scout pilot, running up a tally of eight German planes destroyed, for which he received the DSC.

At the end of WW1 Breadner enlisted in the CAF and in 1920 was made a certificate examiner in the Civil Aviation Branch of the Air Board.

When the RCAF came into being in April 1924 Breadner commanded the Camp Borden Training School in Ontario and, that December, officiated at the service's first Wings Parade. From 1928 to 1932 he served as acting director of the RCAF then commanded Trenton Air Station, Ont., until 1934, when he attended the Imperial Defence College in England. On his return he became Air Staff Officer in 1936 and the air representative of the three military services charged with the joint responsibility of preparing a paper on Canada's future military role, a document that set the guidelines for the policies that followed.

In 1939 Breadner was made CAS, a post he held until 1943; in that position he had the overall responsibility for administration of the BCATP, home defense forces, overseas squadrons, transport and ferry commands. In 1943 he became Commander of the RCAF overseas until the beginning of 1944 and, at the end of March of the following year, he retired. Retaining his interest in the service as a civilian, Breadner organized the RCAF Association in 1948 and became its grand president in 1950.

> CB DSC LoM(Am) OPR(Pol) MC(Bel) Ld'H CdeG(Fr) OWL(Cz) KHCOL(Nor) Capt A/C/M(RCAF) Born July 14 1896 Died March 14 1952
> RefScs: CA 123 235 CCMA 112 app DHist bf OMAP(1) 70 RS&A 207 TBYW 120–21 app

On April 23, 1917, Breadner shot down one of the huge Gotha bombers and landed in a field beside it to find the crew already taken prisoner. He liked to tell the story of arriving back at his base wearing a German flying helmet and carrying a piece of fabric bearing the Iron Cross, which he hung over the fireplace in the mess.

BROWN Arthur Roy

"Shot Down the Red Baron"

R oy Brown was officially credited with shooting down Germany's top air ace, Manfred von Richthofen (the Red Baron), on April 15, 1918; he was awarded a Bar to his DSC for the victory.

RE 18431-24

Born in Carleton Place, Ont., he joined the RNAS in November 1915 after graduating from the Wright Flying School in Dayton, Ohio. By May 1917 Brown was in action with 9 Naval Squadron, flying Sopwith Pups along the coasts of Belgium and France from Dunkirk, where it was attached to the RFC. Brown scored his first victory on July 17 when he was attacked by four German Albatros scouts, one of which he sent crashing into the ground. Up to the time of his encounter with the Red Baron, Brown — by then a flight commander — had twelve German aircraft destroyed to his credit.

The incident with Richthofen took place near Hamel with the German ace leading a patrol of fifteen Fokker triplanes and Albatros biplanes and Brown heading up a flight of eight Sopwith Camels. In the ensuing melee, when an all-red triplane got on the tail of one of his pilots, Brown flew to his rescue, guns blazing. Suddenly the German aircraft faltered then came to a bumpy landing behind the British lines. Soldiers who rushed to the scene found Richthofen dead. He had been struck by two bullets. Brown, suffering from stomach ulcers, shortly afterwards fainted while in the air and crashed. He suffered multiple skull fractures and was lucky to survive.

After the war Brown returned to flying and organized a civil company operating out of Noranda, P.Q., and Haileybury, Ont. But by the 1940s ill health forced him to retire. In 1943 he became advisory editor of *Canadian Aviation* magazine. He died in 1943 in Stouffville, Ont., at age 50.

DSC & Bar Capt Born Dec 23 1893 Died 1943
RefScs: AIC 183 CA 85 DHist bf OMAP(1) 7 TBYW 105 app

Australian infantrymen in the area where Richthofen crashed claimed that one of their riflemen shot the Red Baron down, not Brown. In my opinion the odds weight heavily in Brown's favour. Armed with two synchronized machine guns at close range he was in the ideal position to make the kill as opposed to a pot-shot from a rifle at a plane travelling at 140 miles per hour hundreds of feet above. Roy refused to discuss the subject either privately or publicly.

BROWN Frederick Elliott

"Medical Student Became Ace as Observer and Pilot"

Before training as a pilot in 1917, Frederick Brown was already on his way to becoming an ace, having shot down a German Halberstadt scout on February 25 near Lens as an observer on BE2cs with 2 Squadron RFC. He had also been mentioned in dispatches and awarded the French Croix de Guerre.

Born in Quebec City, P.Q., the former medical student went overseas with the CEF then transferred to the BEF, where he served on the Western Front in 1916 for five months before transferring to the flying service. In October 1917, following his pilot's training, Brown joined 84 Squadron based at Izel-le-Hameau flying SE5s. On November 8 he shared in a kill with another pilot. Early in February 1918 he was made a flight commander and on the twenty-sixth of that month scored a hat-trick. By March he had a score of nine aircraft destroyed and had been awarded the MC. On the thirtieth, following a patrol, he crashed while landing in a heavy mist and was thrown from his plane, suffering a slight concussion and a broken arm. Because he was taken off operations Brown ended the war as an instructor.

During WW2 he served with the RCAF and after that war was employed by the Department of Veterans Affairs. He died in 1971.

MC & Bar MID CdeG(Fr) Capt Born Feb 3 1895 Died Sept 15 1971
RefScs: DHist bf TBYW app

BURDEN Henry John

"Destroyed Five Planes in One Day"

On August 10, 1918, Hank Burden destroyed three enemy aircraft in the morning and, that very evening, added to his day's tally by downing two more, a feat for which he was awarded the DSO.

Born and educated in Toronto, Ont., he initially served with the infantry in 1916 in France before transferring to the RFC as a pilot a year later. In February of 1918 he joined the famous 56 Squadron at the Western Front, a unit that boasted two VC winners. In March he won his first victory. By September, with thirteen victories in the air to his credit and three planes destroyed on the ground, Burden was sent home to Canada.

After leaving the service at the end of WW1 Burden became a partner in an architectural firm as well as a university lecturer. In 1938 he was appointed to the Honorary Air Advisory Committee made up of Canadian war aces. At the outbreak of WW2 he joined the RCAF and, for three years, commanded training schools in Canada. In 1942 he took over command of a fighter-reconnaissance station at Dunsfold in southern England until his return to Canada in 1944, where he became CO of the Repatriation Depot at Trenton, Ont.

L. MacLean (l.) and H.J. Burden (r.) RE 64-522

DSO DFC MID Capt G/C(RCAF) Born Apr 28 1893 Died March 28 1960
RefScs: DHist bf OMAP(1) 72

CARTER Albert Desbrisay

"Sopwith Dolphin Ace"

A native of Pointe de Bute, N.B., Albert Carter shot down twenty-eight German planes, seven of which were shared, in a six-month period while flying French-built Spads and Sopwith Dolphins. A law student when he joined the CEF in 1915, Carter transferred to the RFC in May 1917 and, after qualifying as a pilot, joined 19 Squadron in France. At that time the unit was equipped with Spads but in January 1918 it switched to Dolphins, a plane most pilots regarded as dangerous and difficult to fly. In Carter's hands, however, the Dolphin proved to be a highly effective weapon, one with which his score of aircraft destroyed mounted steadily. In February 1918 he was awarded the DSO and, shortly afterwards, a Bar to the same decoration was added. Then on May 19, with twenty-eight victories to his credit, he was shot down behind German lines and taken prisoner. After the Armistice, Carter was repatriated to England where he joined the newly formed CAF. But on May 22, 1919, while practising dog-fighting in a German Fokker over Shoreham, the wings of his aircraft broke off as he pulled out of a dive and Carter plunged to his death.

DSO & Bar MID(3) CdeG(Bel) Maj Born July 5 1892 KFA May 22 1919
RefScs: CFA 273–75 DHist bf OMAP(1) 72 TBYW app
TSBW 10 19

CARTER Alfred Williams

"Navy Ace First to Carry Out Geological Aerial Reconnaissance"

In 1921 "Nick" Carter, who as an RNAS and RAF scout pilot had destroyed fourteen German planes and shared in the destruction of two more to win the DSC, flew out of Sioux Lookout, Ont., to initiate the first recorded geological reconnaissance from the air. A native of Calgary, Alta., Carter transferred from the CEF in 1916 and flew with No 3 Naval Wing as well as with 3 and 10 (later 210 Squadron RAF) Naval Squadrons on Sopwith Pup triplanes.

One of the closest calls he experienced was when he collided with a balloon-cable, shattering the propeller of his aircraft and winding the wire around the shaft. Carter escaped without a scratch as did the occupants of the balloon basket, who were all but ejected by the jolt.

MBE DSC F/L Born Apr 29 1894 Died Dec 17 1986
RefScs: DHist bf OMAP(1) 72 TBYW 66 122 152 app TSBW 42

CAWS Stanley Winther

"First Canadian Airman Killed in Action"

A veteran of the Boer War, Stan Caws emigrated to Edmonton, Alta., from his birthplace on the Isle of Wight. Prior to WW1 Caws became a Mountie. Enlisting in the Canadian Cavalry at the outbreak of hostilities, he went overseas with the First Contingent of the CEF; then in February of 1915 he transferred to the RFC. Graduating as a pilot in May, he joined 10 Squadron at Chocques, France, flying two-seater BE2cs. On September 21, during a reconnaissance flight over Laiman, Caws and his observer were attacked by a gaggle of German fighters. In a fight that lasted fifteen minutes they kept their assailants at bay until they had expended all their ammunition. Then, completely defenseless, Caws was killed instantly by machine-gun fire; his observer, though wounded in the leg, managed to glide the machine down behind enemy lines, where he was taken prisoner.

Lt   Born Mar 22 1879   KIA Sept 21 1915
RefScs: CA&FWW 352–53   DHist bf   TBYW 29 app

CHISHOLM John Foster

"Submarine Bombing Specialist"

Jack Chisholm's specialty was bombing German U-boats and submarine installations — harbours, lock gates and moles — for which he was twice decorated. A native of Westmount, P.Q., Chisholm joined the RNAS in 1915 after training at the Curtiss Flying School in Toronto, Ont. He served with both 2 Naval Squadron and 218 Squadron flying DH 4s and DH 9s. Zebrugge was one of his principal targets. On December 6, 1917, he won the DSC for photographic reconnaissance work over the submarine base. Returning from one raid on the installation he and his observer were attacked by a Fokker fighter, which they managed to shoot down. During the summer of 1918, in his new role as a flight commander, Chisholm led twenty-five raids in thirty days. On August 1, 1918, he dropped four 50-pound bombs squarely on a submarine just outside the Zebrugge mole. In late September his aircraft was hit by anti-aircraft fire; but Chisholm was able to stay airborne until he got to neutral Holland, where he landed and was interned for the rest of the war. In peacetime he went into law practice in Montreal, P.Q.

DSC DFC   Capt   Born Aug 3 1896   Died 1984
RefScs: LTBW 18–19   TBYW 124 152 app

CLARK Joseph William Greig

"Flight Commander Observer"

Joe Clark, who was born and raised in Toronto, Ont., was one of two Canadians who held the post of flight commander as an observer. Although he went overseas with the CEF in 1916 Clark transferred to the RFC later that year. Within three weeks he found himself with 13 Squadron on the Western Front in the front cockpit of a BE2c reconnaissance machine and later in the rear seat of an RE8, undertaking artillery spotting, directing counter-battery fire and photographing enemy positions. On August 2, 1917, he had his closest call of the war when his aircraft was shot down by a German Albatros. Luckily the pilot was able to make a smooth enough landing to avoid injury to himself and his observer, though the impact pitched Clark forward against a shattered wing strut. After a brief respite Clark returned to the squadron on May 18, where he was made a flight commander. For his work in leading close army support flights he was awarded the DFC in October. Between wars Clark became a journalist; then in WW2 he acted as public relations director of Canada's armed forces. He died in Toronto in 1956.

DFC   Capt   Died Nov 29 1956
RefScs: ST(1) 12   TBYW 211–12 app

CLAXTON William Gordon

"Downed Thirty-Seven Planes in Three Months, Six in One Day"

When Bill Claxton reached age 18 he went straight from high school into the RFC, which had been established in Canada by 1917. A westerner, born in Gladstone, Man., he trained at Camp Borden, Ont., as a pilot. After further flight schooling in England, Claxton joined 41 Squadron in France in March 1918, a time when the Allies faced a new all-out German offensive aimed at a quick end to the war. Within a month he had scored his first victory but, badly hit by ground fire, barely made it across the French lines. He had already been awarded the DFC with eight German planes and an observation balloon to his credit when on July 4 he established a record only equalled by two other Allied pilots. On that date Claxton destroyed six enemy planes, four shortly after breakfast and another two that afternoon, adding a Bar to his DFC. By August 12, the fourth day of the British counteroffensive, Claxton had raised his tally to thirty planes and two balloons, earning him the DSO. Five days later, having added four more to his string of victories in company with fellow Canadian Fred McCall, he accounted for three more before being seriously wounded in the head. He was forced to crash his plane behind enemy lines. He was rushed to a hospital where expert surgery by a German doctor saved his life. Following WW1 Claxton became a newspaperman, eventually publishing his own financial periodical in Montreal, P.Q.

DSO DFC & Bar MID   Capt   Born June 1 1899   Died June 30 1967
RefScs: CFA 251–62   DHist bf   OMAP(1) 73   TBYW 90 93–96 app

CLEMENT Carleton Main

"Set Record in Times and Types of Missions Flown"

His comrades maintained that as a two-seater reconnaissance pilot Steve Clement set a record unequalled by any other airman in WW1. In the fourteen months he fought against the Germans on observation, photographic, combat, bombing, strafing and escort missions he tallied 382 hours and 5 minutes operational flying time and was credited with shooting down five enemy planes. Yet, compared to the publicity afforded the top Canadian aces, he was virtually unknown outside of his own realm. Clement was born in Vancouver, B.C., and went overseas with the CEF. Bored with army life, in 1916 he arranged to take out a private pilot's licence and was accepted by the RFC in May. In June he was posted to 22 Squadron in France, flying FE2bs. By August he had become somewhat of a legend, and not only in the air. On their arrival at the squadron he always challenged newcomers to a wrestling match. By the fall of the year he had become recognized by the 14th Wing as one of its most valuable pilots. When the squadron switched to Bristol fighters in 1917, instead of taking leave he stayed with the unit, which in June moved to Izel-le-Hameau, where he and Billy Bishop of 60 Squadron alternated as leaders of the combined Bristol and SE5 scout patrols. Throughout the summer he continued to distinguish himself. But ironically it was not until after his death on August 19, when he and his observer

were shot down in flames, that the awards of the MC and the French
Croix de Guerre were made.

MC CdeG(Fr)   Capt   Born May 15 1896   KIA Aug 19 1917
RefScs: ST(1) 12   TBYW app

COLLISHAW Raymond

"D'Artagnan of the Air"

Few people ever matched the aerial exploits of Ray Collishaw, who
finished WW1 with sixty victories. Born in Nanaimo, B.C., he exhibited
a taste for adventure from an early age. At 15 he joined the Canadian
merchant marine. A few years later he sailed with the ill-fated Scott
Antarctic Expedition to the South Pole. When the war started he enlisted
in the RNAS and received his flight instruction in England in 1916.

In August 1916 Collishaw joined the 3rd Naval Wing. With this squadron
and flying a Sopwith 1½ Strutter fighter he shot down his first enemy
plane on October 12 over Oberndorf. On October 25 he destroyed two
more near Luneville and the French awarded him their Croix de Guerre.
On December 27 Collishaw was shot down; with his aircraft badly riddled
with bullets he managed to land dead-stick. He had an even closer call
a few weeks later when, while delivering a two-seater to his squadron,
Fokkers attacked him; a bullet smashed his goggles and the shards injured
his eyes, filling them with blood. Temporarily blinded he dived away.
But in the process he landed on a German aerodrome. As bullets erupted
around him he gunned his engine and lifted the Pup into the air, clipping
the tops off trees with his propeller.

Early in 1917 Collishaw transferred to No 3 (Naval) Squadron and
then to No 10 (Naval) Squadron where he was made flight commander.
It was there he had his Sopwith triplanes painted a sinister black, creating
the notorious "Black Flight." By June 5 Collishaw had brought his score
to thirteen. On the following day he shot down three Albatroses in a
single fight. On June 15 he surpassed that feat, this time against three
Halbertstadts and a German two-seater, bringing his total to twenty-three.
By the end of July Collishaw's total had risen to thirty-seven and, sporting
the ribbons of the DSO and DSC under his pilot's wings, he returned
to Canada for two months' leave.

In mid-November of 1917 he was back in France to take command
of 13 Naval Squadron; on December 1 Collishaw added to his tally by
shooting down two seaplanes and a two-seater machine. In January he

PMR 71-788

was given another command, that of No 3 Naval Squadron, where he continued to add to his list of victories. On one occasion however his engine was so badly shot up he barely made it across his own lines. By November 1918, Collishaw's total stood at sixty and he was sent to England to help form the CAF.

That was the last of Collishaw's participation in WW1 but his fighting days were far from over.

After he returned to Canada the RAF offered Collishaw command of No 47 Squadron to fight with the White Russian Army against the Bolsheviks. For a year his fighters and bombers operated from southern Russia. But it was a losing battle. In 1921 Collishaw took 84 Squadron to Persia to battle the Bolshevik menace. But that expedition was also withdrawn and the unit next operated from Mesopotamia to keep order among the Arabs. In 1929 Collishaw was placed in charge of the Fleet Air Arm operating off the carrier *Courageous* to suppress recalcitrant Arab forces in Palestine, an operation that came under the heading of "Tribal Control."

With the outbreak of WW2 Collishaw was given command of 202 Group in Egypt, which, in destroying 1,000 aircraft to defeat the Italian Desert Air Force, played a major role in clearing the Libyan province of Cyrenaica of the Italian Army. In 1942 Collishaw was posted to England and given command of 14 Fighter Group in Scotland. He resigned the following year, undramatically closing out one of the most colourful careers in military aviation history

CB OBE DSO & Bar DSC DFC CdeG(Fr)   Maj   A/V/M(RAF)   Born
Nov 22 1893   Died Sept 29 1976   Ind CAHF 1973
RefScs: CFA 59–102   CFP 76–101   DHist bf   TBYW 53–68 119 122 144
147 149 151 248–49 252 app

One of his comrades told me: "Collie was indifferent to his score. He
loved the fight but the fame meant little. He would give away some of
his victories to new pilots. For example if they'd both fired at a plane
at the same time, when they landed he'd say: 'That was yours.'"

CROIL George Mitchell

"First RCAF Chief of the Air Staff"

A veteran of the Middle East campaigns in WW1, where he served
as a bomber pilot with 47 Squadron and as an instructor, George
Croil, who was born in Milwaukee, Wisc., was one of the original members
of the CAF. In 1924 he became one of sixty-two officers who made
up the newly organized RCAF. After a succession of commands, during
which he attended the Imperial Defense College in Britain (the second
Canadian airman to do so), he was made Senior Air Officer in 1936.
In this post he fought for equal status with the army and navy and,
over the stern objection of the Chief of General Staff, won admission
to the Defense Council. In 1938 Croil succeeded in removing the supervision
over the RCAF by the CGS, and from then on reported directly to the
minister of National Defense. On December 15 that year the title of SAO
was replaced with that of CAS, of which Croil became the first. After
WW2 started he was appointed inspector-general, a position he held until
his retirement, after thirty years of service, in July 1944.

CBE AFC MID CdeG(Fr)   Maj   A/M(RCAF)   Born June 5 1893
Died April 8 1959
RefScs: CCMA 45 app   DHist bf   SY 26–27 464   TSBW 29

CURTIS Wilfred Austin

"Father of the Post-War RCAF"

A WW1 fighter ace, Wilf Curtis molded the post-WW2 RCAF into
one of the world's most effective and efficient fighting forces through
his drive, initiative and foresight. Born in Havelock, Ont., he transferred

Photo courtesy RCAF.

from the army to the RNAS in 1916 and in June 1917 joined 6 Naval Squadron in Flanders. In August he was posted to 10 Naval Squadron, flying Sopwith Camels and a month later scored his first victory. By November, with some ten aircraft to his credit, Curtis was awarded the DSC; in January of 1918 he was promoted to flight commander. By the time he went back to England at the end of the month, Curtis was officially credited with thirteen planes shot down and three probably destroyed, and had been given a Bar to his DSC.

Following the war, Curtis operated his own insurance firm. In 1933 he joined the RCAF Auxiliary, becoming CO of 10 Auxiliary Squadron.

At the beginning of WW2 he went on active service taking charge of No 1 Training Command and serving in a variety of capacities, including member of the RCAF Air Council and Canadian member of the joint Canadian–U.S. Air Council. He was also responsible for selecting airfields for the BCATP. In England Curtis was deputy commander of the RCAF overseas. In 1947 he became CAS and guided the RCAF through the difficult stages of post-war reorganization and its participation in the Korean War. At the same time, it was Curtis who convinced the Canadian Cabinet that the RCAF should make a major contribution to NATO. The result was that, with twelve front-line squadrons in Europe, Canada stood as the principal air defense force on the continent throughout the 1950s.

Retiring in 1953, Curtis became vice-chairman of Hawker Siddeley Canada. Retaining his ties with the service, he was grand chairman of the RCAF Association and also became chairman of the Canadian International Air Show Scholarship Fund. In 1961 Curtis was made Chancellor of York University in Toronto, Ont., which largely came into being due to his efforts.

CB CBE DSC & Bar ED CM Lom(Am) Ld'H(Fr) CdeG(Fr) Capt
A/M(RCAF)   Born Aug 21 1893   Died Aug 14 1977
Ind CAHF 1984
RefScs: CA 253 271   CAHF 115   CCMA app   DHist bf   OMAP(1) 74
RS&A 40 221   SY 48   TBYW 27 244 273

DELHAYE Roger Amadee

"Threw Reconnaissance Machine about Like a Fighter"

Though they were strictly designed for artillery spotting and other reconnaissance chores or at the very most to fight defensively, Roger Delhaye threw the BE2 and RE8 two-seater biplanes about with the abandon of a scout pilot. Born in Chalons, France, Delhaye enlisted in the RFC in Canada and served with both 13 and 19 Squadrons, serving the latter as a flight commander. On June 17, 1918, he was leading his flight of Sopwith Dolphins in pursuit of a squad of Pfalz scouts when twelve Fokker triplanes cut them off from the British lines. In a fight that ranged from 14,000 feet down to 3,000 feet, Delhaye shot one of them down. For this and other duties he was awarded the DFC. By war's end, his score had climbed to nine German planes destroyed.

At the outbreak of WW2, Delhaye had command of No 120 Auxiliary

Squadron RCAF at Sea Island, B.C., equipped with Tiger Moths. On November 18, 1944, Delhaye was killed when the Harvard trainer in which he was flying spun in near Boucherville, P.Q.

DFC   A/C   Born Jan 9 1891   KFA Nov 18, 1944
RefScs: OMAP(1) 75   RS&A 55   TBYW app

DODDS Robert

"Bombed Aerodrome at Zero Feet"

Born and raised in Hamilton, Ont., Bob Dodds joined the army in 1914 and went overseas with the CEF. In 1916 he transferred to the RFC and, upon graduating as a pilot, joined 48 Squadron in France. On August 22, 1917, during one of his first combat flights three German scouts attacked him when, suddenly, his guns jammed. Recocking them, he drove one plane down out of control and damaged another. On March 9, 1918, Dodds led a bombing raid on an enemy aerodrome and, under intense fire, dived to ground level and dropped his bombs on a hangar. Though his machine was badly riddled by bullets, Dodds stayed to orbit the field until the rest of his formation had dropped their loads — an exploit that earned him the MC. These feats, however, overshadowed the fact that he participated in over sixty offensive patrols.

Following his discharge from the RAF he helped form the Hamilton Aero Club in Ontario, managed International Airways, was superintendent of Canadian Airways airmail operations in eastern Canada and, later, became Director of Civil Aviation with DOT. Dodds retired in 1958. During WW2 he participated in the development of the BCATP, for which he was awarded the OBE.

OBE MC   Maj   Born March 11 1893   Died October 1980
RefScs: CA&FWW 165   DHist bf   OMAP(1) 7   TBYW 165 app

DUNCAN William James Arthur

"Ace Became Toronto Maple Leafs' First Coach"

Art Duncan of Sault Ste. Marie, Ont., first distinguished himself as a hockey star before he became an air ace. In 1916 he joined the Canadian Army, transferring to the RFC in England as a pilot. In

September 1917 he joined 60 Squadron, which was equipped with SE5s. Duncan quickly proved to be a superb tactician and, within a few months, was made a flight commander. Of his 8½ victories, none gave him more satisfaction than a combat on April 1, 1918, in which he forced a German pilot down behind Allied lines, who was then taken prisoner. In eight months at the front he flew 223 operational hours and finished the war as an instructor.

After the cessation of hostilities, Duncan pursued a professional hockey career, becoming the first coach of the Toronto Maple Leafs in 1930. He died in 1975.

MC & Bar   Capt   Born July 4 1891   Died Apr 13 1975
RefScs: DHist bf   ST(2) 3

EDWARDS Harold

"Pressed for Overseas RCAF Autonomy"

U ncle Gus, as Harold Edwards was affectionately known in WW2 to those who served under him during his tenure as Air Officer Commanding-in-Chief of the RCAF overseas, was born in Charley, Lancashire, on Christmas Eve, 1892. He emigrated from England to Cape Breton, N.S., as a child and, at the outbreak of WW1, he joined the RCN as an Able Seaman then transferred to the RNAS. Graduating as a pilot, he joined 3 Naval Wing at Luxeuil, France, in April 1916, later moving to Ochey. On April 14, 1917, during a raid on Freiburg across the Rhine, he was shot down behind the German lines and taken prisoner. Released at war's end, he was appointed embarkation officer at Warnemunde, Germany, responsible for the evacuation of 2,500 British POWs.

In March 1919, Edwards joined the RAF Instructional Mission to White Russia, where he also served on operations with 47 Squadron and acted as the unit's adjutant.

Returning to Canada in 1920, he joined the CAF. During the 1930s he served in the Maritimes, where he was instrumental in setting up the organization that made possible effective RCAF anti-submarine operations when WW2 started. A foremost authority on ceremonial procedure, Edwards commanded the RCAF contingent at the coronation of George VI in 1937 and was in charge of air force arrangements for the Royal visit to Canada two years later.

When war started Edwards was made air member for personnel, responsible for logistics of the expanding BCATP. Then in November 1941 he took command of the RCAF overseas for the next two years; during that time he championed Canadianization of RCAF squadrons, which resulted in, among other developments, the formation of a wholly Canadian bomber group. In 1944 Edwards retired from the RCAF. He died in Scottsdale, Ariz., in 1952.

CB MID Ld'H CdeGwC(Fr) OSS(Rus) OSA(Rus) OWL(Cz) Capt
A/M(RCAF)   Born Dec 24 1892   Died Feb 23 1952
RefScs: DHist bf   SY 165   TBYW 150–51 252   TSBW 71

EDWARDS Stearne Tighe

"Navy Pilot Alternated Between Bombing and Fighting Roles"

Switching from bomber to fighter piloting, Stearne Edwards ended WW1 unofficially credited with eight victories of his own and a share in five others. Edwards was born in Franktown, Ont., but raised in Carleton Place, Ont., with Roy Brown (see Arthur Roy Brown). He enlisted in the RNAS in 1915 and by the spring of the following year became one of the originals with 3 Naval Wing.

Formed in England with the objective of crippling munitions production in the Saar, this squadron was one of the original strategic bombing forces. In July the crews flew the unit's two-seater Sopwith Strutter fighters and bombers to Nancy in France from where, on October 16, its first operation — a raid on the Mauser rifle factory at Oberndorf 108 miles away — proved to be one of its most dramatic. Two tons of bombs were dropped. Edwards, who took part as a bomber pilot, spent four hours in the air; much of that time he was under attack by German fighters. In early 1917 he continued to carry out raids, sometimes as a bomber pilot other times as a fighter escort.

After nineteen months of operational flying with three different squadrons and with 430 flight hours on active service in France, however, the wear and tear began to tell on Edwards. In May 1918, while serving with 209 Squadron RAF (formerly 9 Squadron RNAS), he suffered a nervous breakdown. After a spell in hospital he was assigned to instructional duties. On the day after the Armistice, flying a Sopwith Pup, Edwards failed to pull out of a spin in time and crashed into his own airfield. On November 20 one leg had to be amputated; but the operation couldn't save him. He died two days later.

RE 19551-4

DSC & Bar   Capt   Born Feb 13 1893   Died Nov 22 1918
RefScs: DHist bf   OMAP(1) 76   TBYW 106 146 app

ELLIOTT William Boyd

"Flew 100 Daylight Bombing Raids in One Summer"

Between April and September 1918 Bill Elliott of St Catharines, Ont., flew more than 100 bombing missions. In April 1917 he joined the RFC in Canada after being turned down by the RNAS, due to lack of vacancies, and trained at Camp Borden, Ont., and in England. By the time he was posted to 205 Squadron RAF, which was equipped with DH 4 bombers, the German March 1918 offensive had subsided. On June 16 he was made flight commander. From then until August, when he was stricken with typhoid, Elliott led half the squadron's raids, often in the face of stiff resistance from enemy fighters. Following the war Elliott was cofounder of the St. Catharines' Flying Club. He died in his native city in 1979.

DFC   Capt   Born Aug 26 1898   Died March 27 1979
RefScs: ST(1) 6   TBYW 164 250–51 app   TSBW 19

EVANS Henry Cope

"Boer War Veteran One of the RFC's Eldest Air Warriors"

By the time Henry Evans, a British-born rancher from MacLeod, Alta., transferred from the CEF to the RFC in the fall of 1915, first as an observer then as a pilot, he was 37 years old and had already fought with the Canadian Artillery in the Boer War. In the summer of 1916, at the time of the British Somme offensive, he joined the hand-picked 24 Squadron commanded by Lanoe Hawker VC, the first British single-seater unit to go to France. By the time Evans arrived, the squadron was equipped with DH 2s.

On July 20 he scored his first victory. By the end of the summer he had destroyed four German planes, commonplace later in the war but at this time, often against odds of ten to one, highly significant. He had been recommended for the DSO when he was killed in a dogfight against three enemy scouts of a new type on September 3.

His death heralded a new enemy menace — the appearance of the Albatros and Halberstadt single-seater fighters that were to dominate the skies over the Western Front for some time to come.

DSO Lt   Born 1878   KIA Sept 3 1916
RefScs: TBYW 40–42 app

FALKENBERG Carl Frederick

"Wounded as Both Soldier and Airman"

Though wounded twice, once while serving with the CEF and again in a plane crash, neither injury kept Baron Falkenberg out of action for long. Born in Bostwood, Nfld., he joined the First Canadian Division and, while serving at the Western Front in 1916, suffered his first war wound. Transferring to the RFC as a pilot, he joined 84 Squadron at Flez in France on February 28, 1918, flying SE5As at the start of the German spring offensive. On April 29 he shared in the destruction of a German two-seater with another pilot. On May 10 he sustained an injury when he crashed but he was soon back in combat. On October 14 he claimed the last of his fourteen victories, for which he received the DFC and Bar. From May to August 1918 he served with the CAF in England as an instructor before retiring to go into the insurance business.

At the outbreak of WW2, Falkenberg joined the RCAF as an administration officer, serving as CO of 4 Training Headquarters, Calgary, Alta., and 2 ITS Regina, Sask., successively. He died in 1980.

DFC & Bar   Capt   F/L(RCAF)   Born Feb 4 1897   Died Oct 25 1980
RefScs: DHist bf   ST(2) 3

FALL Joseph Stewart Temple

"Only Canadian to Win Three DSCs in the Air"

Only days after joining 3 Naval Squadron in France, Joe Fall earned his first DSC when, on April 11, 1917, while on escort duty flying a Sopwith Pup, he shot down three German Albatros fighters. By the end of June, the Vancouver Islander from Hillbank, B.C., who made his way to England in 1916 to join the RNAS, had run his score up to seven victories. At that time his squadron was re-equipped with Sopwith Camels. On July 7 Fall scored his second triple kill. In August he was posted to 9 Naval Squadron in the Dunkirk area with which his tally had reached 27 1/3 victories and two Bars had been added to his DSC by December 22. In April 1918 he joined the staff of the School of Gunnery and Fighting at Freiston in England, where he spent the remainder of the war instructing. In 1919 he was awarded the AFC and accepted a permanent commission with the RAF in which he served in peacetime and throughout WW2 until 1945, when he retired.

DSC & 2 Bars   AFC   Capt   G/C(RCAF)   Born Nov 17 1895   Died
Dec 1 1988
RefScs: DHist bf   TBYW 100–102 app

FISHER Philip Sidney

"Bomber by Night, Fighter by Day"

A native of Montreal, P.Q., Philip Fisher learned to fly at the Thomas School in Ithica, N.Y., and was commissioned in the RNAS as a pilot in October 1915. After training in England he reported to the Dunkirk Naval seaplane base in June 1916 to fly Short seaplanes. Toward the end of July the unit was also equipped with Sopwith Baby seaplanes, resulting in the formation of the "Baby Seaplane Flight." Fisher was appointed to this formation and varied day patrols on the Babys with night bombing raids on the larger Shorts. On many of his day sorties he frequently had to fend off German fighters and in May 1917 was awarded the DSC. At the end of June Fisher joined No 4 Naval Squadron at Bray Dunes as a flight commander flying Sopwith Camels. Shortly afterward, in a desperate aerial battle, his flight fought twenty Albatros scouts, shooting down five of the enemy. Fisher, whose own machine was riddled with 100 bullet holes, was credited with one of the kills. Fisher brought down another machine on September 10. Then on the twenty-fourth, as leader of five Camels who encountered a force of Albatros scouts, he was severely wounded. He recovered, but his flying days were over. The award of the DSO was announced several weeks later.

DSO DSC   Capt   Born Mar 31 1896   Died Dec 17 1983
RefScs: DHist bf   TBYW 160–62 app

FLAVELLE Gordon Aird

"Roar of Engines Muffled Noise of Tanks Preparing for Offensive"

On the rainy night of August 7, 1918, Gordon Flavelle flew his Handley Page bomber back and forth over a British tank depot in the Amiens area on the Western Front in France to drown out the noise of the armour being readied for a dawn offensive, a feat for which he was awarded the DFC. Born in Lindsay, Ont., Flavelle joined the RNAS and, in 1917, received his training in England before being posted to a Naval Handley Page squadron in the south of France.

On his first raid on October 24, Flavelle came close to losing his life. Having dropped his bombs on the allotted target at Saarbrucken, he lost his way in heavy clouds and crashed; luckily he was on the French side of the lines. But the bomber was reduced to splinters, only the tail and part of the fuselage remained intact. Thrown clear, he only suffered bruises to his head and shoulder. His copilot, however, was not so lucky: a propeller blade had knifed into his back.

In all Flavelle flew thirty-seven raids before returning to Canada. After the war he went into the lumber business. He died in 1987 in Vancouver, B.C.

DFC Capt   Born May 16 1887   Died June 10 1987
RefScs: ST(1) 9   TBYW 168 app

GALBRAITH Daniel Murray Bayne

"Attacked from Behind, Loop-the-Loop Placed Him on His Adversary's Tail"

On July 15, 1916, Murray Galbraith caused a stir at the Admiralty and among his fellow RNAS pilots when a tactic he had developed, albeit out of necessity during his first encounter with an enemy plane, was uncovered. Piloting his Nieuport ten miles out to sea and approaching Ostend at 12,000 feet, Galbraith was suddenly attacked from behind by a German seaplane. Galbraith yanked back hard on the stick at full throttle to put his fighter into a loop and, as he pulled out, found himself dead set on his enemy's tail. From 100 yards he emptied a tray of ammunition into the seaplane, sending it plunging down, streaming flame, into the sea.

Born in Carleton Place, Ont., Galbraith learned to fly at the Wright School of Aeronautics in Dayton, Ohio. In November 1915 he joined the RNAS and was posted to 2 Naval Squadron based at Dunkirk.

Following his first victory, he became embroiled in two more skirmishes before shooting down a second plane on September 28, 1916. For his feats, Galbraith received the DSC and the French awarded him the Croix de Guerre. His third victory came shortly after the squadron switched to Sopwith Pups.

Late in October he transferred to a new squadron, No 8, known as the Naval Eight, which was formed as part of the program for reinforcing the RFC at the Front. In November Galbraith scored another three victories and sent one aircraft down out of control before returning to England for a rest. His next posting was to 66 Wing in Italy, which was engaged in attacking shipping in the Adriatic.

After the war Galbraith joined the CAF and became an instructor at Camp Borden, Ont. On March 29, 1921, he was killed in a car accident.

DSC & Bar CdeG(Fr)   Capt   Born Apr 27 1895   KA Mar 29 1921
RefScs: DHist bf   OMAP(1) 77   TBYW app

RE 19590

GALPIN John Osborne

"Offered Air-Sea Rescue by Pilot Who Shot Him Down"

Minutes after "Tiny" Galpin and a fellow pilot had been shot down in the North Sea on June 5, 1918, following a furious fight with five German seaplanes, one of the enemy pilots landed beside the British flying boat and asked if they would like to be picked up and taken to Zebrugge — and in the process, of course, become prisoners of war. Since they were close to the English coast, the downed airmen peremptorily declined the double-edged offer; they preferred to take their chances of being rescued by the Royal Navy. Thereupon the German flier snapped a photograph of them then promptly took off.

Born in Ottawa, Ont., Galpin joined the RNAS in late 1915 after learning to fly at the Dayton, Ohio, Wright School. He made his first operational flight in 1916 from Felixstowe, spent the early part of 1917 at the Scilly Isles air station, then returned to Felixstowe, where he spent the rest of the war on H12s. During July and November 1917, he made two attacks on submarines and another the following month, apparently with no result. In fact he seemed plagued with bad luck on many of his attacks but nonetheless was decorated twice and twice mentioned in dispatches for his aggressiveness and willingness to engage the enemy. Galpin died in Ceylon in 1950 at the age of 61.

DSC DFC MID(2)   Maj   Born Oct 17 1889   Died 1950
RefScs: DHist bf   TBYW 200–201 app

GLEN James Alpheus

"Participated in First Allied Strategic Air Raid"

On July 30, 1916, James Glen of Enerby, B.C., was one of two Canadians who took part in the first strategic air raid conducted by the Allies. After joining the RNAS, Glen was posted to 3 Naval Wing, the first strategic aerial force formed specifically for the long-range bombing of Germany. Equipped with Sopwith Strutter single- and twin-seater fighters and bombers, the wing was based at Luxeuil-les-Bains in France south of Nancy, only sixty miles west of the Rhine. The objective of the initial raid, undertaken jointly with the 4th French Bomber Group, was to hit gasoline stores at Mulheim. Glen dropped four 650-pound bombs squarely on the target. In the sorties that followed, Glen was a keen participant. At the end of the year he was transferred to 3 Naval Squadron, one of the RNAS units created to bolster RFC strength at the Western Front. Glen was credited with destroying five enemy planes and was decorated three times. Following WW1 he took a permanent commission with the RAF.

DSC & Bar CdeG(Fr) Capt   Born June 23 1896   Died March 7 1962
RefScs: OMAP(1) 77   TBYW 122 142 146 149 app

GODFREY Albert Earl

"Former Drummer Boy, Most Senior RCAF Officer to Open Fire on the Enemy"

Born in Killarney, Man., Earl Godfrey became a drummer boy and bugler in a Vancouver regiment at age 12 and, until his retirement from the RCAF in 1944, never left the service of his country. In 1915 he went overseas with the CEF, transferring to the RFC as an observer then as a pilot. Assigned to 40 Squadron, within nine months he destroyed 13½ enemy planes and two observation balloons, which earned him the MC. During his tour of combat he developed a mounting for twin machine-guns on the Nieuport scout; his own aircraft was the first so equipped. In 1918 he became Commandant of the School of Aerial Fighting at Beamsville, Ont., and at the end of WW1 attended the RAF Staff College and Imperial Defense College. He then retired from the RAF to join the Canadian Civil Aviation Branch, flying fishery patrols off the west coast.

Recalled to the CAF in 1922, Godfrey served at RCAF HQ in Ottawa, Ont., and accompanied Dalzell McKee from Pittsburgh, Pa., on the first trans-Canada seaplane flight in 1926, covering the 3,000 mile route in 35.08 hours. Significantly, Godfrey was one of the first to win the McKee Trophy, inaugurated by the American as a token of appreciation. In September 1928, he carried the first official Canadian air mail — from Ottawa to Vancouver, B.C.

At the outbreak of WW2 Godfrey was given command of Western Air Command; then in 1941 he served with Eastern Air Command. It was in service to the latter, while on convoy patrol in a Liberator as observer, that he took over as air gunner when a U-boat attacked; thus, with the rank of Air Commodore, he became the most senior RCAF officer to fire at the enemy. In 1942 Godfrey was made Deputy Inspector of the RCAF. He retired from the service two years later.

MC AFC VD Maj A/V/M(RCAF)   Born July 27 1890   Died Jan 2
1982 Ind CAHF 1977
RefScs: CA 125   CA&FWW 252–53 CAHF 96 CCMA 18 23 45
CFH 125 164 185 DHist bf 63 OMAP(1) 78 RS&A 208 210
TCNAF 565 625 627–28 TSBW 63

GORDON James Lindsay

*"Member of Felixstowe Flight, One of First Two RCAF
Officers to Be Promoted to Rank of Air Vice-Marshal"*

A Montrealer, Lindsay Gordon learned to fly at the Wright School
in Dayton, Ohio, before being accepted by the RNAS as a pilot
in 1916. A member of the famous Felixstowe Flight, flying Curtiss biplanes,
Gordon was awarded the DFC for attacking German submarines and

PA 117538

enemy aircraft. On May 29, 1917, he rescued a Short seaplane crew from the North Sea by landing in heavy waves. Despite damage to his aircraft, Gordon pulled the survivors aboard then taxied toward the English coast until a cargo ship took the plane in tow. Both he and his observer received the Board of Trade's Silver Sea Gallantry Medal.

After WW1 Gordon took over as CO of Camp Borden, Ont., then was appointed Air Board Assistant Director of Organization, Training, and Operations, as well as Acting Director of the CAF. In 1926–27 Gordon served as Assistant Director of the RCAF, after which he became Director of the Civil Government Operations division, responsible for forest fire protection. In 1933 he was seconded to the militia with the rank of Brigadier as District OC Military District 12 (Regina) and later MD 10 (Winnipeg), the first RCAF officer to hold such an appointment. During that tenure, Gordon attended the RAF Staff and Imperial Defense Colleges. In 1938 he was promoted to Air Vice-Marshal, one of the first of two RCAF officers to be elevated to that rank. Gordon died in 1940.

DFC   Capt A/V/M(RCAF)   Born Dec 11 1892   Died Mar 3 1940
RefScs: CA 83 117   CA&FFW 42   CCMA 20 32–33   DHist bf
TCNAF 63 81 621 623

GOULDING Acheson Gosford Helland

"Forced Enemy Surrender in Mid-Air"

Acheson Goulding had the incredible experience of seeing the observer of an Aviatik two-seater he and another SE5A pilot had been firing on actually stand up in his cockpit and wave a white handkerchief as a signal of surrender. Goulding, a native of Holland, Man., flew with the RNAS in Macedonia in support of the British army fighting the Bulgar forces. With 17 Squadron, which he joined in February 1917, and a newly formed 150 Squadron, to which he was transferred as a flight commander in April 1918, Goulding flew numerous bombing raids, fighter patrols, strafing attacks and reconnaissance missions. In May 1917 he and another pilot bombed a Bulgarian transport column of twenty-six horse-drawn wagons, smashing some of them and causing a general stampede.

It was on patrol on March 20, 1918, that he was party to the mid-air surrender. Goulding and another pilot were on patrol when they spotted the Aviatik photographing British positions. They attacked, causing the pilot to drop 4,000 feet, then dived down still firing. Suddenly the observer signalled his surrender. The SE5A pilots then shepherded the enemy plane to a British landing field at Cerpista.

By the end of his tour, by which time he had been twice decorated, Goulding was unofficially credited with nine planes destroyed, some of them shared.

In WW2 he enlisted in the RCAF and served as CO of No 18 SFTS at Gimli, Man.

MC DFC   Capt   Died Apr 1951
RefScs: OMAP(1) 78   TBYW 231–32 app

GRANGE Edward Rochfort

"First Canadian to Shoot Down Five Planes in Four Days"

On graduating from the Curtiss Flying School at Toronto, Ont., in September 1915, Edward Grange joined the RNAS as a pilot. Born in Lansing, Mich., but raised in Toronto, he served with 1 and 5 Naval Wings, and 8 Naval Squadron in France. It was with the latter at the end of 1916 that he had the distinction of becoming the first Canadian ace to shoot down five enemy machines in four days. Shortly afterward, on January 17, 1917, he was badly wounded in the right elbow during a dogfight and, although he lost the use of his right arm and a great deal of blood, Grange managed to land his aircraft safely and was rushed to hospital. After convalescing Grange became an instructor at Eastbourne, where he taught over 300 pupils the fundamentals of flying before WW1 ended.

DSC CdeG(Fr) Capt   Born Jan 11 1892   Died July 13 1988
RefScs: CA 77 81   DHist bf   OMAP(1) 79   SY 460

HALLAM Theodore Douglas

"Decorated for Both on Land and Air Exploits"

Before becoming a pilot in the RNAS, Ted Hallam had already been decorated with the first of the three DSCs he would earn. But although he served with distinction as a master-gunner at Gallipoli, his heart was in the sky. In the summer of 1914, prior to WW1, the Torontonian took flying lessons at the Curtiss school in Hammonsport, N.Y. When the war started he went overseas with the CEF as a gunner then obtained a commission in the Royal Navy. Hallam became attached to an RNAS

Armoured Car unit in the Dardanelles, where he was wounded and sent back to England. When he recovered Hallam transferred to the naval air service, graduating as a pilot in August 1916, and was posted to the Felixstowe War Flight flying Curtiss H12 flying boats on "Spider Web" patrols against U-boats. His second DSC was awarded for an attack on a German submarine on April 23, 1917, when he dropped four 100-pound bombs causing the vessel to disappear from the surface. By 1918 Hallam had been made commander of the War Flight and had been awarded a Bar to his DSC for his continuous flying boat patrol operations.

DSC & 2 Bars   Maj   Born 1883   Died Dec 14 1948   Author *The Spider Web*
RefScs: DHist bf   TBYW 100 198 203 222 app

HICKEY Charles Robert Reeves

"Injured Dismantling Enemy Plane He Shot Down"

C harles Hickey's closest call to death occurred not in battle, though he had eluded it many times in that milieu, but while trying to wrest a souvenir from a German two-seater he had shot down on April 21, 1918, behind the Allied lines. A time bomb set by enemy airmen exploded, severely burning his face and hands. It was a typical headstrong action by the determined Nanaimo, B.C., native. In 1917, Hickey had transferred from the army to the RNAS and, in August of that year, had joined 4 Naval Squadron in France flying Camels. With this squadron he eventually rose to become a flight commander. By the fall of 1918, Hickey had been credited with 18½ planes destroyed and had been awarded the DFC and Bar. Then on October 5 he was killed on a routine patrol over Nieuport when another pilot in his flight collided with him.

DFC & Bar   Capt   Born Sept 10 1897   KFA   Oct 5 1918
RefScs: DHist bf   ST(2) 3   TBYW app

HOBBS Basil Deacon

"The Ubiquitous Aviator"

B asil Hobbs flew it every which way. Born in England, he moved to Sault Ste. Marie, Ont., as a boy. A graduate of the Wright Flying School, Dayton, Ohio, he joined the RNAS in 1916 as a pilot and was posted to Felixstowe. In Curtiss flying boats, he flew submarine and Zeppelin patrols, succeeding at both. On June 14, 1917, Hobbs and his crew shot down a Zeppelin and on September 28 made two attacks on a submarine that was believed to have been sunk. For such actions he was awarded the DSO and DSC.

After the war, as an RAF officer, Hobbs competed in the 1919 Schneider Trophy seaplane race. He was well in the lead when heavy fog forced him to land on the water. In 1920 he joined the CAF and was employed as certificate examiner by the Canadian Air Board. In 1921 Hobbs was made CO of Winnipeg Air Station, engaging in forestry work and fire patrols. The following year he participated in the trans-Canada flight. In 1923 he was the sole pilot of the first long-range photographic survey undertaken in Canada — over northern Manitoba and Saskatchewan. In 1925 he was made Director of Operations for the RCAF but resigned two years later to form his own wine and spirits import firm in Montreal, P.Q.

At the beginning of WW2 Hobbs was recommissioned in the RCAF and given a succession of commands, eventually taking over Patricia Bay Naval Air Station, B.C., as CO. Following the war he returned to civilian life.

OBE DSO DSC & Bar MID Capt   G/C(RCAF)   Born Dec 20 1894
Ind CAHF 1987
RefScs: CA 83–84 101   CAHF 123   CCMA 5 9   CFH 163–64
DHist bf   TSBW 23–24 62 70–71   OMAP(1) 97

HOIDGE Reginald Theodore

"The Morale Booster"

Reginald Hoidge served with two of the most famous British scout squadrons on the Western Front and, with twenty-five planes shot down to his credit, established himself as one of the leading Canadian aces. In addition, he was acknowledged as a great morale builder. Born and raised in Toronto, Ont., he joined the CEF and went overseas in 1916 and transferred to the RFC. In January 1917 he was posted to Vert Galand in France, home of the notorious 56 Squadron (two VCs). His first victory came on May 5 when, in an SE5, he shot down an Albatros scout. In June the squadron was posted to England briefly to cope with the Gotha bomber daylight raids on London.

Hoidge celebrated his return to the Western Front with a double victory on July 12. On September 23 he took part in the combat in which the German ace Werner Voss was killed. Hoidge claimed to have destroyed

RE 19633-2

one of a pair of planes accompanying Voss during the melee. Next day, after attacking a large formation of enemy aircraft, his plane developed engine and gun trouble. He was driven down from 7,000 to 600 feet and five miles behind enemy lines. With his SE5 badly shot up, Hoidge was able to make it back safely to Vert Galand thanks to his skill and determination. That he accepted such tribulations cheerfully and philosophically did much to boost squadron morale.

On November 19, 1917, having flown eighty-three patrols, Hoidge was posted back to England. In February 1918 he was injured in a flying accident but returned to operational duty with No 1 Squadron, with which he scored his last victory on October 28.

MC & Bar Capt RFC Born Sept 10 1897 Died Mar 1 1963
RefScs: DHist bf OMAP(1) 80 TBYW 102–104 app

HOLLIDAY Frederick Parkinson

"Excelled as 'Brisfit' Ace"

F red Holliday made his name flying two-seater Bristol Fighters known throughout the RFC as "Brisfits." Born in Australia, but a Canadian by adoption, Holliday left his home in Toronto, Ont., in 1914 with the army. After serving for a year as a sapper on the Western Front, he transferred to the flying service in 1915 and, in mid-December of 1916, was posted to France. By March 1917, at the height of the Battle of Arras, he was a member of 48 Squadron based at Bellevue. On April 6 he and his observer shot down their first enemy machine and destroyed another on the twenty-third. On May 11, in a battle with twelve Albatros scouts, they destroyed one of the German fighters and sent another down out of control. By July Holliday was awarded the MC and on the twenty-seventh of that month scored his last victory, bringing his shared total up to an estimated fifteen enemy machines destroyed. In August he was transferred to England as an instructor at Gosport, where he commanded a training flight.

Following the war Holliday went into the electrical business. When WW2 broke out he joined the RCAF where, between 1942 and the end of the war, he served as CO of No 10 Repair Depot in Calgary, Alta. Following the cessation of hostilities Holliday returned to the electrical business as president and managing director of a Swedish firm. He died in 1969.

DSO MC AFC   Maj   G/C   Died Mar 5 1969
RefScs: WIS Oct 1963

HOWSAM George Robert

"Fighter/Test Pilot Became Training Command Efficiency Expert"

George Howsam emerged as an ace from WW1 with an MC and a score of thirteen planes destroyed and two damaged to his credit. He commanded the RCAF's test flight in peacetime and, as CO of a Flying Training Station in WW2, set the highest standard of efficiency of any in Canada. Born in Port Perry, Ont., he joined the CEF as a private in 1915, going overseas the following year. In May 1917 he transferred to the RFC and was posted to 70 Squadron at Poperinge in France that November. On December 28 he scored his first victory. His list of kills mounted until he was wounded in March 1918 and invalided back to England. However, Howsam returned to battle in October.

After the war Howsam joined the CAF, where, in 1923, he was responsible for flight testing lubricants and anti-freeze to find out the effects of cold weather on them at high altitudes. As a member of the RCAF he was appointed Air Staff Officer of MD 2 in 1933; then in 1936 he was made CO of the air force's all-purpose test flight.

G.R. Howsam (r.) AH-341

During WW2, as CO of 11 SFTS Yorkton, Sask., Howsam established such a high level of efficiency that his station became a model training establishment, receiving the Air Minister's Efficiency Award three times in succession. Howsam finished the war as AOC No 4 Training Command and left the RCAF in 1946 to take over as director of a brewery in Edmonton, Alta. He retired to Victoria, B.C., where he died in 1988.

CB MC LoM(Am) CdeG(Bel) OWL(Cz)   Capt   A/V/M(RCAF)   Born
Jan 29 1895   Died Apr 16 1988
RefScs: CCMA 32   DHist bf   TSBW 60   OMAP(1) 80   RS&A 28
SY 107

HUBBARD William Henry

"Flew as Both Reconnaissance and Scout Pilot"

Bill Hubbard began his aerial combat career as a reconnaissance pilot and later flew fighters. A native of Kingston, Ont., he enlisted in the RFC in Canada in 1915, received his pilot's training in England and was posted to France, where he served with both 7 and 5 squadrons, flying BE2cs on artillery observation and photographic missions. In September 1916, his aircraft was attacked by a Fokker monoplane, which his observer destroyed over Landemark. On Boxing Day he was wounded in the calf by anti-aircraft fire, taken off operations and served as an instructor for six months. In March 1918, Hubbard returned to France as a flight commander with 73 Squadron, based at St-Omer, flying Sopwith Camels. On April 11 he scored his first victory. By war's end he had been credited with eleven aircraft destroyed and had been awarded the DFC and Bar. Returning to civvie street after WW1, Hubbard went into the mining business. He died in 1960.

DFC & Bar   Capt   Born May 18 1886   Died June 19 1960
RefScs: DHist bf   ST(2) 4   TBYW app

INCE Arthur Strachan

"First Canadian to Shoot Down a Plane"

A rthur Ince was the first pilot to be licenced by the Curtiss Flying School in Toronto, Ont., and the first to receive the Royal Aero Club certificate. On December 14, 1915, he shot down a German two-seater in flames off the Belgian coast to become the first Canadian to score an aerial victory. This former salesman had enlisted in the RNAS earlier in the year and, on being accepted, was assigned coastal patrols. On the day he scored his victory, Ince acted as the observer/gunner in a two-seater Nieuport hunting for German airplanes bombing a British ship stranded on a sand bar. When he and his pilot spotted an aircraft in the distance, they gave chase. After three attacks Ince's bullets found the mark: the German plane went spiralling down in flames, its bombs exploding in the water. Meanwhile the Nieuport had developed engine trouble and the pilot had to ditch it in the sea. When it hit the water, the aircraft overturned and began to sink. But the two airmen were able to free themselves and swim to a nearby mine sweeper, which hauled them aboard. For that exploit Ince received the DSC, the first decoration awarded a Canadian in the RNAS.

DSO DSC Capt   Born Oct 31 1892
RefScs: CA 77 79   CCMA 3–4   DHist bf   OMAP(1) 12   SY 460
TBYW 116 app

IRWIN William Roy

"Flew in Both World Wars"

B orn in Ripley, Ont., "Sambo" Irwin flew in WW1 as a combat pilot and in the second round as a chief flying instructor. In 1916 he joined the RNAS and was sent to England. But on arrival he was transferred to the RFC and won his wings and commission in April 1917. Posted to 56 Squadron at Baizieux, which had just been re-equipped with SE5A Scouts, he flew his first patrol on March 1, 1918. On September 15, by which time he had run up a score of eleven kills, Irwin was wounded when four Fokkers pounced on him from above while he was attacking a "bait" in the form of a two-seater German machine stooging along below the clouds. Following a short period in the hospital, he was sent to the Central Flying School as an instructor. When the war ended he was discharged from the RAF and returned to Canada.

At the beginning of WW2, Irwin enlisted in the RCAF and was posted to No 3 EFTS, Yorkton, Sask., as an instructor after taking a pilot refresher course; he was eventually promoted to Chief Flying Instructor. Later Irwin assumed command of No 3 SFTS, Calgary, Alta. When the war ended he retired from the service to live in Ottawa, Ont.

MBE DFC & Bar   Capt   G/C(RCAF)   Born June 7 1898   Died Jan 14 1988
RefScs: Dhist bf   OMAP(1) 82   TBYW app

JOHNSON George Owen

"Ex-Fighter Pilot Became Organizing and Training Administrator for BCATP"

W hen WW2 started "Johnny" Johnson, who shot down twelve enemy planes in the earlier world conflict, was made a member of the Air Council and charged with the responsibility of organizing and training of air crews for the BCATP. Born in Woodstock, Ont., Johnson joined the RFC as a pilot and was decorated with the MC and the French Croix de Guerre during his time in combat in France. In 1920, as a member of the CAF, he was navigator for the crew that made the first trans-Canada flight.

Between wars Johnson held many RCAF posts, including Director of Air Operations and Acting Senior Air Officer; in 1934 he became CO of Trenton Air Station, Ont. After attending the Imperial Defense College, he was then given the job of organizing Western Air Command. In 1940 he became Deputy Chief of the Air Staff and was made AOC of No 1 Training Command in Toronto, Ont., two years later. In 1943 he was appointed head of Eastern Air Command. When the war ended, Johnson became AOC-in-C of the RCAF overseas in November 1945, returning to Canada in 1946. He retired the following year to live in Vancouver, B.C., where he died in 1980 at 94 years of age.

CB MC CdeG(Fr) KHCOL(Nor) Capt A/M(RCAF) Born Jan 24
1896 Died March 28 1980
RefScs: CCMA 45 60 app DHist bf RS&A 13 SY 15 TBYW app
TCNAF 62–63 66 229 300 389 400 409 546 558 574 622–23 627
TSBW 47

KERBY Harold Spencer

*"First Canadian to Serve in Dardanelles,
Only One to Account for Two Gothas"*

Harold Kerby, who left Calgary, Alta., in 1915 to join the RNAS, became the first Canadian to serve in the Gallipoli campaign and later to shoot down two of the giant German Gotha bombers. Assigned to 3 Naval Squadron in June 1915, he flew artillery-spotting sorties for the Royal Navy using Voisin two-seaters.

Air fighting in the Dardanelles at this stage of the war amounted to nil; therefore, the aircraft carried only pistols and rifles. Flying missions also extended to bombing Turk positions in Maurice and Henri Farmans. By September the first Fokker scouts appeared over the front, and the British bombers were then armed with machine guns.

In November Kerby succumbed to dysentry and was sent back to England to recuperate. On February 1, 1917, he was posted to 9 Naval Squadron in France flying Nieuports and Sopwith Pups; he was then transferred to 3 Naval Squadron before being sent to the RNAS Defense Flight at Walmar in England. On August 12, 1917, flying a Sopwith Camel over the sea, Kerby encountered a Gotha bomber 4,000 feet below him and dived down, firing as he went. His bullets sent the bomber crashing into the water and, seeing the crew clinging to the wreckage, Kerby threw them his life jacket. Nine days later he accounted for a second of the giant marauders when he and five others attacked a formation of ten Gothas off Ramsgate.

At the end of the war Kerby was made an instructor and eventually took command of the School of Gunnery and Air Fighting at Freiston. Kerby remained in the RAF and commanded the British Advanced Air Striking Force in France during 1939 and 1940. Later he became AOC Air Headquarters, East Africa, and also served with Coastal Command HQ. He retired from the service in 1946 and lived in London, England, where he died in 1963.

CB DSC AFC LoM(Am) Capt A/V/M(RCAF) Born May 14 1893
Died Jan 8 1963
RefScs: TBYW 32 122 193–94 218–22 app

KNIGHT Arthur Gerald

"The Red Baron's Thirteenth Victim"

His fate seems to have been ordained: he learned from the masters only to be killed by the champion of them all. During six months of bitter air combat fighting alongside the brilliant British aerial tactician Lanoe Hawker VC and against Germany's architect of aerial strategy, Oswald Boelcke, Arthur Knight was unofficially credited with nineteen victories. However, he finally fell victim to the gun of the top ace of WW1, Manfred von Richthofen.

Born in Bedford, England, Knight was brought up and educated in Toronto, Ont. After graduating from the Curtiss Flying School at Toronto in 1915 he enlisted in the RFC. In May 1916 he joined Hawker's hand-picked 24 Squadron at Bertangles in France flying DH2s. On July 14 he brought down his first enemy machine, a Fokker. In September he destroyed another, and on October 17 he added a Roland to his score.

Near Bapaume on October 28, Knight and his formation became engaged in a fierce fight in which Boelcke collided with one of his own pilots and crashed to his death. As a result, the Red Baron took his place as head of Germany's most famous *Jagdstaffel*, an ominous turn of events for Knight. In November, after being awarded the MC and DSO for his achievements, he was posted to 29 Squadron, which also flew DH2s, as a flight commander. The fight in which he was killed took place on December 20, 1916, over the Somme. It was Richthofen's thirteenth victory.

DSO MC Capt   Born July 30 1895   KIA Dec 20 1916
RefScs: OMAP(1) 83   TBYW 39 42–43 app   TRKG 103

LALLY Conrad Tohendal

"Long-Range Photographic Reconnaissance and Bombing Specialist"

Conrad Lally spent his entire tour of operations flying long-range reconnaissance and bombing missions at which he became something of a specialist. A native of Wainwright, Alta., Lally joined the RFC in 1916 after serving with the CEF. Following his pilot's training he was sent to 28 Training Squadron in England early in February 1917. On April 11 he was posted to 25 Squadron at Auchel in France where he flew FE2ds and, months later, DH 4s. Together with his observer, Lally accounted for ten German planes shot down. In December he was awarded the MC and received a Bar to the decoration a month later. Early in 1918 he was wounded and taken off operations. Shortly after the end of WW1 he was given the AFC.

MC & Bar AFC Capt Born Apr 3 1888 Died 1919
RefScs: TBYW 173–74 app TSBW 20

LAWSON Walter Brodgen

"Took Part in Notable Bombing Raid"

W alter Lawson first saw action in September 1915 when he flew with the RNAS at Basra on the Persian Gulf in support of General Townshend's campaign in Mesopotamia against the Turks. Lawson was born in Barrie, Ont., and upon graduating from RMC he joined the CEF; in England he was attached to the Canadian Military School at Shorncliffe before transferring to the British air naval service. In the spring of 1916 Lawson was invalided back to England from the Middle East and given instructional duties. During the latter part of 1917 he was posted to the RNAS Gunnery School at Eastchurch, of which he became CO.

In June 1918 Lawson joined 215 Squadron as a flight commander. Equipped with Handley Page O/400 bombers, the unit was part of the Independent Force RAF. On the night of August 25, in appalling weather conditions, Lawson piloted one of two bombers sent to attack the Badische chemical works at Mannheim, a top-priority target. Each of the Handley Pages carried eight 112-pound and five 25-pound bombs. On reaching the target the aircraft glided down to 5,000 feet, where they faced searchlights and heavy anti-aircraft fire. The two planes then swept in low at 200 feet, narrowly missing chimneys, and released their bombs. Having dropped their loads the pilots then flew back over the target area — by now badly damaged and on fire — and raked it with their machine guns. Both planes returned safely despite the vicious flak and frightful flying conditions.

Lawson served in the CAF after the war and returned to Canada in 1928. He was killed in a flying accident June 16 of that year while making his final test flight for a civilian licence.

DFC Capt Born Nov 11 1892 KFA June 16 1928
RefScs: CCMA 7 DHist bf OMAP(1) 40 TBYW 167 app

LECKIE Robert

"Zeppelin Killer to RCAF Chief of the Air Staff"

Though born a Scot, no airman became more dedicated to Canada's role as an air power than Bob Leckie, and few contributed as much toward the RCAF's growth. Leckie came to the Dominion at 16 to work for his uncle in Toronto, Ont. In 1915 he enlisted in the RNAS, graduated from the Curtiss Flying School at Toronto and was posted to Great Yarmouth, Eng., in 1916 where, for the next three years, he operated on HS2L and DH 4 flying boats against the Zeppelins. Leckie was awarded

the DSC after he shot down his first dirigible on May 14, 1917, the first time a flying boat had destroyed a Zeppelin — and the first by a Canadian. A year later he received the DSO after completing 100 reconnaissance trips over Germany where he had been attacked by enemy machines on several occasions. He also bombed two submarines, one of which he severely damaged. On August 15, 1918, he shot down another Zeppelin. As the war came to a close he was assigned to No 1 Wing of the CAF as CO.

After WW1, Leckie returned to Canada on loan from the RAF as director of flying operations for the Air Board. In 1920 he led the first trans-Canada flight, which took ten days although the actual flying time was forty-nine hours and seven minutes. In 1924 Leckie went back to England where he served in various capacities with the RAF including, in 1938, command of the air force in the Mediterranean. In February 1940 he was seconded to the RCAF and given responsibility for setting up schools for the BCATP. He was also made a member of the Air Council for training. In 1942 Leckie transferred to the RCAF and in 1944 became CAS, a post he held until his retirement in 1947. He died in Ottawa, Ont., at age 84.

CB DSO DSC DFC CD SS(Am) LoM(Am) Ld'H(Fr) GOOC(Bel) OWL(Cz) OPR(Pol) KHCOL(Nor) Maj A/M(RCAF) Born Apr 16 1890 Died Mar 31 1975 Ind CAHF 1988
RefScs: AIC 187 CA 83 87 91 CAHF 129 CCMA 6–9 22 DHist bf OMAP(1) 99 SY 466 TBYW 127–38 app TSBW 24 30 35 37–38 44–49 126 244

LESLIE William Alexander

"Flew Three Different Bombing Raids in One Night"

Bill Leslie made sixty-six night bombing raids and during his entire seven months of operations had only one flying accident. Born in Toronto, Ont., he enlisted in the RFC in Canada in 1916. Leslie went overseas, where he flew first with a Home Defense Squadron; then in January 1918 he joined 58 Squadron in France, flying FE2bs. On the night of June 6, Leslie flew on three different raids. On the final sortie he lost a wheel on take-off. Returning from the foray, to ensure an even landing, he had his observer put a burst of machine-gun fire in the other tire. In October the squadron was re-equipped with the sturdier Handley Page bombers. Shortly afterward Leslie crashed his machine into a tree when one of his engines failed and injured his stomach — the only flying accident of his entire tour. In civilian life he became president of the first Canadian firm to manufacture penicillin. In 1982 he died in Toronto, Ont., at age 86.

DFC Capt   Born Sept 19 1896   Died June 20 1982
RefScs: ST(1) 7   TBYW app

MacLAREN Donald Roderick

"Friendly Wrestling Bout Ended Epic Combat Tour"

In a year of steady air fighting Don MacLaren never received as much as a scratch. However, MacLaren, who destroyed forty-eight German planes and six observation planes, ended his career in the hospital with a broken leg sustained in a friendly wrestling match with one of his own pilots. Born in Ottawa, Ont., MacLaren left the family fur-trading firm in Peace River, Alta., to attend McGill University and in 1916 joined the RFC. Because he enlisted shortly after the RFC established a training school at Camp Borden, Ont., MacLaren was one of the first to obtain all his pilot's training in Canada. After receiving his wings, he went overseas and was posted to 46 Squadron in November 1917 at Filescamp Farm. He remained with this squadron during his entire combat tour and eventually became its CO.

Flying a Sopwith Camel, MacLaren scored his first victory in February when he shot down a Pfalz. Then on March 22 he destroyed three LVG two-seaters. Two days later he immobilized a long-range gun by dropping a bomb on it; he also shot down a pair of two-seater German planes and an observation balloon. This mixed bag won him the MC. By April, as his tally began to mount, he was appointed as flight commander and in September received a Bar to his MC.

MacLaren's career also had its amusing side. On one occasion, diving on a two-seater, his guns jammed. Pulling up, he was surprised that the observer hadn't taken advantage of this situation. Then the enemy gunner gestured that his gun wouldn't work either!

After his tour ended and his leg had mended, MacLaren joined the CAF. However, he resigned his commission upon returning to Canada to go into commercial aviation; MacLaren eventually became executive assistant to the president of Trans Canada Airlines. He retired in 1958. Active with the Air Cadet League, he eventually was appointed its president. A trophy was named in his honour. It is awarded annually to the most proficient cadet squadron in B.C.

RE 17890-1

DSO MC & Bar DFC Ld'H(Fr) CdeG(Fr)   Maj   Born May 28 1893
Died July 4 1989   Ind CAHF 1976
RefScs: CA 89   CAHF 93   CFA 185–92 CFP 49–52 109 DHist bf
OMAP(1) 85   TBYW 89 app

MAGOR Norman Ansley

"First Canadian to Sink a Sub"

The fourth submarine to be sent to the bottom by an airplane, the UC-72, was the first credited to a Canadian, Norman Magor of Westmount, P.Q. The action took place in the early morning of September 22, 1917. Magor and his copilot, also a Canadian, while on patrol in a Curtiss flying boat, spotted the U-boat awash and showing some 250 feet of white-painted deck eight miles northeast of the East Hinder Bank near Ostend, Belg. They dived down to 800 feet dropping two 220-pound bombs directly on the vessel. Before it could dive, the submarine exploded just behind the conning tower, throwing up oil and debris; it then keeled over on its side and sank, carrying its crew of thirty-two to a watery grave. For that attack Magor was awarded the DSC. Later the prize money of £160 was divided up between the pilot and Magor's estate (he was killed in 1918).

Magor had joined the RNAS in Canada in 1916 after graduating from the Wright Flying School in Augusta, Ga. Originally stationed at Felixstowe, Magor was flying anti-submarine patrols out of Dunkirk in tandem with Short seaplanes at the time of the UC-72 incident.

DSC Capt Born Jan 16 1891 KIA April 1918
RefScs: CA 84 DHist bf OMAP(1) 97 SY 461 TBYW 202 app
TSBW 23

MALONE John Joseph

"Brought Down Enemy Pilot then Discussed Fight with Him"

John Malone had the unique experience of talking over his combat with the adversary he had brought down only moments before. Malone, who hailed from Regina, Sask., joined the RNAS and in 1916 was posted to 3 Naval Wing. There he completed numerous bombing sorties. Toward the end of January 1917, he was sent to 3 Naval Squadron, one of the RNAS units being formed at Dunkirk to strengthen the RFC fighter forces. On April 24 Malone was flying his Sopwith Pup on patrol when two of his flight managed to cripple a German two-seater. Malone cut the enemy off as he made for his own lines, forcing the pilot down just inside British territory. Then his own engine quit, compelling him to land his plane right beside his downed enemy's. Malone helped the German pilot pull his badly wounded observer from the aircraft; however, the observer died minutes later. Then both friend and foe had to take cover from German shelling until they could reach safety. Eventually Malone escorted his prisoner back to the squadron mess where, over many, many drinks, they held a long, friendly discussion about their combat. The German flier told his captors that he too had been wounded, though very slightly. He also had been under the impression he was landing behind his own lines. Toward the end of the month Malone had run up a score of eight victories and had been recommended for the DSO. However, the decoration had to be awarded posthumously; he was killed in a dogfight on April 30 while escorting FE2bs on reconnaissance.

DSO MC F/S/L Born Dec 12 1889 KIA Apr 30 1917
RefScs: OMAP(1) 85 TBYW 121 149

McCALL Frederick Robert Gordon

"One of Duo in Hour-Long Fight with Forty Enemy Planes"

On June 28, 1918, Fred McCall and another pilot fought forty German fighters for over an hour while escorting a flight of two-seaters. Battling them down to tree-top level, each of the Canadians accounted for three of the enemy. McCall was born in Vernon, B.C., brought up in Calgary, Alta., and went overseas with the CEF in 1916. Transferring to the RFC as a pilot the following year, he was posted to 13 Squadron flying RE8 reconnaissance machines. By April 15, 1918, McCall and his observers had brought down eight planes. At this time he joined 41 Squadron at Sava, flying SE5As as a scout pilot. On May 25 he shot down his first enemy plane with the squadron and four days later destroyed another. His score began to mount rapidly; in a four-day period in June he was credited with nine victories, including those he shot down in his fight with forty fighters. The last day of that month was a record one for McCall, who by nightfall had accounted for five German planes brought down. For this feat he received the DFC. Before taking ill on August 17, McCall scored his final victory and brought his total up to 30½ planes destroyed.

Invalided back to Canada, after the war he engaged in various aviation ventures. At the start of WW2 McCall joined the RCAF, serving at several training schools and becoming CO of No 7 ITS Saskatoon, Sask., as well as of the Administrative Unit, NWAC Edmonton, Alta. He died in Calgary, Alta., in 1949. The airport that opened there in 1956 was named for him.

DSO MC & Bar DFC   Capt   Born Dec 4 1894   Died Jan 22 1949
RefScs: AIC 27   CAHF 98   CFA 263–70   DHist bf 98   OMAP(1) 86
TBYW 92–94 96 app

McDONALD Edwin Richard

"Only Canadian NCO Observer in the RAF"

By the time he joined the RFC in March 1918, Ed McDonald of Sheenboro, P.Q., had already been decorated for bravery. Serving with the Canadian army in France, he was awarded the French Croix de Guerre. Shortly after his transfer McDonald was posted to 98 Squadron, by then an RAF unit. Flying DH 9s, he made forty-one daylight bombing raids and was credited with destroying seven German planes. McDonald himself was shot down and made a POW on August 9, 1918. By that time he had been awarded another French decoration: the Medaille Militaire. After the war McDonald became a railway locomotive engineer, a job he held for forty years. He died in 1960.

MM(Fr) CdeG(Fr)   Sgt   Born Sept 16 1894   Died 1960
RefScs: ST 7   TBYW app

McEWEN Clifford MacKay

"Bomber Chief Devised Fighter-Escort Tactics"

As a WW1 scout pilot, this Commander of Canada's largest aerial combat force in WW2 was instrumental in revising tactics for escorting bombers to and from their targets. "Black Mike" McEwen, who was born in Griswold, Man., went overseas with the Western Universities' Battalion in 1916 and the following year transferred to the RFC. Completing his flying training in October 1917, he was posted to 28 Squadron. Equipped with Sopwith Camels, McEwen's squadron served briefly in France before being sent to Italy. There over Liential, on December 30, McEwen shared in the destruction of an observation balloon and next day shot down his first plane, an Austrian-piloted Albatros. As he gained experience he and his comrades became increasingly frustrated with the close support tactics used to escort bombers. Instead of waiting for the enemy, they evolved a strategy of breaking up enemy formations *before* they could make their attack. With this method the squadron's and McEwen's own tally of Austrian planes began to mount. A successful demonstration of

Photo courtesy Canadian War Museum.

this theory occurred on June 19, 1918, when, with two others, McEwen put a formation of Bergs to flight before they could reach the bombers. Downing one in the process, McEwen found himself alone among five enemy planes and made his escape by flying low through the narrow Astico Valley. By war's end McEwen had 24½ planes to his credit, had been awarded the MC, DFC and Bar, and had been decorated twice — by the French and Italians.

In peacetime he served in the RCAF in a number of posts including CO of Trenton, Ont., which would become a focal point of the BCATP.

In February 1942 McEwen was posted overseas, where he became CO of two bomber stations before being appointed AOC of 6 Group RCAF Bomber Command. To his aircrews he was the inspirational commander who, over the objections of his superiors, often "went along for the ride." Under his command the group had the lowest casualties while delivering the highest number of sorties and the highest amount of destructiveness of any other squadron. By war's end it had dropped 126,122 tons of bombs, destroyed 116 aircraft and sunk or damaged 438 ships. McEwen left the RCAF in 1946 after thirty years of military service. In retirement he served as national vice-president of the Canadian Legion, vice-president of the Dominion Council of the Last Post and as a director of TCA.

CB MC DFC & Bar Ld'H(Fr) LOM(Am) MV(It) CdeG(It) Maj A/V/M(RCAF) Born July 2 1896 Died Aug 6 1967
RefScs: CA 64 87 CFP 19 102–22 140 DHist bf OMAP(1) 97 RS&A 19 26 47 211 213–14 TBYW 77 79 app TSBW 38 41 155 194

When I asked Mike where the prefix "Black" came from he replied, "Nothing sinister. I tan very easily and to a dark shade."

McKEEVER Andrew Edward

" 'Hawkeye,' Top Allied Two-Seater Ace"

Andy McKeever's score of thirty enemy planes destroyed — with his observer's help — was unrivalled by any other two-seater pilot on either side. A native of Listowel, Ont., McKeever joined the CEF at the outbreak of WW1, transferring to the RFC and qualifying as a pilot in December 1916. In May 1917 he was posted to 11 Squadron at Estree-Blanche, which was converting to Bristol Fighters. He shot down his first and second planes on June 26. Then on July 7 he scored a triple kill; and on July 10 and July 13 he accounted for another three, making his tally eight planes destroyed within two weeks. This feat not only won him the MC, it also earned him the nickname "Hawkeye." As he continued to add to his score, a Bar to the decoration followed at the end of August. On September 28 he posted his second triple kill.

But McKeever's outstanding day was November 30. He and his observer were well behind enemy lines strafing troops when suddenly nine German machines confronted them, four in front, five behind. McKeever flew his Bristol headlong at the quartet in front, shooting three of them down while his observer destroyed one and damaged another. Now, with his machine badly riddled and both guns out of action, McKeever side-slipped to within twenty feet of the ground and cut his engine, giving the impression he was about to land. He then gunned the engine, zoomed up and made his escape. Both he and his observer were decorated for this action, McKeever with the DSO, his gunner a Bar to the MC. McKeever ended the war as the first CO of No 1 Squadron CAF.

After the cessation of hostilities, McKeever returned to Listowel. On September 3, 1919, he was on his way to New York to take over as manager of Minneola airport when he had a car accident, sustaining injuries from which he never recovered. He died Christmas Day, 1919.

DSO MC & Bar CdeG(Fr)   Maj   Born Aug 21 1894   Died Dec 25 1919
RefScs: CA 84   CCMA 7   CFA 177–283   CFP 61–65   DHist bf
TBYW 96–98 180

McLEOD Alan Arnott

" 'Devoid of Fear' — Won VC at Age Eighteen"

The youngest man to win the VC in WW1, Alan McLeod showed an affinity for military life at an early age. At 14 he attended summer army camp and when the war started, although he was only 16, tried to join the army but was refused. At 17 he applied for admission to the cadet wing of the RFC in Toronto and was turned down again. But on his eighteenth birthday, April 23, 1917, he was accepted for training as a pilot.

That fall, after training on Curtiss JN4s at Long Branch, Deseronto and Camp Borden, Ont., McLeod sailed for England where he flew BEs and heavy Big Ack biplanes. On November 29, 1917, he joined 2 Squadron at Hesdigneul in France; flying the lumbering Armstrong Whitworth machines, the squadron had been assigned night bombing, photography and artillery cooperation. On many of his first sorties McLeod, whom one of his observers described as being "devoid of fear," encountered enemy fighters and even at the controls of such a cumbersome aircraft as the Armstrong Whitworth was always ready to give battle. On January 14, 1918, he was mentioned in dispatches for shooting down an observation balloon while his aircraft was attacked by an Albatros. By skillfully maneuvering his bomber McLeod placed his observer in a position to destroy the enemy fighter.

In March the Germans began their final offensive of the war and on

RE 18695-1

the morning of the twenty-seventh McLeod's squadron was ordered to bomb enemy installations deep behind the lines. The weather could not have been worse for such an assignment; soon McLeod and his observer were separated from the rest of the formation and lost in thick fog. Turning west, they managed to find one of their own airfields, but on landing the tail skid broke and they had to wait until a tender could bring up a replacement from their own base.

After lunch they took off again and this time were able to find the target area around Albert, close to where the Richthofen Circus was stationed. McLeod and his observer were getting ready to bomb a German battery from 3,000 feet, just under the clouds, when a red Fokker triplane from the Circus pounced on them from above. McLeod put his observer into firing position and after three short bursts the enemy plane spun into the ground. The two airmen were congratulating each other when suddenly the clouds broke to reveal seven triplanes etched against a clear blue sky. One of the planes opened fire. It dived so close, mere feet away, that when McLeod's observer opened fire at point-blank range he couldn't miss and sent it spiralling down in flames.

But at that moment another Fokker swooped up from behind and below the Armstrong Whitworth and bullets struck the fuselage and gas tank, setting the plane on fire and wounding both pilot and observer. The floor of the observer's cockpit and seat fell away, so he climbed up on the ring above it. McLeod wriggled out onto the lower wing; by controlling the joy stick from a standing position he put the machine into a steep side-slip to blow flames away from the two airmen. Another German pilot, thinking them finished, came so close the wounded observer could make out his face. Though one of his arms was useless, he nevertheless managed to shoot the plane down. Now another Fokker attacked, putting the observer's gun out of action; the Fokker's bullets continued striking the bomber again and again as McLeod maneuvered it down to the ground, where he crash-landed in a shell hole. Both men were thrown clear but the blazing wreckage set off eight heavy bombs as well as 1,000 rounds of ammunition. Though neither were hit by the explosion, the observer fainted from loss of blood.   Now caught between the lines the two men were in danger of being targets for German machine-gun fire. Though McLeod had five wounds of his own, he dragged his partner toward their own lines and was again wounded. Finally he collapsed from exhaustion just as members of a South African infantry regiment came to their rescue. They found McLeod unconscious yet still firmly grasping the collar of his observer.

Both McLeod and his observer recuperated from their wounds and, after being invested with the VC by King George V in September, McLeod returned home to Stonewall, Man. He was well on his way to recovery when he fell victim to the influenza epidemic. With the weakened condition of his lungs McLeod quickly succumbed and died in Winnipeg, Man., on November 6, 1918.

VC MID Lt Born Apr 20 1899 Died Nov 6 1918 Ind CAHF 1973
RefScs: CA 83 CAHF 48 CCMA 5 CFA 215–33 CFP 55–61
DHist bf OMAP(1) 32 TBYW 90 175–78 app

MULOCK Redford Henry

"Canada's Most Versatile Airman of WW1"

R ed Mulock held the distinction of being the most experienced combat pilot, aerial leader, administrator, and organizer of any Canadian in WW1. His proficiency ranged from Zeppelin hunting to attacking submarines, dog-fighting, artillery spotting, photographic reconnaissance, and tactical as well as strategic bombing. In fact, by war's end he was the RAF's chief bomber commander.

Born and raised in Winnipeg, Man., in 1915 Mulock transferred to the RNAS from the CEF with the rank of corporal; on March 9 he qualified as the first Canadian in the British air services to receive a pilot's licence. Posted to No 2 Squadron, on the night of May 16/17, flying an Avro biplane, he became the first pilot to fire at a Zeppelin. On July 8 he joined No 1 Naval Wing, equipped with single- and two-seater Nieuports, and began flying such diverse missions as fighter patrols, bombing sorties, photographic reconnaissance flights, as well as directing naval fire. During this time he also earned the notoriety of being the first Canadian to attack a submarine as well as the first pilot to spot for artillery at night — with the use of parachute flares. By the end of the year Mulock had already been mentioned in dispatches. On January 24, 1916, after a second mention, he shot down his first enemy plane and two days later scored another victory. He was again mentioned in dispatches in March and made a flight commander of C Squadron. That same month he was credited with probably destroying three aircraft. Then in June he received the DSO.

In the winter of 1916/1917, when 3 Naval Squadron was formed, Mulock took over as CO. While under his leadership between February and June of 1917, the unit claimed eighty successful combats flying Sopwith Pups. In September Mulock left the squadron to take charge of rebuilding the RNAS depot at St-Pol, which had been destroyed by bombing. Then in March of the following year he was posted to RNAS Dunkirk HQ. On June 13, 1918, 82 Bomber Wing of the Independent Force RAF was formed under his command with the objective of hammering at targets in Belgium and northwest Germany. Late in July Mulock returned to England to organize 27 Group, a special force consisting of two wings of monster "Super" Handley Page four-engine V/1500 bombers designed to strike deep into Germany. On the morning of November 11 one squadron stood ready on the line to take off with Berlin as the intended target. Then shortly before 11:00 a.m. a cancellation order arrived that scrubbed the operation. It read: ARMISTICE.

In 1919 Mulock received the CBE for his wartime service, the only

PMR 71-406

Canadian to do so, and the only one to reach the rank of Colonel in the RAF. He retired from the service that same year and returned to Canada. In peacetime he was active in the aircraft industry and the RCAF reserve, with which he served during WW2. In 1938 he became a member of the Honorary Advisory Air Council made up of noted wartime fliers. He died in Montreal, P.Q., in 1961 at the age of 82.

CBE DSO & Bar MID(3) Ld'H   Col   Hon A/C (RCAF)   ADC(GG)
Born Aug 11 1888   Died Jan 23 1961
RefScs: AIC 27   CA 77 87   DHist bf   OMAP(1) 56 88   SY 460–61
TBYW 112–25 app   TSBW 116

NASH Gerald Ewart

"POW Witnessed Funeral of German Who Shot Him Down the Day Before"

G erry Nash from Stoney Creek, Ont., the "Black Sheep" of Collishaw's "Black Flight" with 10 Naval Squadron, watched from a cell window as the coffin of the pilot who had shot him down less than twenty-four hours earlier was carried to its grave. Nash, who joined the RNAS in 1916, was one of the original five members of the flight formed in late May 1917 that had its Sopwith triplanes partially painted black, each with a white-painted distinctive name, Nash's being "Black Sheep." With a score of five enemy planes destroyed to his credit, Nash was the first one of the flight to be shot down, an event that took place over Quesnoy on June 25 when the flight clashed with a squad of Albatros scouts. Nash was brought down behind enemy lines by Karl Allmenroeder, who had shot down thirty Allied planes. Nash was shaken and he had injured his leg in the crash, but he was unhurt and spent the rest of the war as a prisoner. However, Collishaw himself ended Allmenroeder's career — the day after the German ace shot down Nash. In WW2 Nash served with the RCAF and retired in 1945.

Lt G/C(RCAF)   Born May 12 1896
RefScs: CFP 81–83   DHist bf   OMAP(1) 88   TBYW 59–63 app

PEACE William James

"Played Dual Role: Bomber-Leader and Instructor

T oward the end of his tour as a bomber pilot Bill Peace not only participated in operations but also instructed his squadron's pilots who had had no previous Handley Page experience. Peace joined the

RNAS in 1916 and in the fall of the following year the Hamiltonian was posted to 7 Naval Squadron based at Coudekerque, France. From there it conducted raids on German naval installations at Bruges and Ostend as well as on German airfields and ammunition dumps in Belgium. On Peace's ninth raid he crashed in heavy fog. In the spring of 1918 the squadron was re-equipped with more powerful Handley Pages and returned to France in June to bomb railway lines, bridges and railway stations. Late in August, after making thirty-nine raids, Peace was transferred to 207 Squadron at Ligecourt as a flight commander. Between instructional flights he managed to complete a further sixteen raids; his last, on November 9 against a railway junction, resulted in a forced landing when his engine seized. After the war, in 1930, the Federal Department of Transport hired him to locate airport sites throughout Ontario for its use. In WW2 he served in the RCAF as a pilot instructor. He died in 1981.

DFC   Capt F/L(RCAF)   Born Aug 14 1893   Died Apr 14 1981
RefScs: ST(1) 8   TBYW 168 app

QUIGLEY Frances Granger

"Aerial Duellist-cum-Strafing Specialist"

During the final German offensive of WW1, Frances Quigley, hitherto noted for his aerial combat skills, briefly became one of the deadliest ground attack scout pilots on the Western Front. Before transferring to the RFC in the spring of 1917 he had fought for two years in the trenches with the CEF; he knew full well — from experience — the demoralizing effect aerial attacks made on troops. In July, having completed his pilot's training, he joined 70 Squadron at Estree-Blanche, which had just been equipped with Sopwith Camels. From the outset Quigley showed an aptitude for air fighting that quickly brought him a mention in dispatches and, as he began to run up a score of planes destroyed, also brought him the MC that fall. At the time of the German offensive in March 1918, by which time the squadron had moved to Vert Galand, Quigley was engaged in troop strafing and in four days fired 3,000 rounds of ammunition and dropped over thirty bombs. In the process he also brought down several German airplanes. An award of the DSO quickly followed. Shortly afterward he destroyed an observation balloon, for which he received a Bar to his MC. By May 1 Quigley's score totalled thirty-four aircraft shot down. A few days later, however, his ankle was shattered by an enemy bullet and he ended up in hospital.

Sent back to Canada, that summer Quigley became an instructor with the RAF in his native Toronto, Ont. Fully recovered from his wounds by September, he requested a return to combat duty. Though it was granted he never made it. With the global influenza epidemic at its zenith, he contracted the virus while aboard ship enroute to England and died in a Liverpool hospital.

DSO MC & Bar MID Born July 10 1894 Died Oct 18 1918
RefScs: AIC 187 CFA 271–72 DHist bf OMAP(1) 89 TBYW app
TSBW 10

REDPATH Ronald Francis

"Starred in War's First Combined British-French Strategic Bombing Raid"

On October 12, 1916, Ronald Redpath saved his flight and probably countless others from internment in Switzerland when, through a navigational error on their way home from a raid on the Mauser arm works at Oberndorf, the planes were inadvertantly headed for neutral territory. Redpath calmly cut sharply in front of the formation heading it off in the right direction.

Born in Montreal, P.Q., Redpath graduated from the Curtiss Flying School in Toronto, Ont. On joining the RNAS, he was posted in the late summer of 1916 to 3 Naval Wing at Luxeuil-les-Bains in France, where he flew Sopwith Strutter fighters as bomber escort. The Oberndorf mission marked the Wing's first large-scale raid and the first combined strategic raid by the Allies. Made up of eighty British and French fighters and bombers, the formation dropped 3,900 pounds of bombs and, along the 233-mile route to and from the target, encountered German fighters. Redpath flew with the wing until March 1917 when he was posted to several RNAS fighter squadrons in the Dunkirk area. At the end of 1917, by which time Redpath had received the Croix de Guerre from the French, he was assigned instructional duty for the remainder of the war. Following the Armistice Redpath joined the CAF and became its second Director from March 22 to July 12, 1921.

CdeG(Fr) Lt W/C(RCAF) Born July 7 1888 Died Jan 11 1970
RefScs: CCMA app TBYW 145 147 149 150 app

REID Ellis Vair

"Baby of the Black Flight"

Ellis Reid, the youngest member of the "Black Flight" — Ray Collishaw's covey of five black-painted Sopwith triplanes — ran up his record of eighteen kills in only two months of aerial combat. Born in Belleville, Ont., he enlisted in the RNAS in 1916 and in November was posted to 3 Wing in France. In May 1917 he joined 10 Naval Squadron at Dorglandt. For the next 2½ months, until his death, he flew his "Black Roger." His first victory came on June 1 when he shot down over Menen a German Albatros DIII from 16,000 feet. A month later he had been recommended for the DSC. On July 27, the day before he was killed, he destroyed two planes and sent another out of control. Next day Reid added another to his string before he went missing, the second Black Flight pilot to lose his life. With one other a POW and only two of five originals left the flight *per se* ceased to exist.

DSC Lt   Born Oct 31 1889   KIA July 28 1917
RefScs: CFP 81   DHist bf   OMAP(1) 90   TBYW 59–61 64–67 152

ROGERS George Clarence

"Unfazed by Dangers of Reconnaissance Missions"

George Rogers was so impervious to the hazards of German flak while directing artillery fire that he would take on any task. Time after time Rogers returned with his BE2c or RE8 two-seater machine so shredded by enemy gun-fire that often observers refused to fly with him. Undaunted, he flew missions by himself. A native of Brandon, Man., when WW1 broke out Rogers left his job as an engineer to enlist in the CEF. Sent overseas, in September 1916 he became attached to the RFC in France before returning to England to train as a pilot. When 52 Squadron arrived in France at Christmas that year, Rogers was one of its eighteen members. His aggressiveness earned him the admiration of his fellow officers — even those who wouldn't fly with him — all of whom he outlasted. But on October 27, 1917, his luck finally ran out. While on an artillery observation patrol Rogers' aircraft was attacked by a German fighter and a bullet struck him in the thigh.

Although he lost a great deal of blood, he nevertheless managed to get his shot-up RE8 back to his field. But Rogers never recovered from his wound and died three days later.

MC Lt Born 1892 DOW Oct 30 1917
RefScs: ST(1) 10 TBYW 36 app

ROGERS William Wendell

"Conquered Gotha Impregnability"

W illiam Rogers shot down the first Gotha bomber to be destroyed over the Western Front. No mean feat in itself, but its significance lay in the fact that he had uncovered the huge German bomber's vulnerability. Born in Alberton, P.E.I., in 1916 Rogers was recruited by the RFC in Canada and sailed to England where he received his pilot's training. On May 18, 1917, he joined 1 Squadron, a scout unit flying Nieuports at Bailleul. By the end of November he had shot down eight enemy planes and was a flight commander. At this time the British had been concerned about the appearance of the Gothas over France. This was the "English" Squadron, originally formed to bomb London, now employed in the additional role of bombing troops. Although the raids were made in daylight, the Gotha crews regarded British fighters as little more than an annoyance. Bristling with guns, the crews relied on crossfire from their formations to protect them from attack. To the scout pilots they were considered unassailable.

Rogers had other ideas. He had studied the construction of the huge aircraft and found that while the rear gunner could fire above and, through an opening in the underbelly, below as well, he could not fire horizontally without shooting off his own tail. Rogers calculated that if he attacked at the same level from behind he could aim with comparative safety. On December 12 he had the chance to put his theory into action. Leading a patrol of two other Nieuports, Rogers climbed to attack a formation of Gothas at 10,000 feet over Armentieres. As they came within range the contrast between the fighters and their targets was startling: the Gothas were three times the size of the Nieuports. However, Rogers was not put off. Just as he had planned Rogers closed in behind the tail of one of the bombers lagging behind the others. The move called for precise flying to avoid being hit by the bullets being fired above and below him from the rear turret. When he was within thirty feet, after firing more than sixty rounds, Rogers saw the bomber veer left and start a

RE 64-2932

slow glide. Then black smoke belched from it and the gas tank caught fire. At 4,000 feet two of its occupants leapt from the plane to their deaths. Then it exploded and flaming wreckage fluttered down between the trenches.

This victory was viewed with the utmost importance by the RFC because it showed that the Gothas could now be successfully attacked. It also had an effect on the morale of the Gotha crews who could no longer regard their bombing behemoths as impregnable. Rogers was awarded the MC and shortly after took up instructional duties with the RAF in Canada for the rest of the war. In peacetime he operated a car business and became the moving spirit behind the Saint John Flying Club in New Brunswick. In WW2 Rogers enlisted in the RCAF, attaining the rank of Squadron Leader.

MC Capt S/L(RCAF) Born Nov 10 1896 Died Jan 11 1967
RefScs: CFA 237–46 DHist bf OMAP(1) 90 TBYW 194 app

A week after Rogers' Gotha victory an Australian army colonel was a guest at dinner in the 1 Squadron mess. He told of having seen the fight and how his troops had recovered some of the wreckage; the colonel wished he could find the pilot responsible so he could give him some of the pieces as a souvenir. Whereupon one of his hosts told him the victor was the man sitting next to him. A canvas from the wing displaying the Black Cross was later donated by Rogers to the Byng Boys' Club in Saint John where it adorned the ceiling of the lounge.

ROSEVEAR Stanley Wallace

"Destroyed Entire German Company"

In October 1917, flying close support to a British infantry attack in Flanders, Stan Rosevear of Walkerton, Ont., wiped out an entire German company. At the time Rosevear, who was officially credited with shooting down twenty-four German planes by the end of the war, already had six to his credit. For that and for his army cooperation work he was awarded the DSC. After joining the RNAS in 1916 and completing his pilot's training, he was posted to 1 Naval Squadron in 1917 (later 201 RAF when the RFC and RNAS merged); the squadron was then flying Sopwith triplanes and later Camels. A strong advocate of target practice, he nearly lost his life in his first combat when he approached an enemy scout at too-close range. By March 1918 he was made a flight commander. His career came to an end on April 25, 1918, when, while diving vertically on a ground target, his aircraft failed to flatten out.

DSC & Bar MID(3) Capt Born Mar 1896 KFA Apr 25 1918
RefScs: DHist bf ST(2) 4 TBYW app

RUSSELL John Bernard

"Achieved Ace Status as an Observer"

John Russell was one of the few Canadian observers to become an ace in WW1. After joining the RFC he was posted to 103 Squadron and, flying DH 9s, made eighty-three long-range bombing raids into Germany within a period of four months; on many of these raids he and his pilot were heavily engaged by German fighters. On September 18, 1918, the pair participated in a lone attack on a train and mechanical transport deep inside enemy territory. A particularly daring exploit; they not only had to face heavy anti-aircraft and machine-gun fire but the sortie was carried out at low level, for which their DH 9 was totally unsuited. During his tour Russell shot down five planes and was awarded the DFC.

DFC Lt Born June 5 1894 Died 1960
RefScs: DHist bf TBYW 213 app TSBW 21

SCOTT James Stanley

"Train-Buster Became Second RCAF Director"

J immy Scott, who was born in Roberval, P.Q., began his military career
as an army gunner but soon switched to flying. He transferred to
the RFC as a pilot in 1915 and quickly distinguished himself as an artillery
observation pilot on the Western Front. In July 1916 Scott was decorated
with the MC for his work in attacking trains. In the fall of that year
he returned to Canada as an instructor and eventually became CO of
Camp Borden Flying Training School in Ontario.

In 1919 Scott was appointed Superintendent of the Certificate Branch
of the Air Board; from 1921 to 1922 he commanded the CAF. After
attending the RAF Staff College he became the second Director of the
RCAF, a post he held from May 1924 to February 1928, when he retired
from the service. Re-enlisting in 1940, he was given various training
commands during WW2, including SASO of Nos 1 and 2 Training
Commands in Toronto, Ont., and Winnipeg, Man., successively. Scott
retired in 1944 and at age 86 died in Ketch Harbor, N.S.

MC AFC ED Maj G/C(RCAF) Born Feb 18 1889 Died July 19 1975
RefScs: CA 103 119 CCMA 7 29 22 CFH 145 DHist bf SY 27
TBYW app TSBW 22 35 37 46 53 59

SHARMAN John Edward

"Black Flight Elder"

T hough he was never a member of Ray Collishaw's "Black Flight",
Sharman flew with him in the same unit and his Sopwith triplane
was ominously christened the "Black Death." A native of Oak Lake,
Man., Sharman had already distinguished himself before joining 10 Naval
Squadron. Having enlisted in the RNAS in February 1916, that summer
he reported to 3 Naval Wing. On October 12 Sharman participated in
a raid on the Oberndorf munitions plant, the unit's first large-scale bombing
raid. During a raid on the Burbach blast furnaces in the Saar in January
he shot down a German monoplane. On April 14 he became the only
pilot to fly both attacks on Freiburg im Breisgau, leading the raids on
each occasion. By the time he joined No 10 Squadron at Dorglandt

in May he had been awarded the DSC. In July, as his score of victories began to mount, he received a Bar to the decoration. Then on July 22, in a dogfight between Ypres and Messines, his aircraft was hit by anti-aircraft fire and exploded. By the time he met his death he had shot down nine enemy machines.

DSC & Bar CdeG(Fr) Capt Born Sept 11 1892 KIA July 22 1917
RefScs: DHist bf OMAP(1) 91 TBYW 59–60 64–66 149–51 app

SHERREN Percy Clark

"One of the Original Train-Busters"

Percy Sherren excelled at attacks on ammunition trains. An example was a raid on Hirson junction on November 16, 1916, when he led a squad of six Martinsyde Elephant single-seaters eighty miles behind the lines, a flight of over two hours. Two of the aircraft acted as escort while the other four dropped eight 112-pound bombs on their targets from 1,000 feet. Six railway coaches were blown off the tracks, rolling stock on the sidings were destroyed and two station buildings were demolished. Such actions won Sherren, who was born in Crapaud, P.E.I., the MC and Bar. Early in the war he had gone to Europe with the CEF. Transferring to the RFC in 1916 he joined 27 Squadron on the Western Front in August with which he flew until early 1917. Several months before the war ended he was given command of 98 Squadron, flying DH 9s on bombing raids. Sherren remained in the RAF after the war and saw service in Waziristan during the 1920s. He was killed in 1937 while flying in the King's Cup Race.

MC & Bar Maj W/C(RCAF) Born July 20 1893 KFA Sept 10 1937
RefScs: DHist bf TBYW 162–63 app TSBW 21

SHIELDS William Ernest

"Took on Fourteen Fokkers and Got Away with It"

On September 18, 1918, on a lone offensive patrol, William Shields was attacked by fourteen German Fokker triplane scouts. He not only extricated himself from his predicament but in the process shot one of the enemy fighters down before making his escape. Born in Lipton, Sask., Shields joined the RFC and served with 41 Squadron on the Western Front, with which he won the DFC and Bar.

By the end of WW1 his number of victories stood at twenty-three, which included several observation balloons. In 1921 Shields was killed in a flying accident at High River, Alta.

DFC & Bar   Capt   Born Oct 15 1892   KFA Aug 1 1921
RefScs: OMAP(1) 91   TBYW app

SHOEBOTTOM Lionel Robert

"Made Two Successive Raids Lasting Ten Hours"

In the summer of 1918 Lionel Shoebottom, flying Handley Page bombers with 217 Squadron of the Independent Force RAF, returned from a daylight raid to find that another long-distance attack had been planned for that night. Though he had just spent 4¼ hours in the air he immediately volunteered for the night sortie and put in another 5¾ hours. His total flying time within that twelve-hour period was ten hours.

Shoey, who was known as the "little train," was born in Lucknow, Ont., and in 1916 was accepted by the RNAS for pilot training. By the fall of 1917 he was in action in France with 7 Naval Squadron at Coudekerque making regular bombing raids on German naval installations, airfields and ammunition dumps. During a six-month tour he flew twenty-seven night raids. His second tour was with 216 Squadron based in the southern sector of the French Front. All sixteen of the raids he made with that unit were in conjunction with the American and French armies.

While still on operations Shoebottom was asked to lend his expertise to develop modifications to the Handley Page bombers at an experimental station in England. Following the war he worked in England for an American-owned steel company, rising to become director of the British subsidiary that, during the Blitz of 1940/41, was the target of Nazi bombs. During one raid the explosions sent Shoebottom into shock from which he never fully recovered and he died on May 5, 1941.

DFC   Capt   Born July 28 1895   Died May 5 1941
RefScs: ST(1) 8   TBYW 165 app

SHOOK Alexander Macdonald

"Navy Pilot Star Leader"

A lexander Shook proved to be one of the great Canadian air leaders in WW1. From Tioga, Ont., he joined the RNAS at the beginning of the war and was posted to 5 Naval Wing in April 1916. He flew Caudrons on a number of bombing missions before illness forced him to return to England to convalesce. In October he went back into combat and became a flight commander in 4 Naval Squadron with which he shot down six enemy planes and led bombing attacks on enemy airfields, harbour installations and shipping. On July 4 he led a flight of five Sopwith Camels from his base at Bray Dunes near Dunkirk to intercept sixteen Gotha bombers. A running fight ensued in which Shook was certain he had shot one of the giant bombers down in flames. On July 27 he and two other pilots intercepted and headed off a Gotha, ostensibly on its way to bomb British naval ships. They were well inside enemy territory and despite heavy anti-aircraft fire Shook and one of his wingmen managed to attack the bomber and send it down. Though it was not seen to crash it was presumed to have been destroyed. Shook flew with the unit until July 1918 at which time he was posted to England as an instructor with the newly formed RAF.

DSO DSC AFC CdeG(Fr) Maj Born Dec 2 1888 Died May 30 1966
RefScs: DHist bf OMAP(1) 91 TBYW 156–57 193 app

STANGER Stanley

"Used Boots as Wheel Chocks to Assist Take-Off Escape from Austrians"

O n patrol over the Austrian lines in Italy on October 17, 1918, Stan Stanger suddenly lost consciousness. When he came to, he was less than 100 feet over a field, into which he promptly landed, only to discover he was in enemy territory. His first impulse was to burn his aircraft, but he opted instead to attempt a take-off even though space was limited. However, by using his flying boots as wheel chocks he was able to rev the engine sufficiently to get his Camel off the ground just as Austrian troops rushed him from less than fifteen yards away. When he landed at his base he passed out again. With 390 aerial combat hours to his credit, Stanger's fighting days were over.

Stanger, who was born in Montreal, P.Q., enlisted in the CEF and served in 1916 on the Somme as a dispatch rider. He then transferred to the RFC, trained as a pilot and was posted to 66 Squadron in France. When the unit moved to the Italian Front he quickly established a reputation as the smoothest Camel pilot in that theatre as well as an exceptional tactician in combat. After the incident in October 1918 he never flew again, but by that time he had tallied a score of 12½ aircraft shot down and had been awarded the MC and DFC. Following the war, in partnership with his brother, he formed the Guardian Trust Company. He died in 1967.

MC DFC   Capt   Born July 10 1894   Died Sept 10 1967
RefScs: DHist bf   ST(2) 4   TBYW 80 app

STEELE Robert Crawford

"Played Key Role in Allenby's Capture of Jerusalem"

R obert Steele became the star Canadian fighting pilot on the Palestinian Front. Born in Enniskillen, Ont., he joined the RFC in Canada in September 1916. After completing his pilot's training in England in March 1917 he was posted to 14 Squadron based at Deir el Balah in Egypt in support of Allenby's British forces against the Turks. Flying Martinsyde scouts, Steele was frequently called upon to play a bombing role on Turkish positions during the unsuccessful Battles of Gaza. In August he was transferred to 111 Squadron, then being formed as a fighter unit in preparation for an offensive into Palestine. On October 8 Steele and his observer scored the squadron's first victory when they brought down an Albatros D III behind the British lines. It was captured and flew with the squadron under British markings. For that feat Steele was awarded the DSO. A week later he and his observer attacked three Albatros fighters, shooting the wings off one of them to send it crashing into the ground. When the offensive to the north began at the end of the month Steele's squadron was engaged in escort work as well as fighter patrols. In December the unit moved to Jerusalem and was re-equipped with SE 5s. Steele remained with the squadron until mid-February 1918, when he was sent back to England.

DSO   Capt   Born Apr 12 1890
RefScs: TBYW 229–30 app

STEPHENSON William Samuel

"The Man They Called Intrepid"

As a scout pilot in WW1 Bill Stephenson well lived up to the code name given him for his espionage activities a generation later. Born in Winnipeg, Man., he went overseas with the CEF to serve in the trenches; there he was gassed and invalided back to England. However, in 1917 he was accepted by the RFC and joined 73 Squadron on February 9, 1918; with this squadron he rose to become a flight commander flying Sopwith Camels. By the summer Stephenson had been credited with shooting down eight German planes and had been awarded the MC and DFC. The French added to his laurels by conferring upon him the Croix de Guerre.

On July 18 he flew to the rescue of a French reconnaissance machine being attacked by seven Fokker DVIIs. Although he successfully broke up the formation he was wounded in the leg and forced to crash-land behind enemy lines, where he was taken prisoner. In October he managed to escape. But by then the war was coming to a close and he never again flew in combat.

In peacetime Stephenson became wealthy as a businessman. When the prospects of war again loomed, he began organizing the intelligence network, known as the British Security Co-ordination office, in New York City, N.Y., which he headed up in WW2. From this office he directed all British counter-espionage, anti-espionage, economic warfare, and political and secret intelligence operations in North and South America. Churchill gave him the code name Intrepid. He was knighted for this contribution in 1945 and received the U.S. Medal of Merit. After the war Stephenson retired to Bermuda where, at age 93, he died.

MC DFC CdeG(Fr) MM(Am) Capt Born Jan 11 1896 Died Jan 31 1989
RefScs: AMCI 4–12 DHist bf TBYW app

STEVENSON William Gordon

"One of Independent Force's Most Durable Day-Bomber Pilots"

Many IF RAF aircrews regarded Bill Stevenson as an idol, calling him brave to a fault. "Steve," as his colleagues called him, was born in North Bay, Ont., and in December 1917 enlisted in the RFC.

After completing his pilot's training he was posted to 99 Squadron, the Independent Force RAF, flying DH 9s on daylight missions, Stevenson made his first air raid on May 20, 1918, against the Metz-Sablon railway triangle. His superiors were quick to recognize both his determination and his talents and on August 22, by which time he had flown twenty-two raids, he was given responsibility for leading the next one. This was the first of thirteen missions he would fly as leader. In all Stevenson made forty-two sorties; on four of these occasions he had to return without dropping his bombs.

Between wars Stevenson worked for the Toronto Department of Works and in WW2 served with the RCAF. Following the cessation of hostilities he returned to the TDW, where he stayed until his retirement.

DFC Capt F/L(RCAF) Born Nov 2 1891
RefScs: ST(1) 6 TBYW app

STEWART James Alexander

"Instructor-Turned-Bomber-Pilot Led His Squadron in Number of Raids"

A lex Stewart began his career as an RFC instructor at the Camp Borden school of aerial gunnery before becoming one of Canada's leading WW1 bomber pilots. Early in 1918 he was posted overseas where, in England, he joined 97 Squadron RAF, which was then being formed. In August the unit flew its Handley Pages to France. When it began operations on the night of August 19, Stewart was one of the five pilots who participated. By the end of the month he had flown on five raids. One of his most notable sorties was on September 13 in an attack on Frankfurt that lasted six hours. The squadron encountered vicious anti-aircraft fire. In the final months of the war heavy fog shrouded the front and reduced activity to a minimum; still, by the time his tour ended Stewart had logged nineteen raids, the record number for his squadron. Stewart left the RAF and returned to his native Montreal, P.Q. There, he worked for a men's dress shirt manufacturer and during WW2 was active with the Royal Canadian Air Cadets. In 1962 he retired and that same year died of a heart attack at Hudson Heights, P.Q.

DFC Lt Born 1895 Died 1962
RefScs: ST(1) 9 TBYW app

THOMSON George

"Scored Two Double Kills as an Observer"

On two separate occasions and from the back seat of his Bristol Fighter, RFC observer George Thomson of Celista, B.C., scored a double victory against attacking German fighters. The first incident occurred on July 10, 1918, when, as a member of 22 Squadron in France flying with eight others, he and his pilot were pounced upon by twenty German Fokker triplanes and Pfalz biplane fighters. The Bristols came out on top by knocking down ten of their assailants, two of them credited to Thomson. Ten days later while escorting bombers Thomson again shot two of the enemy out of the sky as well as driving down out of control a third. By war's end Thomson's score had reached nine planes destroyed, for which he was awarded the DFC.

DFC Lt S/L(RCAF)
RefScs: OMAP(1) 93 TBYW 214 app

THOMSON William MacKenzie

"Third-Ranking Canadian Two-Seater Ace"

With fifteen planes shot down to his credit, William Thomson ranked as the third-highest Canadian two-seater pilot in number of victories. Thomson came from Toronto, Ont., and enlisted in the RFC in Canada in 1917. On arrival overseas he was posted to 20 Squadron in France, which was equipped with Bristol Fighters. Several of his victories came against odds of three and four to one. During WW2 Thomson served with the RCAF and continued to do so until 1954.

MC DFC Lt Born Sept 15 1898 Died July 9 1987
RefScs: DHist bf OMAP(1) 93 TBYW 215 app

TURNBULL George Mark

" 'Busiest' Canadian on 'Busiest' Bomber Squadron"

In the spring of 1917 George Turnbull, who hailed from Mannville, Alta., joined 100 Squadron. The squadron became known as one of the busiest RFC bomber units at the Western Front, flying incessant night raids against German airfields. Turnbull proved to be one of its busiest pilots, making a total of forty raids that summer and fall, and was appointed a flight commander. For his efforts Turnbull was awarded the Belgian Croix de Guerre and later the AFC.

AFC CdeG(Bel) Capt Born April 19 1897 Died 1944
RefScs: DHist bf TBYW 163 app

WANKLYN Frederick Angus

"First Canadian Warbird"

M ontrealer Fred Wanklyn became the first Canadian to see operational service with the RFC. A graduate of RMC, he received a commission in the Royal Artillery in 1909 and quickly grasped the possibilities of military use for flying machines. In 1910 he visited Manchuria to study the battleground of the Russo-Japanese war of 1904/5. After assessing the costly Japanese capture of a hill overlooking Port Arthur to observe Russian naval activity, Wanklyn noted that "in days to come a man-lifting kite, a balloon or aeroplane could do the job."

With the formation of the RFC in May 1912 Wanklyn applied for transfer, received his pilot's certificate and was seconded to the British flying service. At the outbreak of WW1 he took over command of 4 Squadron at St Omer, France. Wanklyn then transferred to 5 Squadron flying the Vickers "Gun Bus," the first truly aerial fighting machine. In June 1915 headquarters mentioned him in dispatches and awarded him the MC. That December he joined 15 Squadron, which was engaged in artillery spotting with Henri Farmans. His final command at the Western Front was as CO of 9 Squadron, which was equipped with BE2c reconnaissance machines and with which he remained until mid-1916; Wanklyn then received orders to take over an experimental station in England.

In July 1917 he returned to Canada as a staff officer with the RFC training scheme. Following the cessation of hostilities Canada's earliest air warrior returned to the Royal Artillery. He retired in 1928

MC MID Lt/Col Born Aug 14 1888
RefScs: DHist bf TBYW 25–26 app

WATKINS Loudon Pierce

"First Canadian to Down a Zeppelin Over England"

Pierce Watkins joined the RFC in 1915 after graduating from the Curtiss Flying School in his native Toronto, Ont. In 1916 he served with Nos 7 and 21 Squadrons in France before being assigned to 37 Home Defense Squadron stationed at Goldhanger that December.

After two unsuccessful attempts to track down Zeppelins in March and May, Watkins finally scored his major triumph on June 17, 1917. That night he took off and climbed to 8,000 feet over his field then, still climbing, flew east toward Harwich on the coast, just south of Felixstowe. When he reached 11,000 feet he sighted a Zeppelin 2,000 feet above him. After climbing another 500 feet he tilted his twin Lewis guns upward and opened fire — to no effect. He fired again. Still no result. Now he waited until he came within 500 feet of the dirigible and emptied the remainder of his drums into the Zeppelin's tail. Suddenly the rear portion caught fire. Then flames sizzled along both sides, quickly turning the airship into a burning hulk of wreckage as it crashed into a field just outside of town. Miraculously two of the five-man crew survived. Another pilot had joined in the attack but Watkins was given credit for the kill and awarded the MC. After his home duty tour Watkins returned to France flying FE2b night-bombers with 48 Squadron. He was killed returning from a raid in July 1918.

MC   Capt   Born Sept 7 1892   KIA July 1 1918
RefScs: DHist bf   OMAP(1) 100   TBYW 187–88 app

This marked the first time a Canadian had shot down a Zeppelin over Britain, although until now that feat has been hitherto erroneously accredited to Wulstan Tempest, who destroyed a Zeppelin on the night of October 12, 1916. Tempest was born in England and homesteaded in Perdue, Sask., for three years before the war. In 1914 he returned to England to join the British army. That hardly qualifies him as a Canadian.

WEMP Bert Stirling

"First Canadian DFC Recipient Became Toronto Mayor"

In 1918 Bert Wemp of Tweed, Ont., became the first Canadian to win the DFC, a medal struck especially for the newly amalgamated RAF.

AH 591

Wemp received the award for his numerous bombing and reconnaissance flights. In 1915, having graduated from the Curtiss Flying School in Toronto, Ont., he joined the RNAS. One of his first missions came on April 25, 1916, when, while flying from Great Yarmouth air station, he bombed a German battle cruiser squadron sailing off Yarmouth. In 1918, when 218 Squadron RAF was formed at Dover, Wemp was given command with instructions to take it to Petit Synthe on the continent. Equipped with DH 9s, the squadron engaged in daylight raids on German bases and airfields in Belgium and around Lille. By war's end he had also been decorated with the French Croix de Guerre and the Belgian Order of Leopold in addition to the DFC.

After the war Wemp returned to his original vocation, newspaper reporting, in Toronto. In 1929, after having served as a member of the board of education, as alderman, and as controller, he was elected mayor of the city. In WW2 he became a war correspondent. He died in 1976 from emphysema.

DFC CdeG(Fr) OL(Bel)   Maj   Born July 3 1889   Died Feb 6 1976
RefScs: DHist bf   TBYW 123 app

WHEALY Arthur Trealor

"Flew Record Number of Combat Hours"

W ith a total of 521 hours and 35 minutes flown on operations, Art Whealy of Toronto, Ont., posted one of the highest records of time spent in combat of any pilot in WW1. A graduate of the Curtiss Flying School in Toronto and Newport News, Va., Whealy joined the RNAS and in February 1916 sailed for England to complete his training. Later that year he joined 3 Naval Wing, a strategic bombing force stationed in the south of France, where he made one bombing raid into Germany before the wing was disbanded. He was then posted to 3 Squadron flying Sopwith Pup scouts. In July 1917 he became a flight commander with 203 Squadron flying Camels and was decorated with the DSC and Bar, and the DFC for destroying 21½ German aircraft. After an exceptionally long tour he was taken off operations in September 1918. Whealy died in St Marguerite, P.Q., in 1945.

DSC & Bar DFC MID   Capt   Born Nov 2 1895   Died Dec 23 1945
RefScs: DHist bf   ST(2) 5   TBYW 122 149 app

WHITE Joseph Leonard

"All Round Scout Pilot"

J oseph White from Halifax, N.S., not only showed exceptional air fighting prowess but also showed equal ability in strafing missions and in rendering valuable reconnaissance services. Going overseas with the Canadian Machine Gun Corps, he transferred to the RFC in September 1917 and, after completing his pilot training, was posted to 65 Squadron.

In one of his first encounters White and another pilot he was flying with were attacked by fourteen enemy scouts: one he shot down in flames and a second he shot down out of control. By the time his tour ended he had been credited with thirteen machines destroyed and had been decorated with the DFC and Bar as well as the French Croix de Guerre. Following the war White joined the CAF. On February 2, 1925, he was killed in a mid-air collision at Camp Borden, Ont.

DFC & Bar CdeG(Fr)   Capt   Born Jan 6 1897   KA Feb 2 1925
RefScs: OMAP(1) 95

WHITESIDE Arthur Barlow

"Made Night-Bombing Missions at Low Level"

B etween October 1917 and the end of April 1918 Arthur Whiteside flew some 100 night bombing raids, most of them in adverse weather conditions. Thus he was often forced to make some of his attacks well under 1,000 feet in the face of German anti-aircraft fire to assure placing his bombs accurately on the target. He often accompanied his incursions with machine-gun fire of his own. Born in Inverness, P.Q., Whiteside went overseas with the CEF and was wounded in Flanders in 1916 before joining the RFC. In 1917 he was posted to the Western Front to 102 Squadron, which was equipped with FE2bs. Their main targets were German ammunition dumps, rail centres and airfields. For his feats he was awarded the MC and Bar. Whiteside was killed in an accident in England in 1919 when his Handley Page failed to clear some buildings adjacent to the field from which he was taking off.

MC & Bar   Capt   Born Dec 13 1891   KFA Apr 23 1919
RefScs: ST(1) 7   TBYW 164 app

WILLIAMS Thomas Frederick

"Elderly Flight Commander Became World's Oldest Pilot"

I n 1971 at age 87 WW1 ace Tom Williams was still flying. But then he never did let age stand in his way. Born in Ingersoll, Ont., he joined 45 Squadron at the Western Front in 1917 having already served on

T.F. Williams (l.) 1577-295

the line for two years as an infantryman. The 31-year-old novice was elderly by RFC standards; however, he showed a ready aptitude for flying by soloing after less than four hours of instruction.

In December 1917, 45 Squadron was posted to the Italian Front and by the end of March Williams had destroyed ten aircraft with his Sopwith Camel, had received the MC, and was transferred to 28 Squadron as a flight commander. His main duty was escorting bombers on long-distance bombing and reconnaissance missions and, although he was shot-up three times, while under his protection not one bomber or fighter was lost. In July he had his narrowest escape when, having scored his final victory, he had to glide home twenty-one miles through mountain passes with his engine out of commission. Credited with eleven aircraft destroyed and three probables Williams, whom the Italians awarded their Medaglio Valori, was posted to Canada in August 1918 as an instructor.

Between wars Williams maintained his keen interest in aviation as a commercial pilot. In 1939 he became chief test pilot for the Fleet Aircraft Company and also test-dropped parachutes for Irvin Airchute Ltd. On retirement he bought a Fleet for pleasure. At 87 he finally relinquished his unofficial title as the world's oldest pilot when he let his licence lapse after fifty-six years as an aviator. He died in 1985, only a few months short of his one hundredth birthday.

MC MV(It) Capt Born Oct 12 1885 Died July 26 1985 Ind CAHF 1973
RefScs: CA 243 CAHF 80 DHist bf OMAP(1) 95 SY 454

We always invited Tom to our Canadian Fighter Pilots (WW2) reunions. He seldom came but always acknowledged the gesture, always in writing and always addressed to "You young whipper-snappers."

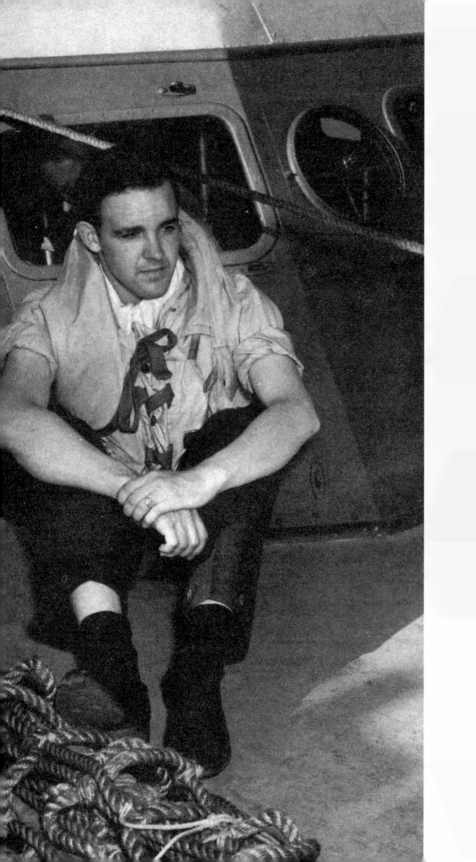

I n her brief military history Canada's principal contribution to the cause of freedom was the British Commonwealth Air Training Plan during World War II. During the period of 1939–45 this vast university of the air produced an arsenal of trained air crews from Australia, Britain and New Zealand, as well as from Canada herself. It inspired President Roosevelt to praise the Dominion as the "aerodrome of democracy."

The Royal Canadian Air Force (formed in 1924), which at the outbreak of hostilities numbered a mere 4,000 officers and men, grew to 249,662 men and women of all ranks to become the fourth largest air force in the world. In five years it trained a total of 131,553 aircrews — pilots, observers, navigators, gunners, wireless operators, flight engineers — from the Commonwealth as well as from some occupied countries. That aside, the RCAF posted a combat record of 38 squadrons that served overseas and another 28,500 Canadian airmen who served with the Royal Air Force. This is an impressive accomplishment even for a country that in two world wars produced more warriors per capita than any other nation.

AIKMAN Alan Frederick

"Served in Three Theatres"

A l Aikman of Toronto, Ont., served in the European and North African theatres on fighters as well as in Burma as a transport pilot. His operational career began with 134 Squadron RAF flying Spitfires over France. As a member of 154 Squadron he took part in operation Torch, the Allied invasion of northwest Africa in November 1942; by the end of the month Aikman had shot down three German bombers, shared in the destruction of two others and was credited with a probable and a damaged. Throughout the Tunisian campaign he continued to add to his list of aircraft destroyed. Except for a Junkers Ju 87 Stuka dive bomber, which he shot down on April 5, 1943, all his victories were single-seater fighters. As a flight commander, he destroyed a Focke-Wulf 190 and two Messerschmitt 109s between January 13 and April 25. His final victory came over Sicily on July 17 when he downed a Macchi C202 fighter, bringing his tally to 9½ destroyed, two probables and three damaged for which he received the DFC and Bar. In 1944–45 he flew another tour in Burma with 436 Transport Squadron RCAF flying Dakotas. He received his discharge from the air force in 1945.

DFC & Bar   F/L   Died 1991
RefScs: OMAP(2) 103   RCTFFY 335 f349   TDS 211   TTS 284

ANGELL Henry Ellis

"Led Transports in Three Major Airborne Operations"

F lying four-engine Stirling bombers, Henry Angell led his unit, 295 Squadron RAF, in three different airborne invasions: Normandy, the Arnhem campaign and the Rhine aerial crossing. A native of Bassano, Alta., Angell joined the RAF in 1937. After a lengthy career as a combat pilot he was made CO of 295 Squadron RAF in September 1944 then promoted to the rank of Wing Commander. In August 1945 he was awarded the DFC. After the war Angell remained in the service.

DFC   W/C
RefScs: DHist bf   RAW 423

ANGUS Allen Benjamin

"First Canadian WW2 Ace"

Allen Angus of Winnipeg, Man., became the first Canadian in WW2 to shoot down five German planes, making him the first of his countrymen to rank as an ace. Angus joined the RAF on September 27, 1937, as a student pilot and received his commission on November 28. On July 8 of the following year he joined 85 Squadron, the only RAF unit in WW1 to boast two VC COs: Billy Bishop (who formed it) and Mick Mannock. By May 1940 the squadron, by then equipped with Hurricane fighters, was assigned patrols covering the BEF advance into Belgium to meet the German invasion. On May 10, the opening day of the battle, Angus shot down a twin-engine Junkers Ju 88 bomber. Two days later he scored a double victory by bringing down a pair of Heinkel 111s. Then on May 14 he destroyed two more enemy planes. But his promising career came to an abrupt end when, two days later, he was shot down and killed.

DFC F/O Born May 10 1918 KIA May 16 1940
RefScs: DHist bf OMAP(2) 103 TTS 280

ANNIS Clare

"Made First RCAF Air Attack on a U-boat in North Atlantic Waters"

On October 25, 1941, Clare Annis of the North Atlantic Squadron 10 Bomber Reconnaissance RCAF made the first attack by Eastern Air Command on a German submarine. The assault failed because a crewman back at Digby left the depth-charges on safe; his target, the U-573, escaped unharmed. But the experience proved invaluable. Annis, who was born in Pickering, Ont., joined the RCAF in 1936; he soon established himself as the foremost expert on anti-submarine warfare. From April to August 1943, as CO of 10 BR, Annis supervised the squadron's conversion to Liberators. Subsequently he commanded the RCAF Station at Gander, Nfld., the air force's largest operational base at that time. In March 1944 Annis was sent overseas to command the RCAF bomber station at Linton-on-Ouse in Yorkshire. In 1945, after attending the RAF Staff College in London, he returned to Canada to become chief instructor of its counterpart in Toronto, Ont. Following the war he held several senior appointments and in January 1958 was made AOC Air Material Command.

OBE CD A/V/M   Born Jan 1912
RefScs: DHist bf   RAW 106–107   TCNAF 442 481–82 525 538 547
SY 466

ARTHUR Ian

"Three Fighter Tours with Seven Different Squadrons"

W ith a total of 448 operations in 717 hours and 30 minutes, "Duke" Arthur was the third-ranking Canadian fighter pilot in terms of operational sorties and hours flown. A native of Fort Garry, Man., Arthur joined the RAF in 1938 and shortly after WW2 broke out was posted to 141 Squadron with which he flew thirty operational sorties. The squadron flew Blenheims and Defiants; the latter, which resembled a Hurricane, had a gun turret in the rear but no forward firing armament. In its first encounter with German Messerschmitt 109s the squadron was cut to ribbons: four pilots and six air gunners were killed. Arthur was one of the few survivors.

In December 1940 he was transferred to 242 Squadron RAF, with which he finally flew his first bona fide fighter: the Hurricane. His duties included Rhubarbs — small-formation low-level raids against enemy coastal targets — as well as convoy patrols. By the following May, although he had logged another ninety-five operational sorties, Arthur had seen virtually no action. He next joined 145 Squadron RAF where he became a flight commander as part of the Tangmere wing under the legendary legless ace Douglas Bader. Flying a Spitfire with this outfit on June 25, 1941, during his 151st sortie, Arthur scored his first victory — over an ME 109 just inland from Le Touquet on a fighter sweep. Two days later his flight latched on to twelve other aircraft over France that they thought were friendly but discovered, to their horror, that they were Messerschmitts.

In October Arthur finished his first tour and, after a stint as an instructor, joined 411 Squadron; this the only time that he flew with an RCAF unit. By March 1943 he was posted to his old squadron 242 in Tunisia and spent the rest of his operational career in that theatre, first helping to clear North Africa of the Germans then aiding in the invasions of Sicily and Italy by following the Allied armies into Rome and beyond.

Arthur finished his second tour in February 1944 but returned to combat in April as CO of 72 Squadron RAF where he completed a third tour of sixty-nine operational flights. Following the war Arthur stayed in the RAF until 1954 then returned to Canada where he operated a water transport business in B.C. until 1971.

DFC & Bar W/C
RefScs: CWC 1–21

AUDET Richard Joseph

"Only Allied Pilot to Shoot Down Five German Planes in One Combat"

Two days before New Year's Day 1945 Dick Audet set a record never equalled by any other pilot in the RAF or RCAF by destroying five German aircraft in a single combat. As a section leader with 411 Squadron RCAF flying Spitfires, while leading a patrol at 10,500 feet between Osnabrück and Rheine over Germany, Audet spotted a Messerschmitt 262, the first jet fighter ever to see combat. At the same time he also sighted a dozen Focke-Wulf 190s and ME 109s. Audet bored right in to pick out the rear Messerschmitt, which he quickly sent down in flames. He then turned his attention to one of the 190s, setting it on fire. Now he slipped in behind a 109, sending it into a dive and forcing the pilot to bail out. Next he went to the rescue of another Spitfire pilot being chased by an FW 190. Audet closed to within 250 yards and let go a short burst. In seconds the enemy plane was plunging down on fire.

Still he wasn't through. The fight had brought him down to 4,000 feet. Now below him he saw a lone 190, which turned to face him head on. At 200 yards Audet pressed the gun button and a fifth victim fell crashing to the ground from his cannon and machine-gun fire. For his feat Audet received an immediate DFC.

Two days afterward he scored again shooting down a pair of FW 190s. Then on January 4, 1945, he brought down one FW 190 himself and shared another. Nine days later he destroyed another Focke-Wulf. On January 23 he decimated an ME 262 on the ground at Rheine airfield and another in the air on the way home, thus achieving the distinction of being the only RCAF pilot of the war to destroy two jet fighters. On the following day he damaged another. But with 11½ aircraft destroyed and one damaged to his credit, Audet's luck had begun to run out. On February 8 his aircraft was hit by flak and he had to bail out. Then on March 3, while attacking a train in the Münster area, his Spitfire

PL 41717

received a direct hit, burst into flames and fell from 500 feet to crash into a wood near Coesfeld, killing the pilot.

Audet's career was as ironic as it had been meteoric. Born in Lethbridge, Alta., he had graduated as a pilot in October 1942 but had to wait more than two years before bringing his guns to bear on an enemy plane, although by that time he had already completed fifty-two sorties. Then suddenly in one day he had become an ace. And in little over two months he had earned a Bar to his DFC only to lose his life, not in aerial combat but against a ground target.

DFC & Bar   F/L   Born Mar 13 1922   KIA Mar 3 1945
RefScs: AIC 201   CA 241   DHist bf   CCMA 73   OMAP(2) 33 104
RCTSY 239 244   TDS 29–31   TSBW 211   TTS 23–28 app

AVANT Alan Fredrick

"Flew Lancaster Back from Berlin with Wing on Fire and Plane Riddled"

On the night of March 29/30, 1943, while starting his bombing run over Berlin, Alan Avant of Hughton, Sask., a bomber captain with 115 Squadron RAF, suddenly found his Lancaster trapped in a concentration of searchlights. Because straight and level flight had to be maintained if the bombs were to be dropped accurately, Avant kept on an even course while flak began to burst all around his aircraft. By the time the cargo had been unloaded the perspex covering the front and mid-upper gun turrets, and the windshield in front of the pilot's face had all been shattered. Then a shell smashed through the starboard wing between the two engines cutting all controls and gas to the outer motor and setting the wing on fire. Avant feathered the engine and put out the flames. He decided to try to make it back to England with only the three engines still operating. Suddenly the outer port engine began running out of control from flak damage to the throttle mechanism. Avant had to feather it. As he approached home base he had only two engines running, yet he managed to make a perfect landing. For his night's work Avant received a DFC.

After finishing his tour Avant served as an instructor to 6 Bomber Group RCAF and then completed a second tour with 426 Squadron RCAF, adding a DSO to his laurels.

After the war Avant resigned from the air force to take a course in mechanical engineering then re-enlisted. After several senior appointments, which included Commandant of Royal Roads Military College, Avant served as CO of No 1 Wing of the NATO Air Division in France from August 1963 to August 1966. He retired in December 1976.

DSO DFC CD   G/C   Col(CF)   Born Sept 20 1922
RefScs: DHist bf   RCTSY 66   RS&A 126 216

BANNOCK Russell

"Premier RCAF Night-Fighter Pilot"

With a score of eleven German aircraft shot down, four damaged and eighteen V1 flying bombs destroyed to his credit, Russ Bannock ranked as the RCAF's top night-fighter ace in terms of aerial objects destroyed (see page 102). Born in Edmonton, Alta., he began flying in 1937 and already held both his private and commercial pilot's licences by the time he joined the RCAF in 1939. Ironically that very expertise prevented him from seeing combat for four years; the air force considered him too valuable as an instructors' instructor to be spared for overseas duties. Bannock found himself assigned to the Central Flying School in Trenton, Ont., for two years before being made Chief Flying Instructor of No 3 Flying Instructors' School at Arnprior, Ont., in 1942.

Finally on June 7, 1944, Bannock joined 418 Squadron RCAF at Helmsley, Hants., flying Mosquitos on night intrusions over Europe. A

R. Bannock (l.) PL 31295

week later he scored his first victory: a Messerschmitt 110 over Avorde airfield in France. On June 18 he made the first sighting of a V-1 achieved from the air and between June 19 and August 12 he and his navigator accounted for eighteen of the flying bombs. On one occasion they shot down four in an hour. By September he had been awarded the DFC and Bar. In October Bannock was given command of 406 Squadron RCAF based at Colerne, Wilts., which under his leadership became the most effective intruder squadron in RAF Fighter Command.

In May 1945 he became Director of Operations at RCAF Overseas Headquarters. Bannock then retired from the service in 1946 to join de Havilland Aircraft of Canada Limited, where he later became president. In 1978 he left the company to set up his own consulting firm. He was appointed Associate Fellow of the Canadian Aeronautical Institute in 1956. Bannock also served as chairman of the Export Committee for Aerospace Industries Association, as president of the Canadian Fighter Pilots Association and as president of the Canadian Air Show.

DSO DFC & Bar W/C Born Nov 1 1919 Ind CAHF 1983
RefScs: AIC 125 CAHF 110 CCMA 71 DHist bf OMAP(2) 105
RAW 178 264 SY 340 TDS 32–36

Moose Fumerton's score of fourteen planes shot down (see Fumerton) bested Bannock's eleven; but the latter's total, including eighteen V-1s, came to twenty-nine missiles destroyed, hence the qualification.

BARTLETT Christopher

"Transport Pilot Extraordinaire"

In 1941, when a revolt against British forces in Iraq got out of hand, Chris Bartlett of Fort Qu'Appelle, Sask., was called upon to fly a secret mission into neutral neighbouring Syria; the plan was to blow up a bridge and prevent a German invasion of the country. On May 24, flying a Valentia transport, he landed a platoon of British sappers in the desert and completed the operation in only forty-five minutes. Both the bridge and the Valentia were gone from the scene just as an enemy armoured car rolled up. This feat earned Bartlett the DFC. It was for such exploits that he quickly became recognized as the first Canadian to distinguish himself as a transport pilot.

Bartlett, who had joined the RAF in 1937, was sent to the Middle East after completing his pilot's training. When war broke out he joined 216 Squadron flying supplies and troops into shifting trouble spots in Egypt, Lebanon and the Sudan. By 1940 bombing operations had been added to the unit's duties, and Bartlett took part in the squadron's first bombing raid, which was on Tobruk. When the Germans invaded Greece and Crete in the spring of 1941 Bartlett flew troop evacuation sorties from forward bases.

From the desert Bartlett was posted to England where, on his second tour as a bomber pilot, he became CO of 434 Squadron RCAF flying Lancasters from Croft in Yorkshire. He was killed in a raid on Arras, France, in June 1944.

DFC & Bar   W/C   KIA June 12 1944
RefScs: CITR 51 10574   RAW 368–69 423   TDS 172

BARTON Robert Alexander

"Canadian Battles of Britain/Malta Ace"

"**B**utch" Barton, one of the first Canadians to fly a Spitfire, distinguished himself in the two major fight-against-odds aerial tussles of WW2: the battles of Britain and Malta. Born in Kamloops, B.C., Barton enlisted in the RAF in 1936 and joined 41 Squadron after pilot training. On May 16, 1940, he was posted as a flight commander to a new Hurricane squadron being formed, 249 RAF, with which he served his entire operational career.

On August 15 — the follow-up to the German Eagle Day in which the Luftwaffe hurled itself against the British Isles from bases stretching from Brittany to Norway — Barton scored his first victory by destroying a twin-engine Messerschmitt 110 and damaging another. Eight days later he was credited with probably destroying an ME 109, and on September 2 he shared in the destruction of a Dornier 17 bomber. Three days later Barton himself was shot down but managed to bail out of his burning aircraft. Next day, because the CO was wounded, he took temporary command of the squadron. On September 11, when the unit attacked a gaggle of Heinkel 111 bombers, Barton fired at four of them seeing strikes on all of his targets. By the time Barton received the DFC in October, he had shot down six aircraft, and damaged and probably destroyed others. He was made CO of 249 by the end of the year, and on December 29 he led one of the first offensive patrols of the war by the RAF on an escort patrol over Boulogne.

In mid-April 1941 the squadron was taken off operations in England and sent to Ta Kali, Malta, to bolster that island's defenses. There Barton shot down six enemy planes, one of them shared, to bring his total to thirteen destroyed, 4½ probably destroyed and nine damaged. On July 31 he crashed when his engine failed, suffering second degree burns. After that he was chiefly assigned to staff chores, although he continued as

CO of the squadron until December. Following the war Barton remained in the RAF until August 1958, returning to Canada in 1965 to live in retirement at Hedley, B.C.

OBE   DFC & Bar   W/C   Born June 7 1916
RefScs: DHist bf   OMAP(2) 105   RCTFFY 38   TTS 38–43

BAUDOUX Everett L.

"Bomber Pilot Attacked Nine Submarines, Shot Down One German Fighter, Probably Destroyed Another"

On October 25, 1940, three Hudson bombers of 233 RAF Squadron took off from Leuchars, Scotland, on an offensive patrol looking for shipping and submarines. Just before noon off the coast of Norway flying at 6,500 feet, they spotted the U-46 submarine heading home after weeks in the Atlantic. "Shan" Baudoux was the first to attack, facing brisk machine-gun fire as he approached. One fuel tank was punctured, the fuselage holed and the elevator controls disabled, thus forcing the crew to use the trim tabs to regulate the altitude. Regardless, the Hudson dropped ten 100-pound bombs, one scoring a direct hit on the conning tower. By then the anti-aircraft had stopped. This was just one of Baudoux's typical feats during his 2½ tours of operations, during which he attacked a total of nine U-boats as well as destroying one enemy fighter and probably trashing another.

His war career included flying the first operational land-based aircraft with radar, teaching operational combat techniques over the Bay of Biscay and flying in the first air raid of the North African landings, dropping leaflets on Casablanca.

A native of Stellarton, N.S., who had enlisted in the RAF, Baudoux was also engaged in the Atlantic ferry service. At the end of the war he joined the RCAF. His postwar career was filled with firsts: he was the first to make jet flights in Canada, the first to fly a Vampire in the Dominion and he was the first to test the CF-100 Canuck. In 1954 he became Assistant Chief Superintendent of the Canadian Armament Research and Development Establishment. Baudoux retired from the military as Commander of the Anti-Submarine Warfare Canadian Force Base at Greenwood, N.S.

DSO DFC CD   W/C   Born June 14 1919
RefScs: DHist bf   OMAP(2) 79   RAW 342

BAZELGETTE Ian Willoughby

"Pressed Home Attack in Blazing Bomber; Remained at Controls in Attempt to Save Crew"

On the night of August 4, 1944, Ian Bazelgette was the Master Bomber of 635 Pathfinder Squadron RAF detailed to mark the target — a V-1 flying bomb storage depot at Trossy St Maximin in Northern France

PL 37038

— for the main bomber force. As he approached the objective his Lancaster came under heavy anti-aircraft fire. Both starboard engines were put out of action. Fires broke out in the fuselage and along the starboard wing. The bomb aimer had an arm and part of a shoulder torn away. Smoke and fumes overcame the mid-upper gunner who had to be given morphia. Because the deputy Master Bomber had been shot down "Baz" knew the success of the raid depended on him and his crew so, despite the appalling conditions, he pressed on, bombing and marking the target with precision. After the bombs had been dropped, however, the Lancaster dived out of control. Bazelgette managed to right it, but then the port engine packed up and the whole of the starboard wing became a mass of flames. At 1,000 feet, without any hope of gaining height and with one of the crew mortally wounded and another suffocating, Bazelgette told the remaining crewmen to bail out. Spiralling down in a wide arc to circumvent the village of Senantes, he hoped to land in a field nearby and haul his comrades to safety. But before he could touch down the Lancaster exploded, killing all those aboard. For his courage and total disregard for his own safety Bazelgette was awarded the VC.

Bazelgette was born in Calgary, Alta., and went to school in Toronto, Ont., until he was nine, when the family moved to England. Completing his education there, in 1940 he joined the British army, transferring to the RAF the following year. In 1942 he was posted to 115 Squadron RAF with which he completed a tour of operations and earned the DFC. He then served a stint as an operational training instructor, joining 635 as a flight commander in April 1944.

There is a plaque to his memory at Downham Market in the U.K., the former home of 635 Squadron. But he is also appropriately honoured and remembered in Canada. In 1949 a mountain in Jasper National Park, Alta., was named after him.

VC DFC S/L Born Oct 19 1918 KIA Aug 4 1944 Ind CAHF 1973
RefScs: DHist bf CAHF 13 VM 178

BEIRNES John Rife

"Typhoon Dive-Bombing Specialist"

John Beirnes made a specialty out of dive-bombing against a variety of targets, including German gun emplacements, tanks, trains and shipping. Born in Edmonton, Alta., he joined the RCAF in 1940 and upon graduation became a staff pilot at an air navigation school. In June 1942 he was posted to the Aleutians on fighters. In October of the following year he joined 438 Squadron RCAF in England. Flying Typhoons, the unit was assigned reconnaissance and dive-bombing duties.

Typical of the sorties carried out by Beirnes was a dive-bombing attack on a German gun placement at the Chateau de Bosmalet near Dieppe in May 1944 in preparation for the Allied invasion of France. A few days later he bombed a radar station at Abbeville. Early in June he caved in a railway tunnel with his bombs. It was dangerous work that had the ever-present threat of ground fire and heavy flak, but Beirnes seemed impervious to it. Later in June the squadron moved to an airstrip at Lantheiul in Normandy, the principal bombing targets being bridges that the enemy troops could use to move into the bridgehead area. On August 3 Beirnes, who had joined the unit as a Sergeant-Pilot, became CO. In mid-October he had completed his tour and been awarded the DFC.

In April 1945 Beirnes returned to take over his old command. Six days later a new twist was added to Typhoon dive-bombing: attacking German shipping. Beirnes led his squadron against vessels anchored off Wilhelmshaven and sank a light cruiser, which earned him a Bar to his DFC. He now developed a new procedure for reconnaissance flights, that of carrying bombs in case targets of opportunity presented themselves. On April 21, flying as part of a Typhoon wing, the squadron completely wiped out the town of Achim. On May 3 his squadron again attacked enemy shipping, this time in the Kiel Canal. The following day the war in Europe ended and Beirnes' fighting days were over. Ironically, on June 1 during a routine flight over Denmark his engine stopped; in Beirnes' attempts to force-land in a field one wingtip dug into the ground. The Typhoon cartwheeled and disintegrated, killing the pilot instantly.

DFC & Bar   S/L   KIA June 1 1945
RefScs: DHist bf   RCTFY 233 255–57   SY 145   TDS 139–45

BEURLING George Frederick

"Aerial Knight of Malta"

G eorge Beurling, who became Canada's top fighter pilot in WW2, scored all but four of his victories over Malta in a period of less than five months. Credited with being the best deflection shot in the world he had the surest eyesight of any man alive. Born in Verdun, P.Q., Beurling learned to fly at age 14 and soloed at 16. Anxious to put his talents to war he volunteered to join the Chinese forces against the Japanese

PL 14940

invaders. Instead Beurling ended up in a Seattle jail for illegal entry into the U.S.

When WW2 broke out he applied to the RCAF but was turned down because of his lack of education. When the Russians invaded Finland he was accepted by the Finns; but because he was still under 21 Beurling's father refused his consent. Beurling then signed on as a deckhand and sailed to England; but the RAF turned him down because he forgot his birth certificate. He returned to Verdun, retrieved it, made a second Atlantic crossing and was finally accepted.

In the spring of 1941 he began pilot training and by mid-December was flying Spitfires with 403 Squadron RCAF from Martlesham Heath in Suffolk. However the posting did not last long. As a member of the RAF he was not allowed to stay on strength in a designated Canadian unit and was transferred to 41 Squadron. Shortly afterward he scored his first two victories — over Focke-Wulf 190s. But because he had broken formation his fellow pilots shunned him.

When an opportunity arose to be sent to Malta in May 1942 Beurling jumped at the chance. On June 7, along with thirty-two others in Spitfires equipped with long-range tanks, he took off from the carrier *Eagle* in the Mediterranean off Algeria. He headed for the beleaguered isle where he joined 249 Squadron RAF. Shortly after his arrival in Malta he was credited with damaging a Messerschmitt 109. But it was on July 6 that he exhibited the fighting quality that quickly established him as Malta's leading ace. In two different combats he shot down a Messerschmitt 109 and two Italian Macchi fighters, and damaged a Cant bomber. Four days later he shot down another ME 109 and a Macchi. Day after day he continued to add to his score — on one occasion shooting down two planes within an incredible ten seconds. By July 17 his victories totalled eighteen and he had been twice decorated.

Beurling's outstanding gunnery was not just the result of phenomenal eyesight. That certainly gave him an edge, particularly in spotting the enemy first. But it was practice and mathematical ability that counted most. He practised by shooting at lizards from different distances with a revolver. He memorized aircraft angles with the use of models. He kept note of all his attacks, angle, distance, speed, amount of ammunition expended (his bursts rarely exceeded two seconds). He even exercised his eye muscles by staring at an object 300 yards away then focussing on something at close range. Beurling was a professional fighter pilot to the *n*th degree.

During most of August he was out of action with the "dog," a weakening form of dysentry. In any case the Germans had taken a breather. But they were back again at the end of September and Beurling, in the thick of the fighting, soon became the island's highest scorer. During October he was only in action twice, but those two days could not have provided a greater finale to his Malta tour. On October 13 in a head-on attack with twenty Messerschmitts, he brought down two of them as well as a German bomber. Next day he added another two 109s to his score and a twin-engine Junkers Ju 88 bomber. But this time he failed to notice a Messerschmitt on his tail. Suddenly his Spitfire was raked with cannon shells. With his aircraft on fire he climbed out on the wing at 2,000 feet and parachuted into the sea.

His tour in Malta was over, but during that time Beurling had accounted for twenty-seven planes destroyed, plus one shared with two other pilots, nine probably destroyed and three damaged.

For the two weeks following his jump Beurling was hospitalized until he was well enough to be flown out. Then the Liberator in which he was a passenger crashed at Gibraltar. Beurling survived by diving out of an emergency exit.

After a hero's welcome in Canada he transferred to the RCAF and returned to England for another tour of operations with 403 and 412 Squadrons RAF, the latter as flight commander, adding two more enemy planes destroyed to his tally.

Following the war, after trying his hand at several jobs, he joined the Israeli Air Force in 1948 to fight against the Arabs. On May 20 at Urbe airport outside Rome, Italy, Beurling and a co-pilot took off in a Norseman on a shakedown flight before ferrying it to Israel. Coming in to land the plane crashed, killing both occupants. Several days later Beurling was buried at Varano cemetery by a people against whom he had fought so valiantly but who in the end had come to revere him as a fighter for freedom.

> DSO DFC DFM & Bar   F/L   Born Dec 26 1921   KFA May 20 1948
> Co-author *Malta Spitfire*
> RefScs: CFP 14–64   DHist bf H(biog)   MS(biog)   RAW 160 171 366
> 372 375–76 392   TDS 1–6   TFAOR 21–28

I once had a practice dog fight with Beurling when we were both stationed at Biggin Hill in England during the winter of 1943–44. I'm glad he was on our side. No matter how hard I tried I couldn't shake him off my tail. Nor could I get on his. His control of his aircraft was phenomenal, his reflexes and coordination were incredible. And not only in the air: he was adept at golf, squash, swimming and riding.

But back to air fighting. He once told me: "I'd sacrifice anything for speed. It's the essential." As a footnote, very few people knew he was something of an artist. I remember him applying a skilled touch to painting little black crosses on his plane to denote his victories. He came by the talent naturally. His father was a commercial artist.

BIRCHALL Leonard Joseph

"Saviour of Ceylon"

Winston Churchill called it "one of the most important individual contributions to victory." Len Birchall and his crew had been flying their Catalina flying boat all day in search of the Japanese fleet that was intent on capturing Ceylon and the Dutch East Indies to threaten communications between the U.S. and Australia. The date was April 4, 1942, and Birchall and 413 Squadron RCAF had arrived in Ceylon from the Shetland Islands only two days earlier. There they had been flying convoy patrols over the North Sea and the Atlantic — seemingly endless and cold sorties. At least flying over the Indian Ocean was warm.

As it turned to night the moon began to rise. Then, 500 miles south of Ceylon, the airmen spotted the Japanese convoy. Birchall began to recite to a count to his radio man: "Four battleships, five carriers, many cruisers and destroyers, speed and course, heading for Ceylon." The radio man managed to get off three messages to Colombo, Ceylon, before Japanese fighters shot the Catalina down in flames. Then, as the crew struggled in the water, enemy planes strafed them. Only Birchall and five of his crew survived, three of them wounded. They were taken aboard a Japanese destroyer and held prisoner. But their efforts had saved Ceylon.

Admiral Chuichi Nagumo attacked on Easter Sunday April 5 with ninety-one bombers plus fighter escort. But the British had heeded Birchall's warnings and had cleared the harbour at Colombo of all merchant vessels and British fighters. The Allies then shot down eighteen of the Japanese planes; another five were lost to anti-aircraft fire. Nagumo withdrew and, in the Battle of the Coral Sea that followed, could only muster three carriers out of his original five.

Birchall, who was awarded the DFC for his action and who spent the rest of the war in a prison camp, was born in St Catharines, Ont., and attended RMC before joining the RCAF in 1937. By 1939 he was a flying boat pilot with 5 Bomber Reconnaissance Squadron flying anti-submarine and convoy patrols from Dartmouth, N.S. In May 1940 he was responsible for capturing an Italian merchant ship, netting Canada her first Italian POWs. In 1941 he served a brief stint as a staff officer with 2 Training Command in Winnipeg, Man., before being posted to Trans-Atlantic Ferry Command in Bermuda and then joining 413 Squadron in the Shetlands. For his leadership while a POW Birchall was awarded the OBE. On one occasion as Senior British Officer at Niigato Camp he called a sit-down strike in protest against the ill treatment of his men. On another he physically prevented the Japanese from making sick prisoners work; for that action he was given solitary confinement. Birchall remained with the RCAF and later the Canadian Forces after the war. He held many senior appointments, including that of Commandant of RMC, Kingston, Ont.

OBE DFC CD ADC   A/C   B/G(CF)   Born July 1915
RefScs: CA 221   CCMA 60   CSA   DHist bf   P 102–103 120–28
RAW 397 399 445 451   RCTFFY 305 321 354   SY 180   TDS 116–26
152   TSBW   150

BISHOP Arthur Albert

"Persisted in Submarine Attack in Face of Fierce Return Fire"

On the morning of August 4, 1943, Albert Bishop of 423 Squadron RCAF flew out of Reykjavik, Iceland, over the North Atlantic to attack a U-489. Despite heavy flak from the submarine that crippled the Sutherland flying boat's controls and set fire to a wing root and the galley, Bishop continued his barrage.

Attacked by Hudson bombers the day before — and escaping virtually unscathed — the submarine had resurfaced to recharge its batteries when Bishop spotted it from four miles away and from an altitude of 4,000 feet. As he closed to within one mile at 600 feet the submarine made no move to submerge. Though Bishop had no way of knowing it, the U-boat was immobilized until the batteries had been at least partially revitalized. Bishop circled into position to attack the bow and so avoid fire from the flak battery behind the conning tower. But the submarine deftly swing about to present its stern to the Sutherland. Bishop decided to give up trying for the ideal position and attacked from out of the sun. At 1,200 feet range the aircraft opened fire with its nose cannon. When he had closed to within 500 yards Bishop levelled out at 50 feet and opened up the gas-operated upper turret cannon. Strikes could be seen all around the conning tower.

Suddenly from 300 yards away the Sutherland was rocked by return fire from the submarine's flak battery. It became more intense as the aircraft dropped its depth-charges right over the target. Flames erupted along the port wing root and in the galley. The ailerons and trim tabs had become useless, the outer engine controls unserviceable. Bishop proceeded to land as best he could. He bounced the aircraft twice then the port wing dug into the water causing the aircraft to swerve to the right and nose in. Six of the crew of eleven managed to escape from the stricken, burning hull, which sank in less than four minutes. But damage to the U-489 had also been severe and it began to go under, its crew climbing into dinghies. With only its bow visible at a 30-degree angle the submarine exploded and disappeared. Twenty minutes later a British destroyer rescued airmen and seamen alike.

For the attack Bishop, a native of Erskine, Alta., received the DFC, the citation for which noted that after ditching Bishop had helped a wounded comrade who had no life jacket and supported him until the warship arrived. One other member of the crew was also decorated and another mentioned in dispatches.

DFC F/L
RefScs: CA 231   CCMA 66   RAW   345   TSBW 230

BLATCHFORD Howard Peter

"First WW2 Victory by a Canadian"

On October 17, 1939, "Cowboy" Blatchford shared in shooting down a German Heinkel 111 twin-engine bomber over the North Sea to become the first Canadian to file a combat report in WW2. Later he starred in blunting Mussolini's abortive attempt to launch his Regia Aeronautica against the British Isles.

Born in Edmonton, Alta., Blatchford obtained his pilot's licence in 1930 when he was eighteen years old; for the next five years he worked as a bush pilot in northern Canada. In 1935 he joined the RAF and two years later joined 41 Squadron, then flying Hawker Demons. By war's outbreak the unit had been equipped with Spitfires and its duties were to guard the naval station at Scapa Flow. Early in 1940 he joined the Photographic Reconnaissance Unit, which moved to Bricy near Orleans to make reconnaissance flights of enemy troop positions when the Germans invaded France and Belgium. With the imminent French defeat Blatchford escaped to England in a Fairey Battle, an aircraft he had never flown before. He later returned to the continent several times in a Hudson to evacuate French aircrews. At the end of September he was posted to 17 then to 257 Squadrons, both RAF Hurricane units. The latter posting was as a flight commander.

In the summer of 1940 Mussolini had ordered his air force to participate in the aerial assault on England in retaliation for RAF raids on Italian factories. On Armistice Day, November 11, a force of BR20 medium bombers escorted by Fiat CR24 biplane fighters as well as G50 monoplane fighters clashed with British fighters over England for the first time. Leading his squadron Blatchford shot down one of the bombers, shared in the destruction of another and damaged two fighters, chopping a piece of one fighter's wing off with his propeller when his ammunition ran out. The Italians took such a mauling that day the Duce called off any further participation against Britain. For his entire performance Blatchford was awarded the DFC.

Later Blatchford and the CO, Bob Stanford Tuck, flew the first Rhubarb, a low-level reconnaissance, over the coast of France. May 12, 1941, Blatchford scored his one and only victory at night, against an He 111. In mid-July he was made CO of the squadron, leading fighter sweeps over France, and at the beginning of September was given command of the Canadian Digby Wing. At the end of April 1942 he was taken off operations to serve as a staff officer at Fighter Command HQ. Following this he returned to combat as commander of the Coltishall Wing; his duties consisted of leading his squadrons as escort to medium bombers. On May 3, 1943, on one such sortie the formation was heavily attacked by Focke-Wulf 190s, which wiped out an entire Ventura bomber squadron. In the melee Blatchford's Spitfire was badly shot up and he crashed into the sea.

DFC MID   W/C   Born Feb 12 1912   KIA May 3 1943
RefScs: CWC 22–40   DHist bf   OMAP(2) 106   TTS app

BOOMER Kenneth Arthur

"Only North-American RCAF Aerial Victory Over Japanese"

E arly in June 1942 the Japanese seized Kiska and Attu at the extreme western tip of the Aleutians as a diversion for the attack on Midway. RCAF and USAAF units were quickly moved into the area. On September 20 a joint raid was launched by nine Liberators, twelve Lightnings and twenty Kittyhawks, four piloted by Canadians — one of them Ken Boomer, CO of 111 Squadron then stationed at Adak. The island was defended by a handful of Rufes — Zero fighters on floats — three of which rose to meet the attack. Boomer pulled up under one of the enemy planes and opened fire then watched as it plummeted down in flames. It represented the only RCAF air victory over the Japanese, indeed the only RCAF air combat in the North American Theatre.

Boomer then led a group of the Kittyhawks in strafing submarines in the harbour. He was awarded the DFC for his victory and the U.S. Army Air Medal for his part in the raid.

A native of Ottawa, Ont., Boomer saw his first action with 411 Squadron RCAF on an escort sortie over France on September 2, 1941, when he damaged a German Messerschmitt 109. In November while on convoy patrol off Lincolnshire he destroyed a Junkers 88 bomber. On April 27 he took over command of 132 Squadron based at Patricia Bay, B.C., and on August 20 he became CO of 111 Squadron, then at Unmak Island in the Aleutians. In October 1944 he was killed in action serving overseas.

DFC AM(Am)   S/L   KIA Oct 2 1944
RefScs: CA 223   DHist bf   OMAP(2) 38   RAW 116   RCTFFY 47 117
RS&A 42 62   TDS 134

BRETZ Norman Hobson

"Versatile Fighter Career Included Combat, Bomber Escort, Dive-Bombing, Shipping Strikes, Rescue Operations"

In his four-year career as a fighter pilot, Norm Bretz of Toronto, Ont., flew just about every type of combat sortie. A graduate of the first BCATP course, on arrival overseas in December 1940 he was posted to No 2 Fighter Squadron RCAF at Digby, Lincolnshire, for combat training; the squadron's CO, Gordon McGregor, was a veteran of the Battle of Britain. On March 1, 1941, the squadron, which was flying Hurricanes, was officially numbered 402 Squadron RCAF and declared operational. It then became engaged in standing readiness duties, fighter sweeps over France, as well as bomber-escort sorties.

On one occasion in company with the CO, Bretz flew a search mission for a pilot who had been shot down in the English Channel. When they found the downed flier in his dinghy, the pair orbited above him to provide a fix for the Air Sea Rescue Service, a routine that became standard procedure.

In October the Hurricanes were armed with 250-pound bombs and during the following month the squadron raided aerodromes in France. In December Bretz was made a flight commander and early in the new year the unit was employed in shipping strikes. In March the squadron was re-equipped with Spitfires and by May had moved to Redhill in Surrey to fly as part of the Kenley Wing. On June 8 Bretz had his first successful combat when he damaged a Focke-Wulf 190 and on August 17 he became CO of the unit. Two days later he led his squadron on four different sorties during the raid on Dieppe by the Canadian army. During the raid he destroyed an FW 190 and damaged another. In September Bretz received the DFC. He scored his final success of the war that same month by destroying an FW 190 while escorting Flying Fortresses on a bombing mission.

Bretz's tour ended in March 1943 when he returned to Canada to serve with an Operational Training Unit. On December 31, after attending the RAF Staff College, he took over the Digby Wing as Wing Commander Flying. In April 1944 he was repatriated to Canada and served with 1 OTU at Bagotville, P.Q. Then Bretz successively became CO of No 1 Repatriation Depot and of RCAF Station Whitehorse, Yukon. He retired from service in June 1946. He died in December 1956 in Toronto.

DFC W/C Born May 5 1913 Died Dec 1956
RefScs: CWC 41–48 RAW 447 RCTFFY 61 66 68 96 354
RCTFY 116 RS&A 84 98 215

BROWN Alan Coatsworth

"Shot Down Three Times Before Battle of Britain Began"

As a Blenheim bomber pilot, Alan Brown of Winnipeg, Man., was shot down three times within three weeks during the German attack on the West in May and June 1940. Brown joined the RAF in February 1934. By the outbreak of WW2 in September 1939 he was serving with 53 Squadron, which was originally based at Odiham but moved to France later in the month.

When the invasion started in May 1940 the squadron was assigned tactical targets to slow down the Wehrmacht's advance, a hopeless, losing venture. On May 13 Brown's bomber lost an engine from enemy ground fire and he barely made it back to his base in England to which the squadron had been evacuated. Then on June 1 his bomber was again hit. This time he was forced to crash-land at Manston on the British southeast coast. Next day Brown's Blenheim was so badly damaged he had to belly-land on the Dunkirk beach; he and his crew were rescued by boat.

On January 7, 1942, Brown became CO of 407 Squadron RCAF based at Bircham Newton in Norfolk, flying twin-engine Hudson Bombers, which he commanded until September. At dawn on May 7 Brown led twelve of the Hudsons on a shipping strike off the Dutch coast near Terschelling, sinking seven of twelve vessels they attacked. Following the war Brown remained with the RAF.

OBE DSO DFC MID W/C CdeG(Fr) OL(Bel) G/C
RefScs: CITR 113   RCTFFY 113 256 258–60 263   RS&A 92

BROWN Mark Henry

"First Canadian Airman to Land in France in WW2"

On September 8, 1930, when 1 Squadron RAF flew its Hurricanes from Tangmere in the south of England to Norrent Fontes airfield near St Omer, "Hilly" Brown of Portage la Prairie, Man., became the first Canadian fighter pilot in WW2 to land in France. Then on November 23 when he shared in the destruction of a German twin-engine Dornier 17 bomber, he became the first Canadian to score a victory from the continent.

Brown learned to fly at the Russel Flying Club in Brandon, Man., and enlisted in the RAF in 1936. By the time the war started he had already logged 623 hours and 40 minutes flying time.

In France his squadron saw some of the fiercest fighting of the war in May and June of 1940 when the Germans invaded France and the Lowlands. On June 14 Brown, by then a flight commander, was hit by enemy fire and forced to take to his parachute. After a three-day walk he arrived at his base to find that the squadron had been evacuated to England. Brown managed to hop aboard the last boatload of troops to leave Brest.

After a hiatus of two months rest and practice No 1 Squadron joined in the Battle of Britain. Brown began to run up his score enough to make him an ace — but not before he was shot down again. This time, as the plane fell in flames, Brown suffered burn wounds to his face. However he was soon back in action and by November had been made CO of his unit.

In April 1941, with a score of 7½ aircraft destroyed, 5½ damaged and three probables to his credit, Brown was taken off operations and assigned the post of Squadron Leader Flying at an operational training unit in Scotland. Then in October he was posted to Malta as Wing Commander Flying. On November 12, during a sweep over Sicily, Brown's Spitfire was hit by flak; he was killed instantly when his plane crashed.

DFC & Bar CzWC   W/C   Born Oct 9 1911   KIA Nov 28 1941
RefScs: CWC 49–72   DHist bf   OMAP(2) 107   TSBW 202
TTS 280–81

BRUNEAU Arthur Andrew

"Last Canadian to Sink a U-boat"

Arthur Bruneau of Westmount, P.Q., had the distinction of being the last Canadian to sink a German submarine in WW2, a feat for which he received the DFC.

By early May 1945 the German armies were in retreat, the Luftwaffe had been decimated and of their own volition the U-boats were trying to escape through the narrow Kattegat waterway from Denmark to Norway. The unknown quantity was whether, when discovered from the air, they would still put up a fight. RAF Coastal Command crews decided to take no chances. On May 5, 1945, flying from Leuchars in Scotland across the North Sea as captain of a Liberator, Bruneau cut the risk to a minimum by flying at deck level to stay under the German radar screen search. Over Denmark, enjoying its first day of freedom from the Nazi yoke, he and his crew were treated to the rare sight of flags flying and people waving. Then back to business as they emerged over the Kattegat.

A short time later the crew picked up their own radar contact fourteen miles distant. As they approached the Danish coast two submarines came into view, one of them firing a warning flare. Although it was too late for them to crash-dive one of the submarines opened fire. While his front-gunner responded, Bruneau's bomb-aimer concentrated on the aiming point — the water-line at the bow. Bombs away! Four 250-pound depth charges to port and one on the starboard side straddled the U-boat just ahead of the conning tower. As the Liberator pulled up in a climbing turn the submarine exploded; the bow rose above the water at a 40-degree angle then rapidly sank stern first. A second Liberator destroyed the other U-boat. Bruneau circled for fifteen minutes as bodies, debris, and oil rose to the surface. His victory confirmed, he then set course for home.

Joining the RCAF in June 1942 Bruneau was posted to 547 Squadron RAF in July 1944 as a second pilot. He was made captain on March 2, 1945. With the end of hostilities in Europe he returned to Canada to await a posting to the Tiger Force, Canada's contribution to the war in the Pacific, for which he had volunteered. But VJ-Day arrived before he could be posted and he retired from the service in September 1945.

DFC F/O Born Oct 28 1923
RefScs: DHist bf TDS 126–29

BUCKHAM Robert Andrew

"Rhubarb Specialist"

During the winter of 1942/43 Bob Buckham of Golden, B.C., made a specialty out of Rhubarbs — low-level fighter attacks in pairs against German ground targets on the French coast, usually in poor weather to take advantage of low cloud cover protection against anti-aircraft fire. When Buckham joined the RCAF in October 1940 he already had his private pilot's licence and was something of a skilled aerobatic flyer. In November 1941 he joined 416 Squadron RCAF then being formed in Scotland. On August 14, 1942, the unit moved to Hawkinge on the English south coast. Five days later, while participating in the air cover for the Canadian army assault on Dieppe, Buckham made his first score: a Focke-Wulf 190 destroyed and another damaged.

On October 17, 1942, Buckham led the squadron's first Rhubarb, destroying a locomotive, a railway signal box and a flak tower. In December he was appointed as flight commander of the squadron then stationed

PL 22285

at Kenley. With the poor weather that winter — lots of low cloud cover — he was mainly engaged in Rhubarbs, at which he had become expert. It was not until February 1943 that he shot down another plane, an FW 190 in a head-on attack. By May 16, 1943, he had run his score up to four enemy aircraft destroyed, several others damaged and five locomotives destroyed. Awarded the DFC as well as the contemporary U.S. decoration he was temporarily taken off operations.

In September Buckham joined 421 Squadron RCAF as a flight commander. On October 6, 1943, by which time he had added two more aircraft destroyed to his tally, he was posted to 403 Squadron RCAF as CO. At first the squadron was engaged mostly in flying escort sweeps to American bombers over the occupied countries; later they engaged in dive-bombing the German V-1 flying bomb sites under construction.

On June 13, a week after D-Day, Buckham became Wing Commander Flying of 127 RCAF Wing; he moved his four squadrons to an airstrip in Normandy near Crepon several days later. His operational career ended in August when he turned the wing over to his successor and was awarded a Bar to his DFC.

After the war Buckham stayed in the air force, taking over as CO of the Northwest Air Command RCAF Station at Whitehorse, Yukon. On September 6, 1947, Buckham was killed when the Beechcraft in which he was travelling as a passenger with five others crashed into Marsh Lake thirty miles from his base.

DFC & Bar DFC(Am) W/C Born Oct 15 1914 KFA Sept 6 1947
RefScs: CWC 73–83 DHist bf OMAP(2) 108 TTS app

BURNETT Wilfred Jasper

"Special Services Pilot"

In 1944, as CO of 138 Squadron RAF, Wilf Burnett flew four-engine Halifax and Stirling bomber missions to drop agents and arms for the resistance all over Europe. A native of Garden Creek, N.B., Burnett enlisted in the RAF in 1937 and by war's outbreak was flying twin-engine Hampden bombers with 76 Squadron at Upper Heyford in Oxfordshire. After a brief posting to 106 RAF Squadron he joined 49 Squadron RAF at Scampton, Lincolnshire, in January 1940, finishing his first tour — on Hampdens — at the time the Germans invaded Europe in May. After serving as an OTU instructor Burnett joined 408 Squadron RCAF as a flight commander shortly after it was formed at Lindholme, Yorkshire, in July 1941.

On the night of January 16, 1942, Burnett's Hampden was hit by enemy fire, killing three of his crew. But after ten hours in the air he managed to reach England, where he crashed near West Burton. Burnett spent the next seven months in hospital. On August 26 he was appointed tactics officer with 6 Group RCAF Bomber Command. For his special services work Burnett was awarded the DSO. Following the war he remained with the RAF, reaching the rank of Air Commodore.

DSO DFC AFC CdeG(Fr) A/C
RefScs: CITR 114–15 RCTFFY 155

CAINE John Todd

"Day-Ranger Champion"

W hile Johnnie Caine shot down two German planes at night as a Mosquito intruder pilot, it was on Day-Ranger operations that he showed his real expertise by destroying three aircraft in the air and fifteen on the ground, and damaging seven others.

Caine, who was born in Edmonton, Alta., joined the RCAF in 1942. By October 1943 he joined 418 Squadron RCAF at Ford in the south of England, where he quickly proved his métier. On the night of December 20/21 he destroyed his first enemy aircraft while over northeast France. But because of the difficulty of finding German night-fighter fields at night the squadron switched to Day Rangers — long distance forays deep into enemy territory using drop tanks — and that brought Caine and his observer distinction.

Caine's career in that milieu began on the afternoon of January 27, 1944, when, near Bourges, he shot down a Junkers 88 and shared in the destruction of two Ju W34 transports, sending one down in a sheet of flame. On April 14 his promising career nearly came to an end when, after shooting down three aircraft and damaging another, his Mosquito was heavily attacked by two Focke-Wulf 190s.

Caine's most successful Day Ranger sortie came on May 2 when he destroyed six planes and damaged two more. Again his aircraft was hit by enemy fire and he had to struggle back to base. A week later his first tour ended with sixteen aircraft destroyed and five damaged, for which he received the DFC and Bar. After an instructional stint in Canada, he returned to action with 406 Squadron RCAF, flying the latest Mosquito-types from Manston on the British southeast coast. During that tour he added four more aircraft destroyed and two damaged to his tally and was awarded a second Bar to his DFC, one of only six Canadians to be so decorated in WW2. After the war he operated one of the largest fur ranching operations in Western Canada then retired to Vancouver, B.C.

DFC & 2 Bars F/L Born Aug 20 1920
RefScs: CA 237 CCMA 69 OMAP(2) 108 RAW 262 RCTFY 158–61
163–66 168 f174 TTS 55–61 app

CAMERON Lorne Maxwell

"Used Seine Bridges to Foil Enemy Fighters"

O ne usually associated Lorne Cameron with being on the offensive. But on the evening of June 30, 1944, when his wingman deserted him, Cameron had to take desperate defensive measures to shake fifteen German Focke-Wulf 190 fighters off his tail. Diving down to deck level — literally — he waggled his Spitfire along the Seine River, flying under its bridges. It did the trick. The German fighters had no stomach for such risky maneuvers and soon gave up the chase.

A native of Roland, Man., Cameron enlisted in the RCAF in January 1941. After completing his training he joined 402 Squadron RCAF at Warmwell, which were flying Spitfires that January 1942. After an injury sustained in a crash in July he rejoined the squadron that September at Kenley in Surrey. His first tour ended in April 1943 and for the next six months Cameron served as an operational training instructor. On November 12 he was posted to 401 Squadron at Biggin Hill. Cameron had been made flight commander by December 20, the day he scored his first kill — a Junkers 188 bomber in a fight near Brussels. Several days later he was appointed CO.

Cameron became recognized not only for his fighting ability — he was an excellent shot — but also for his leadership qualities, which earned him the DFC. On June 7, D-Day plus one, with four victories and two aircraft damaged to his credit, he made a double score over the Normandy beachhead by shooting down two Ju 88s. Other members of his squadron accounted for five more destroyed.

In the early morning of July 3 Cameron was shot down behind enemy lines near Falaise while strafing a truck convoy. Successfully belly-landing in a field, he hid out all day and tried to get through the lines that night. When that proved impossible he travelled south, finally teaming up with an individual who claimed to be a member of the French Resistance but turned out to be a traitor. When they reached Bordeaux he handed Cameron over to the Gestapo. He was put in irons and thrown into a jail. Afterward, enroute to a prison camp in Germany, he and several other captives overcame their guards and escaped. Cameron was later liberated by the Americans.

Following WW2 Cameron went into the investment business and for two years, 1948–50, was CO of 402 Auxiliary Squadron in Winnipeg, Man. He later retired to Victoria, B.C.

DFC S/L Born Feb 22 1922
RefScs: DHist bf OMAP(2) 108 RCTFY 114–15 119–20 126 f127 127
134 229 241–42 246 253 RS&A 82 153 TTS app

Dick Stayner, Lorne Cameron and Jack Sheppard (l. to r.). PL 28535

Cam lost none of his forthrightness or authority even when shot down. As soon as he had safely landed wheels-up someone from our squadron called on the radio transmitter to ask if he was alright. His reply was predictable: "Get the hell away from here." He spoke evenly, almost contemptibly. He wanted to avoid any chance of the Germans picking up his position.

CHADBURN Lloyd Vernon

"A Quintessential RCAF Fighter Wing Leader"

L loyd Chadburn became the first BCATP graduate to command a squadron. At 21 years old he was the youngest Squadron Leader in the RCAF at that time. He was also the first RCAF officer to win a Bar to the DSO, one of only four Canadians to receive the award. His score of victories was equally commendable: nine destroyed including four shared, seven probably destroyed as well as two shared, and eight damaged. But what Chad was best remembered for most by those who knew and flew with him was what Lloyd Breadner, who commanded the RCAF overseas, said of him; he was described as "one of the best-loved members of the force." One pilot who served under him said: "He seemed to know every officer and airman in the unit by his first name and made a point of drawing each of us out into personal conversation." Indeed the quintessential fighter wing leader.

Chadburn was born in Montreal, P.Q. Before WW2 he tried unsuccessfully to join the peacetime RCAF, the RAF and the RCN. But when war broke out he was finally accepted by the RCAF and after receiving his wings was posted overseas in November 1940. He joined No 2 (later 402) Squadron RCAF, converting from Lysanders to Hurricanes. On April 15, 1941, Chadburn participated in the first offensive sweep by an RCAF squadron over enemy territory. In June he was transferred to 412 Squadron RCAF at Digby, equipped with Spitfires, where he flew reconnaissance patrols. Later he transferred to 19 Squadron RAF at Coltishall. There he was made a flight commander. On November 20 he scored his first victory by sinking a German E-boat. In February 1942 he was given command of 416 Squadron RCAF flying shipping strikes and fighter sweeps over the occupied countries. On August 19, while over the Dieppe landings, Chadburn shot down a Junkers 88 and damaged another, for which he was awarded the DFC.

The squadron was now engaged in escorting American bombers on raids in France and Belgium. In January 1943 Chadburn ended his first tour of operations. In April he returned to take over command of 402, his original squadron. Then shortly afterward he was given command of the Digby wing, which consisted of his own squadron and 416. In August he was awarded the DSO. In November 1943, when his second tour ended, he was given a Bar to the DSO and returned to Canada for a victory bond tour. He was then posted back to England in 1944 where he took over the Kenley wing, made up of 403 and 421 Squadrons. Chadburn led his wing on fighter sweeps and dive-bombing attacks on No-ball targets — flying bomb sites — and his unit was among the three Canadian Spitfire wings that helped cover the D-day landings. Ironically, on the morning of June 13, 1944, he was killed in a collision with another Spitfire pilot while taking off from a landing strip in Normandy.

DSO & Bar DFC CdeG(Fr) Ld'H(Fr) W/C Born Aug 21 1919
KIA June 13 1944
RefScs: CCMA 60 CWC 84–93 DHist bf BS 25–28 OMAP(2) 108
RAW 180 184 RCTFFY 56 68 90 f96 98 102 106–108 112 114 353–54
RCTFY 101 102 105–107 110–11 114 116 124 f126 226 227 231–32
RS&A 84 102 215 222 TTS app

CHAPMAN Cecil George William

"Headed Squadron that Sank Five U-boats in One Month"

During the European invasion of June 1944, 162 Squadron RCAF commanded by Cecil Chapman sank four German submarines and shared in the destruction of a fifth, a record for a RCAF unit. At this time the Canso crews of the outfit operated from Wick, Scotland, in an effort to attack the southern flank of the route used by the U-boats to reach the North Atlantic from Norway. By war's end they could boast a VC, two DSOs, seven DFCs and three DFMs. Chapman himself accounted for one of the submarines and became one of the squadron's two DSO recipients.

On this occasion Chapman's Canso was so crippled by fire from the sinking U-boat he had to ditch it in the sea, forcing him and his crew to abandon ship and take to their dinghies. There they waited for nine hours before being rescued; he lost three of his crew to the wet and cold.

Born in Hillsborough, N.B., Chapman joined the RCAF in June 1939 as a permanent officer. When WW2 started he was appointed Command Navigation Officer at Eastern Air Command before being posted to 162 Squadron. Following the war he stayed in the service and held such posts as CO of 426 Transport Squadron; Director of Operational Requirements; Chief Staff Officer, Canadian Joint Staff Headquarters in Washington, D.C.; and Air Commander with the United Nations in the Congo. In June 1963 he was appointed Air Attache in Stockholm, Sweden.

DSO CD G/C Born Aug 17 1918
RefScs: DHist bf RCTFY f287 297 305–307 RS&A 185

CHARLES Edward Francis John

"Shared in Record-Breaking Kill"

With 15½ German planes destroyed, 6½ probables and 5 damaged to his credit, Jack Charles ranked as one of the leading Canadian air aces of WW2. But his most memorable victory was one he shared with the CO of the Free French Alsace Squadron on May 15, 1943.

PL 22043

On that date both Spitfire pilots had shot down a Focke-Wulf 190 at precisely the same moment in the same area so that they decided to divide the honour of scoring the one thousandth victory for Biggin Hill, Britain's most famous fighter base.

Born in Coventry, England, Charles emigrated to Canada with his parents as a child and was brought up in Lashburn, Sask. In 1937 he joined the Saskatchewan Horse Militia and then was commissioned in the RCAF. In May 1939 he transferred to the RAF in England. By December of that year he flew with 81 Squadron and transferred to No 2 Squadron RAF in June 1940. That August Charles was posted to an operational training school. He then served with 54 and 64 Squadrons RAF, running up a score of 7½ destroyed, a string of probables and aircraft damaged; he was awarded the DFC. His next posting, toward the end of 1942, was 52 OTU in Gloucester where he was appointed gunnery officer, an apt assignment; Charles was a fabulous shot. In the spring of 1943 he joined 616 Squadron RAF at Biggin Hill as a flight commander. On April 22 he took over as CO and in early August was promoted to Wing Commander; by this time he had been awarded the DSO, a Bar to his DFC and the U.S. Silver Medal. In May 1944 he transferred to the RCAF, retiring at the end of the war to take up residence in B.C.

DSO DFC & Bar SM(Am)   W/C   Born Feb 6 1918
RefScs: CWC 94–102   DHist bf   OMAP(2) 108   RBH 285   TTS app

Though Jack was crack shot with a tremendous eye for deflection, when I was at 52 OTU his advice as gunnery officer to me was: "Forget all that theory about angles. Just get in so close you can't miss."

CHRISTIE George Patterson

"First Canadian to Go on Offensive Over Europe"

On December 20, 1940, with another Spitfire pilot, George Christie attacked Le Touquet airfield near the French coast. This was the first RAF aerial offensive action over Europe since the Dunkirk evacuation. Born in Westmount, P.Q., Christie joined the RAF in 1937 and by April 1940 was attached to 212 Squadron, an independent squadron that was a Photographic Development Unit in France. On May 24 he damaged a German Messerschmitt 109 fighter. Late in July he joined 242 Squadron RAF led by the legless ace Douglas Bader; with this squadron he shot down two aircraft and probably destroyed another to win the DFC. On September 3 Christie was posted to 66 Squadron RAF as a flight commander. Next day he chased an ME 109 across the Strait of Dover forcing the pilot to bail out. But by then, only ten miles from the French coast and almost out of ammunition, he was attacked by two other 109s. He managed to escape intact. Later that day, in a fight with another ME 109, which he claimed as probably destroyed, a cannon shell wounded him when it went through his starboard wing. Christie was kept out of action until October 30. But before he was sent back to Canada at the end of 1940, he had added two more enemy planes destroyed, one probable and two damaged to his tally. And he became one of the first Canadians to receive a Bar to the DFC. In 1942 he was killed in a flying accident at Lake St Louis, P.Q.

DSO & Bar F/L Born Oct 1 1917 KFA July 6 1942
RefScs: DHist bf RCTFFY 8 38 TSBW 143 147

CHRISTIE Ralph MacLaren

"Winner of First RCAF DSO"

R alph Christie, of L'Orignal, Ont., was the RCAF's first recipient of the DSO; it was awarded him for an attack on German shipping off the Dutch coast. On January 5, 1942, as a Hudson pilot with 407 Squadron RCAF at North Coates in Lincolnshire, he had already exhibited his derring-do in this type of operation when, after setting fire to a 6,000-ton vessel, his aircraft was hit by flak. His starboard engine caught fire and shortly packed up. Despite this damage and the imminent danger Christie managed to limp home to base.

On May 15, flying from Bircham Newton in Norfolk, Christie led two formations against a strongly escorted convoy of ten German ships. As he pressed home his attack at deck level fierce cannon and gun fire riddled his Hudson, shot out the instruments, put the hydraulic system out of action and wounded the observer. But Christie's bombs hit his target and created a huge explosion in the rear of the ship. In the engagement four Hudsons were shot down. But three merchant vessels had been hit and left burning, and two more received direct hits, while another was badly damaged. Christie's Hudson suffered such punishment that on reaching base he had to crash-land.

DSO W/C   .
RefScs: DHist bf RCTFFY f241 258 259–60 353 RS&A 92 SY 466

CLAYTON Arthur Chamberlain Pitt

"Bomber Leader Headed Demobilization Operation"

A rthur Clayton, who commanded two RCAF bomber squadrons and flew over fifty-seven sorties himself, ended WW2 as Director of Demobilization at Air Force HQ in Ottawa, Ont. A native of Victoria,

B.C., Clayton joined the RAF in 1938. By the time the war started he was serving with 83 Squadron flying twin-engine Hampdens. Its earliest assignment — to find the German fleet — ended in failure. Clayton's first action came when the Germans invaded the West in May 1940; the squadron was given the job of attacking tactical targets — trains, transport troops. On the night of August 25/26, Clayton took part in the first British air raid on Berlin, a force consisting of 100 planes. When his tour ended he was awarded the DFC.

After serving as an instructor Clayton rejoined his old squadron in 1941. He was later transferred to 408 Squadron RCAF, which was being formed at Lindholme in Yorkshire, where he became a flight commander. Less than a year later, in March 1942, he was made CO of the unit; by that time the squadron had turned its Hampdens in for four-engine Halifaxes. Clayton relinquished his command in April.

After a leave in Canada he returned to the U.K. to take over as CO of 405 Squadron RCAF in November. Flying Halifaxes from Beaulieu, Hants., the unit was chiefly engaged that winter in patrols over the Bay of Biscay protecting shipping geared for the Allied invasion of North Africa.

When his tour ended in April 1943 Clayton became Air Staff Officer at 6 Group RCAF Bomber Command. He next attended the RAF Staff College before transferring to the RCAF in September 1944 and returning to Canada to take over demobilization duties.

OBE DFC & Bar   G/C
RefScs: DHist bf   RAW 272 281 284   RCTFFY 155 157 286–87 288
RS&A 89 94

CLEMENTS William Isaac

"First in the RCAF to Fly Into Germany"

On the night of September 29/30, 1939, William Clements became the first member of the RCAF to fly into Germany when he piloted a Blenheim twin-engine bomber on a deep reconnaissance from Metz in France to the Hamm-Hanover area. A native of North Devon, N.B., Clements was a graduate of RMC who enlisted in the RCAF, serving first with 5 Coastal Reconnaissance Squadron then with No 2 Army Co-operation Squadron as a flight commander. Posted to the U.K. on exchange duties with the RAF in 1939 he served in that same capacity with 53 Squadron with which he made his flight over Germany. In 1940 he returned to England to command 112 Squadron RCAF then was transferred to Air Force HQ in Ottawa until 1943. At that time he was named RCAF representative on a British Military Mission engaged in duties in the Pacific and Far East. Returning to AFHQ in 1944 he became CO first of RCAF Station Uplands, Ottawa, Ont., and then of Gander, Nfld. After the war he held a number of senior posts, including Chief of Staff No 1 Air Division HQ in France and AOC Maritime Air Command.

OBE CD CdeGWgc(Fr) A/C Born Aug 2 1909
RefScs: CA 207 CCMA 52 DHist bf SY 465 TSBW 134

CLEVELAND Howard Douglas

"Star Day-Intruder Pilot"

Howie Cleveland of Vancouver, B.C., proved to be one of the outstanding Mosquito day intruder pilots of the war. Though he only flew some thirty Day Ranger missions and was on operations little more than five months, with the help of his navigator he accounted for ten German planes destroyed and two damaged. These forays called for precise flying at low level.

On two occasions Cleveland was the catalyst of what can only be called a carnage. On February 26, 1944, when he scored his first success in company with another Mosquito, he attacked two German airfields at St Yan and Dole, setting a Heinkel 177 bomber on fire and destroying a Junkers 87, and sharing in the destruction of a glider-towing five-engine He 111Z (two twin-engine He 111s joined together with one engine added) as well as one of the Gotha 242 gliders it was hauling behind. He also damaged another Gotha on the ground. On another sortie Cleveland and the crew of an accompanying Mosquito accounted for six enemy destroyed in the air and two on the ground.

On May 16, while attempting to strafe some seaplanes in Kubitzer Bay, Cleveland's Mosquito was caught in a cross-fire between two Bofors 37-mm guns. Both he and his observer were wounded, the instruments of the aircraft blown away, the starboard engine riddled and a hole blown in the wing. Cleveland managed to ditch his aircraft in the Baltic but his observer drowned before a Swedish ship arrived to rescue them. Cleveland was interned for a month and upon repatriation rejoined his unit. He accounted for one more aircraft destroyed before being sent home on leave and assigned ground duty.

Cleveland had joined the RCAF in 1940 and spent two years as an instructor before being posted to 418 Squadron RCAF based at Ford in January 1944. In January 1945 he was attached to American 9th Air Force HQ in the U.K. until May 24, 1945, when he was assigned to 418 Squadron RCAF as CO to close up shop and send the men home. After the war he joined a sign company he had worked for before the war, eventually becoming president before he retired.

DFC   W/C   Born July 7 1913
RefScs: CA 237   CCMA 69   DHist bf   OMAP(2) 109   RCTFFY
161–62 165–66 168–69 f270   TTS 75–80 app

CONRAD Walter Allen Grenville

"Bailed out Twice, Returned to Unit Each Time"

Twice Wally Conrad was forced to bail out, once when he was shot down in the desert and again when he collided with another Spitfire over France. But on both occasions he returned safely to his unit.

Born in Melrose, Ont., Conrad joined the RCAF in 1940 and, on completing his pilot's training the following year, was sent overseas. After operational instruction he was posted to 247 Squadron RAF at Sidi Haneish North in Egypt flying Hurricanes. On December 1, 1941, he scored his first victory by shooting down a Messerschmitt 109 fighter. Before being transferred on July 16, 1942, to 145 Squadron RAF, a Spitfire outfit based at Garbert, Conrad's tally stood at three German aircraft destroyed, two probably destroyed and one damaged.

On June 16, just prior to his transfer, Conrad was shot down when a cannon shell exploded in his cockpit and forced him to bail out. Despite a wounded wrist he made it back to his squadron. In September he completed his first tour and returned to England.

In May 1943 Conrad joined 403 Squadron RCAF at Kenley in Surrey where he became a flight commander. He was made CO on August 12. By August 17 he had added three more enemy aircraft destroyed and one damaged to his score. However on that day Conrad was forced to bail out over France. He jumped out at such a low height he was lucky to land in a haystack just as his parachute opened. Conrad hid in a trench for four days before he finally made contact with the French underground. They shepherded him into Spain and, after six months in a prison there, he eventually arrived at Gibraltar.

Conrad went to Canada on leave. Then at the beginning of 1944 he took over as CO of 421 Squadron RCAF at Kenley. Before relinquishing his command of that unit in July, which was then based at Bazainville in Normandy, he had damaged another enemy aircraft. Conrad returned to Canada and was discharged from the RCAF in October 1945.

DFC & Bar   W/C   Born Apr 3 1920
RefScs: DHist bf   OMAP(2) 109   RAW 370   RCTFFY 105 111–12 354
RCTFY 115 235 f239 240   RS&A 86 115   WL 163 176–79

COONS Herbert Lindsay

"Dog-Fought Japanese Fighters with a Transport"

On January 14, 1945, seven unarmed twin-engine Dakota transports of 435 Squadron RCAF, led by Herb Coons, were about to drop gasoline and other supplies to British forces behind the Japanese lines at Schwebo in Burma when they were attacked by a dozen Zero fighters over the drop zone. As one of the Zeros bored down on Coons' aircraft he waited until it was only 400 yards away then, with super-human effort, he yanked the lumbering transport around into as tight and steep a turn as he could. It worked! The fighter skidded by. But the Zero attacked again and again — four more times. And four more times Coons repeated his evasive maneuver to elude the fighter. The Zero then turned its attention to another one of the Dakotas. Coons swung toward the Zero to draw fire away from the other transport. In so doing he again became the target. His encounters had lost him precious height but now, hugging the ground, he once more turned to meet the attack. Too low. His starboard wing struck a tree top. Fortunately the Japanese called off their attacks and Coons somehow managed to right his machine, which he flew back to his base at Tulihal in Manipur, India, minus four feet of wing and with a fuselage full of holes. For his feat Coons received a Bar to the DFC he had won earlier while serving with RAF Coastal Command. He seemed to have been equally oblivious to danger there.

Coons joined the RCAF in 1940 and trained as an observer. After graduation he joined 93 Squadron in RAF Coastal Command in September 1941 flying Sunderland flying boats. There he took part in three air-to-air battles. During one of these battles the crew claimed a four-engine Focke-Wulf Kurrier destroyed. On another sortie the bomb compartment caught fire and Coons was instrumental in dousing the flames. Twice during his tour the Sunderland was forced down in the sea. But Coons calculated his position for radio transmission so accurately that Air Sea Rescue Service ships reached the downed plane in short order. In October 1943 he remustered as a pilot and, after receiving his wings in April 1944, was posted for transport duties to the India-Burma Theatre. As a graduate engineer, Coons became a mining consultant following the war.

H. Coons (l.) PL 60119

DFC & Bar   S/L   Born Feb 17 1918
RefScs: AIC 210   DHist bf   RCTSY 410   SY 158   TDS 182–84

When I asked Herb what on earth he thought he was doing mixing it up with a Zero — one of the most nimble fighters of WW2 — in a clumsy Dak, he shrugged it off. "It just seemed like the natural thing to do," he said.

CORBETT Vaughan Bowerman

"One of the First RCAF Pilots Wounded in Combat"

A ugust 31, 1940, was the height of the Battle of Britain. Vaughan Corbett's section of Hurricanes was patrolling over the English coast near Dover at 20,000 feet. Suddenly they were bounced from out of the sun by a host of German Messerschmitt 109s. Three of the Canadian pilots were forced to take to their parachutes, including Corbett, who suffered serious burns when his aircraft caught fire.

Born in Toronto, Ont., Corbett took summer pilot training with the RCAF at Camp Borden while attending RMC. While working in Montreal,

P.Q., after graduation Corbett was one of the first to join 115 RCAF Auxiliary Squadron when it was formed in 1936. In May 1940 he was posted to No 1 Squadron RCAF, with which he went overseas in June. He went into combat at Northolt during the third week of August. On the twenty-fourth of the month he damaged a Dornier 215 twin-engine bomber.

After a lengthy stay in hospital recovering from the wounds he suffered when he was shot down Corbett was appointed CO of 402 Squadron RCAF, originally 112 Army Co-operation Squadron. Based at Digby in Lincolnshire it was one of the first to become a fighter-bomber outfit, its Hurricanes fitted with 250-pound missiles. Corbett served as its squadron leader from April to December 1941. During that time he shared in shooting down a Focke-Wulf 190. After a lengthy service career Corbett was killed in a flying accident at No 1 RCAF OTU, Bagotville, P.Q., of which he was Station Commander, in 1945.

DFC G/C Born Mar 24 1911 KFA 1945
RefScs: DHist bf HBB 24 31 35 RAW 167 202 RCTFFY 14 f33 46
62–63 355 RCTFY 121 RS&A 167 202

DALE Robert Gordon

"Snooper Navigation Specialist"

During the air power offensive in preparation for the D-Day landings in the spring of 1944, Bob Dale became a specialist in navigating Mosquito Snooper sorties — reconnaissance missions at low level in daylight providing immediate assessment and photographic proof of the effectiveness (or lack of it) of a raid once the bombers had left their targets.

Dale, who was born and raised in Toronto, Ont., joined the RCAF in 1940 as a navigator. Upon graduation he was posted overseas in 1941 where in March he joined 150 Squadron RAF flying twin-engine Wellington bombers from bases in Nottingham and Yorkshire. On his sixth sortie his bomber was coned by searchlights over the German Ruhr and badly shot up. The pilot had to take such violent evasive action the aircraft dropped from 12,000 feet down to 5,000 feet. Then the bomber was attacked by a Junkers 88 night fighter, which riddled it and wounded the rear gunner. Yet somehow the crew got home.

Bob Dale. Photo courtesy Bob Dale.

Dale survived thirty missions, considered to be somewhat of a miracle on Wellingtons, and was awarded the DFC.

In the middle of 1942 he returned to Canada for Specialist Navigator Training at Port Albert, Ont. In 1943 he was back in England as Navigation Officer of No 1 Group RAF. In December he joined 1409 Flight, part of No 8 Group Pathfinder Force RAF, which was equipped with Mosquitos. There Dale made his mark carrying out Snooper Raids. His work on meteorological missions was outstanding also. His unit's reports were responsible for postponing D-Day for twenty-four hours. As a pathfinder Dale completed two tours and was awarded the DSO.

Returning to Canada in 1945 he spent two months as CO of No 10 Observers School at Chatham, N.B., and then posted to Air Force HQ in Ottawa, Ont., to the planning department for the Pacific Theatre. Discharged late in 1945, Dale retained his association with the RCAF, first as CO of 180 Air Cadet Squadron; then as president of the Air Cadet League and as president of the National Executive Committee; and as Honorary Colonel of 400 Auxiliary Squadron. In 1982 he was appointed ADC to the Lieutenant Governor of Ontario. In business he became chairman and executive officer of Maple Leaf Mills, retiring in 1987.

DSO DFC CD   S/L   Lt/Col (Hon) ADC(LG)   Born Nov 1, 1920
RefScs: WWIC(1984-5) D3-4

Some quotes from Bob's D-Day address to the Royal Canadian Military Institute on June 6, 1991, reflect his own experiences and cast an interesting insight into RAF bomber operations:

"Writers and historians with the benefit of hindsight have claimed that casualties (only four percent of us would survive our first tour of operations) in the air war might have been considerably less if training standards had been high. But . . . the demand for aircrew, at least in the early stages, was so incredibly urgent that the Air Force had no alternative but to speed up training."

"[As] to whether the results of bombing raids, from a strategic point of view, justified the heavy loss of life and aircraft . . . two crews out of five were able to deliver their bombs on the specific targets!"

"During the Battle of Berlin (November 1943–February 1944) 30,000 sorties were flown . . . and 1,300 aircraft were lost."

"To move from Wellingtons to Mosquitos was like stepping into another world."

DAVIDSON Robert Tremayne Pillsbury

"Only Canadian to Shoot Down Aircraft in All Three Theatres"

B ob Davidson held the distinction of being the only Canadian to shoot down aircraft of all three Axis powers — Germany, Italy and Japan — as well as a French-built fighter.

Born in Vancouver, B.C., Davidson joined the RAF in 1937 and flew four tours of operations in Egypt, Greece, Crete, Libya, Ceylon, France and northwest Europe. His first victory was over an Italian Cant seaplane, which he shot down in Greece in 1940 while flying a Blenheim with 30 Squadron RAF. He made his next score in January 1942 by bringing down a German Junkers 52 transport with a Hurricane.

The squadron then moved to Ceylon. Flying out of there on April 5 he shot down a Val Bomber. Then on April 24 Davidson destroyed a Japanese Zero fighter and a bomber. From December 1942 to March 1943 he served in Ferry Command. Then in May he became CO of 175 Squadron RAF in England flying Typhoons. Later he was made Wing Commander Flying of 124 RAF Wing; in December he destroyed a French Leo 45 in service with the Luftwaffe. On May 8, 1944, Davidson was shot down in France where he teamed up with the Resistance. He

PL 50508

engaged in espionage as well as producing valuable information on German V-1 installations.

Following the war Davidson transferred to the RCAF. In 1952/53 he went back into combat in Korea with the American 4th Fighter Group. In 1961 he was posted to the Canadian Joint Staff in Washington, D.C. He retired to Kemptville, Ont., in 1967 and died five years later.

DFC CD AM(Am) CdeG(Fr)   G/C   Born Feb 1917   Died 1971
RefScs: CITR 125–16   DHist bf   OMAP(2) 110   RAW 237   RCTFY
122–26 135–36 f255   SY 259   TDS 27   TTS 283

While hiding out in France Davidson had the unusual experience of breaking bread with the foe — incognito albeit — when a German soldier arrived at the farm house in which Davidson was sheltered and asked the farmer's wife for a meal. Over lunch Davidson and his antagonist chatted in faltering French about this and that, all the while the Wehrmacht infantryman unaware he was sharing a repast with an enemy airman.

DAVOUD Paul Yettvart

"Night-Fighter Leader Devoted Fifty Years to Aviation"

Few men came to the wartime RCAF as well equipped and trained as Paul Davoud. And few contributed as much to Canadian aviation. A native of Provo, Utah, Davoud was educated in Kingston, Ont., attending RMC from 1928 to 1932, where he won the Van Smissen award. During the summers of 1929–31 he trained with the RCAF at Camp Borden; he graduated as a PPO and received the Sword of Honour as the best all-round cadet. In February 1933 he joined the RAF and obtained a permanent commission. Davoud served with 17 Fighter Squadron until March 1935, when he resigned to take up commercial flying. Davoud flew first with Canadian Airways then later with the Hudson's Bay Company as a bush pilot.

In 1940 he joined the RCAF and was posted to Trenton, Ont., as Assistant Chief Flying Instructor. On May 27, 1941, Davoud was one of the first pilots to ferry a Hudson across the Atlantic to England where, on June 30, he was selected to form 410 Night Fighter Squadron RCAF.

Paul Davoud (c.) and Dal Russel (r.) at presentation of the Dutch Command Order of Orange Nassau, 1945. PL 51780

On September 5, 1941, he was given command of 409 Squadron RCAF equipped with Beaufighters. That November Davoud shot down his first German aircraft — a Dornier 217 bomber — over the North Sea. By early 1944, Davoud had been awarded the DFC. However in February of that year Davoud was badly burned in a crash and taken off operations.

In June he became CO of 418 Intruder Squadron RCAF. Flying Mosquitos, the unit was assigned to maintaining night patrols over German night-fighter fields as well as daylight raids on training fields and ground targets. Davoud's leadership in these operations earned him the DSO. From January 9 to July 13, 1944, he commanded 22 Sector RAF Second Tactical Air Force. He was then given command of 143 RCAF Fighter Bombing Wing, made up of three squadrons of Typhoons. This post he held until January 1945.

Following the war Davoud joined TCA then held various aviation positions, among them vice-president of Hawker Siddeley Canada Ltd. From 1959 to 1963 he served as chairman of the Air Transport board and in 1971 became Director of Aviation Services for the Ontario Ministry of Transportation and Communications until his retirement in 1978. He died in 1987 at Kingston, Ont.

OBE DSO DFC MID CdeG(Fr) Ld'H(Bel) OONK(Dch)   G/C   Born
Nov 25 1911   Died Mar 24 1987   Ind CAHF 1985
RefScs: CAHF 119 DHist bf   RAW 17 37 255 268 281   RCTFFY 128
146–47 149 f288 355   RCTFY 155 160 254   RS&A 95–96 214 223
TDS 37–39

DAY Robert William Rouviere

"Only Canadian Ace Against the Japanese"

Bob Day shot down more Japanese planes than any of his countrymen and became the only Canadian ace to fight against the Nipponese. Born in Victoria, B.C., he joined the RCAF in 1940, graduated as a pilot and for two years served as an instructor. In November of 1942 he was posted overseas and in February 1943 he joined 416 Squadron RCAF flying Spitfires from Kenley. Day flew his first sortie on March 7 and a month later had his first dogfight. In April he was transferred to 402 Squadron RCAF at Digby then in June returned to Kenley to join 421 Squadron RCAF. Toward the end of the year Day was posted to the Far East, arriving in Bombay in December. He went straight to 81 Squadron RAF, operating from Imphal, India, with red-nosed Spitfires.

Though in all his time on fighter sweeps and bomber escort sorties over northwest Europe he had failed to score against the Luftwaffe, his experience as a fully operational pilot now proved invaluable. On February 15, 1944, Day shot down a Japanese A6M Zero, marking his first victory. Early in March the British flew four army brigades in behind enemy lines, an operation heavily supported by air power; 81 Squadron moved to an advanced airstrip near to the action on March 13. By now a flight commander, Day bagged his second victim that afternoon, an Oscar fighter-bomber. On March 28 Day raised his score to three by destroying another Oscar. On August 15 Day was promoted squadron leader; three days later he was taken off operations and assigned to staff duties.

In December Day was given command of 67 Squadron RAF. At the beginning of 1945 the unit moved to the island of Akyab off the Burmese coast, which the Japanese had abandoned some days earlier. On January 9 six Oscars tried to bomb the harbour. Day led a flight of Spitfires to intercept them and shot down two of the fighter-bombers. This brought his total Japanese aircraft destroyed to five and made him the only Canadian to attain ace status against the fliers of the Rising Sun.

DFC   S/L   Born Sept 14 1916
RefScs: DHist bf   OMAP(2) 110   TTS 287

DUNLAP Clarence Rupert

"Last CAS, Only RCAF Officer to Command RAF Bomber Wing"

On November 22, 1943, Larry Dunlap, last to hold the post of RCAF Chief of the Air Staff, took command of 139 Wing, 2nd Tactical Air Force, which comprised Nos 98, 180 and 320 Squadrons flying American-built Mitchell medium bombers. He thus became the only Canadian air force officer to head up an operational RAF wing. A native of Sydney Mines, N.S., Dunlap joined the RCAF in 1928. At the outbreak of WW2 he was serving as Director of Armament at Air Force HQ, Ottawa, Ont. Posted overseas in 1942 he took up duties as CO of RCAF Station Leeming in Yorkshire, a 6 Group Bomber Command base. In mid-May of 1943 Dunlap became CO of 331 Wing, made up of three RCAF Wellington bomber squadrons: 420, 424 and 425. They flew to North Africa to take part in the softening-up campaign for the invasions of Sicily and Italy.

Based in the Kairouan area of Tunisia the wing began operations on June 26 and made its last raid on October 5 when Grosetto aerodrome was bombed. By that time the unit had made 2,127 sorties, dropped 3,745 bombs and unloaded ten million leaflets. Small wonder Dunlap was picked to command 139 Tactical Air Force Wing with which he flew thirty-five sorties. Under his leadership the unit scored outstanding successes against German V-1 and V-2 sites as well as in support of the Allied ground forces; for this Dunlap was awarded the American Silver Star.

At the end of the war Dunlap commanded 64 Base of the Canadian Bomber Group. In May 1945 he returned to Canada as Deputy Air Member for Air Staff. In 1946 he represented the RCAF at the Bikini atomic bomb tests. Dunlap held a number of senior appointments, including Deputy Chief of Staff Operations at SHAEF. Appointed CAS in April 1962, Dunlap was the last officer to hold that post. He relinquished it in 1964 to become Deputy Commander of NORAD.

CBE CD SS(Am) A/M Born Jan 1 1908
RefScs: CA 229 233 293 299 CCMA 65 67 app DHist bf RAW 23 330 385 RS&A 207–208 210 214 224 SY 51 296 366 463 467 472

EDWARDS James Francis

"Kittyhawk Ace Became Desert Air Force's Top Scorer"

In the fall of 1942, after the British 8th Army retreat to El 'Alamain in North Africa, "Stocky" Edwards of Nokomis, Sask., had become the top Allied scorer in the desert. Edwards joined the RCAF in October 1940. After completing his pilot's training he was posted to the Middle East in November 1941 to join 94 Squadron RAF flying Kittyhawk fighters. On his first operational flight, March 2, 1942, he shot down his first enemy plane, a Messerschmitt 109. In June he was posted to 260 Squadron RAF where his score continued to mount and in December he became a flight commander. Shortly afterward he was awarded both the DFC and the DFM.

In June 1942 he was taken out of action for six months as a gunnery instructor. This was hardly surprising: he was a phenomenal shot. Having completed that stint he joined 417 RCAF Squadron, a Spitfire unit in Italy, first as a flight commander then as squadron commander. In February 1944 he was made CO of 92 Squadron RAF with which, on the nineteenth of the month, he destroyed three German fighters, two ME 109s and a Focke-Wulf 190. On March 17 Edwards survived a crash in which he was thrown clear. Although badly battered he returned to duty a week later. In the spring the squadron was posted to England to become part of a Spitfire fighter wing that saw action during the Normandy invasion and the breakout that followed.

In the fall of 1944 Edwards went to Canada on leave and took part in a war bond tour. He returned to the U.K. to take over command of 127 RCAF Wing, equipped with Tempests. On May 5 Edwards flew sortie 373 of his career, one that turned out to be his last. During his final engagement he damaged two German aircraft and shared in the destruction of a third; that brought his score to fifteen aircraft shot down, eight probables and many more damaged. He had also destroyed eight more aircraft on the ground and destroyed or damaged 300 vehicles.

Following the war Edwards stayed in the service. In October 1954 he led the first RCAF wing to return to Continental Europe since the end of WW2.

DFC & Bar   DFM   W/C
RefScs: CWC 112–18   DHist bf   RAW 374   RCTSY 261–62
SY 108 267   TTS app

ENGBRECHT Peter

"Only Air Gunner to Become an Ace"

Shortly before his retirement from the military in 1972, Russian-born Pete Engbrecht received the NORAD Plaque for distinguished service in the defence of North America against air attack, the climax of a thirty-year career with the RCAF. During this career he was the only bomber air gunner to become an ace in WW2. Born in Poltwaks, Engbrecht emigrated to Canada at age three and lived in Manitoba. He joined the RCAF in 1942 as the lowest-of-the-low: a GD2, General Duties Air-

PL 30466

craftsman Second Class, and as such he was posted overseas as a maintenance assistant. In 1943 he remustered to aircrew and, after graduating as an air gunner, was assigned to 424 Squadron RCAF based at Skipton-on-Swale in Yorkshire to become a mid-upper gunner of a Halifax.

Engbrecht's first raid was on May 26, 1944, on Bourg-Leopold in Belgium. His bomber was attacked fourteen times by enemy fighters. As the pilot corkscrewed the machine to evade his assailants Engbrecht coolly shot down two of them: a Focke-Wulf 190 and a Messerschmitt 109. On June 10, four days after D-Day, Engbrecht repeated his tandem performance by destroying an ME 190 and a twin-engine ME 110 night-fighter. On August 13, with the help of the tail gunner, he shared in the destruction of another ME 110. Before his tour was over he shot down his fifth enemy plane and achieved ace status — an unprecedented feat for an air gunner — and scored two more probables.

During his service with NORAD following WW2 Engbrecht distin-guished himself as a back-up crew chief. He was also in charge of training at the long-range Canadian radar site in Colorado.

CGM   Sgt
RefScs: DHist   OMAP(2) 111   RAW 313   SY 165bf   TDS 65–67

FAIRBANKS David Charles

"Top Canadian Tempest Pilot"

With fourteen German aircraft destroyed, one probable and four damaged to his credit, along with two V-1 flying bombs destroyed, Dave Fairbanks emerged as the top Canadian pilot flying Tempests, the peak of British wartime piston designs, and became one of only four members of the RCAF to be decorated with the DFC three times.

Born in Ithica, N.Y., Fairbanks enlisted in the Canadian air force in February 1941 and, after graduating as a pilot, spent two years as an instructor. In January 1944 he joined 501 Squadron RAF, which was flying Spitfires. In July he was transferred to the Tempest-equipped 274 Squadron RAF.

During the summer of 1944 he shot down two of the flying bombs over England. Fairbanks' unit then joined the 2nd Tactical Air Force in France in September. Flying from there on December 17 Fairbanks ran up his first score: two Messerschmitt 109 fighters destroyed and another shot down, which he shared with an anti-aircraft battery.

In January 1945 he was sent to 3 Squadron RAF as a flight commander; that month Fairbanks destroyed three German aircraft, shared in the destruction of another, probably destroyed two Junkers 88 twin-engine bombers on the ground and damaged one other. He had already been awarded the DFC and Bar by February 9 when he took over as squadron CO. In the next fortnight he accounted for seven enemy fighters destroyed, among them a Messerschmitt Ar234 jet, the first of its type to be brought down.

On February 28 his squadron engaged in a melee in which they fought forty Focke-Wulf 190s and ME 109s. Fairbanks sent one of his attackers to earth in flames before he was shot down and forced to take to his parachute. On alighting he was seized by angry citizens who were about to lynch him when a German gun-battery officer came to his rescue and commandeered him to a POW camp.

After being released Fairbanks was repatriated to Canada and discharged from the service. He pursued a civilian career that paralleled his war record: in 1955 he joined de Havilland of Canada as a test pilot; he eventually became manager of flight operations, responsible for the company's operations around the world. He died in Toronto in 1975 and was posthumously awarded the McKee Trophy for his services to Canadian aviation.

DFC & 2 Bars   S/L   Born Aug 22 1922   Died Feb 20 1975   McKTw
RefScs: AIC 203   DHist bf   OMAP(2) 77   RAW 181   TTS 87–91

FAUQUIER John Emilius

"King of the Pathfinders — Saviour of London"

J ohnny Fauquier ranked as the leading Canadian bomber pilot of WW2. In three tours he flew over 200 bombing sorties against Germany, including such historic raids as the fire-bombing of Hamburg, the one thousandth plane attack — on Cologne — and the devastation of the Peenemünde rocket station. He became the only member of the RCAF to win the DSO three times. Before the war Fauquier, who was born in Ottawa, Ont., learned to fly in Montreal and became a bush pilot. By the time WW2 began he had logged more than 300,000 air miles. In November 1939 he enlisted in the RCAF but with the BCATP just getting underway his flying experience was more urgently needed as an instructor than in combat.

In June 1941 Fauquier was posted to England and joined 405 Squadron RCAF, the first Canadian bomber unit to be formed overseas and the initial RCAF force to carry the attack into Germany. Fauquier made his first raid in October, on Emden. By January 17, 1942, he had proven himself to be such a capable bomber pilot he was made flight commander. In February he was promoted to CO and became the first RCAF officer to lead a bomber squadron into battle.

By this time his aggressiveness had become something of a legend. One night in June, over Bremen, heavy flak and night-fighters created a havoc among his bombers. Fauquier picked out an assembly of searchlights and flak guns below him and dived his Lancaster down to deck level. He twisted and turned his plane like a fighter, not only drawing fire away from his squadron but also giving his gunners a chance to shoot out the lights and still the batteries.

Fauquier's first tour ended in August that year, at which time he received the DFC. After a stint at 6 Group RCAF Bomber Command HQ he returned to operations in April 1943 and took command of his old squadron. By that time, however, the unit had been transferred to the elite Pathfinder Force — the RAF's most skilled and prestigious bombing group. Its job was to find targets in the dead of night and light them up with flares to ensure greater accuracy. This style of bombing made the bomber stream obsolete and allowed many aircraft to be over the target at once; this lessened the time spent in the area and made it more difficult for night-fighters to find the raiders in the dark.

Early in 1943 spies and special agents as well as aerial reconnaissance photos revealed that German scientists at Peenemünde were working on two revolutionary secret weapons: the V-1 jet-propelled pilotless bomb-plane and the V-2 guided rocket. There was little doubt at Bomber Headquarters as to who should lead a raid on such a vital target. On August 17 Fauquier flew his force to the Baltic seaport with explicit orders that the target had to be utterly wasted on the first go. Over the target Fauquier spent thirty-five minutes dodging flak while he made seventeen passes directing the bombers and assessing the bomb damage. By the time the raid ended Peenemünde was a mass of blazing wreckage and the V-weapon program had been set back a year. By then, June of 1944, the Allies had landed in Europe and, although the British capital suffered heavily, it had been saved from total destruction. Recognizing this, the Fleet Street press dubbed Fauquier "The Saviour of London."

At the end of January 1944 Fauquier had completed his second tour, was given a desk job at 6 Group Headquarters and in June was promoted to the rank of Air Commodore. When he learned there was an opening as CO of 617 Squadron RAF Fauquier voluntarily dropped two ranks temporarily to take on the job. The Dam Busters needed somebody like the hard, tough Canadian to lead them. Their many successes — breaching

PL 112734

the Ruhr dams, sinking the *Tirpitz* — had made the aircrews cocky prima donnas who needed a heavy dose of discipline. Fauquier quickly straightened them out. He got them up early every morning for PT (physical training); when winter grounded operations he lectured them on formation flying then sent them out to shovel snow off the runways. In 1945 the squadron was assigned raids on communications and supply lines, and was equipped with a spectacular new 22,000-pound bomb known as the "Grand Slam." With it the Dam Busters destroyed the U-boat pens at Bremen, sank the pocket-battleship *Lutzow*, knocked out bridges, oil refineries, railways and, finally, Hitler's mountain retreat at Berchtesgaden. As usual Fauquier took part in almost every raid in which they assigned his squadron, continuing to follow his formula for leadership of never asking another man to do something he wasn't willing to do himself.

Fauquier completed his third tour of operations a few weeks before the war ended then came home and resigned from the air force. He became involved in several commercial enterprises before finding his niche in the real estate business. During his civilian years he rarely looked back on his heroic flying days. In fact the bush pilot who had fought flames to rescue men from a forest fire, the bomber pilot who had flown over 1,200 hours through the flak- and fighter-infested nights over Germany never again took the controls of an airplane after leaving the RCAF. He died in 1981.

> DSO & 2 Bars   DFC   CdeG(Fr) Ld'H(Fr)   A/C   Born 1919   Died
> April 3 1981 Ind CAHF 1973
> RefScs: CAHF 22   CCMA 60–61   DHist bf   RAW 288 293 294
> RCTFFY 164 167 f227 353 356   RCTFY 11 f15 26 66 81 183
> RS&A 62 89 214   TDS 49–52

A lot of people thought Johnny was absolutely fearless. He was far from it. Where his bravery showed was in the record he achieved while he learned to live with fear. He once told me: "A fellow who isn't afraid lacks imagination. And a guy who has no imagination can't be much of a combat pilot, and certainly never a leader."

FEE John Clark

"Led Squadron After Only One Month in Combat, Won Two DFCs Within Five Months"

In April 1942, after only one month on operations, "Nobby" Fee of Toronto, Ont., was given command of a Spitfire unit: 41 Squadron RAF. Few pilots, if any, adapted so quickly to battle conditions and needs;

before he was killed in action Fee had been awarded the DFC and Bar within five months of one another.

Fee joined the RCAF in 1937. In the spring of 1939 he was posted to 115 Auxiliary Squadron in Montreal, P.Q., as instructor and adjutant. When WW2 started Fee's squadron went overseas, although he did not accompany it. The BCATP was beginning to take shape and Fee's services were needed at home as an instructor.

In 1942, after having put in over 800 instructional hours, he was sent to England to join 41 Squadron. Although he held a Squadron Leader's rank, as a "sprog" (fledgling) he rated the equivalent status on operations as a Sergeant-Pilot. Fee accepted this cheerfully, but within 30 days he was made CO of the unit. During the next three months he led the unit on forty-eight sweeps over France, the most notable being a low-level line-abreast attack on Abbeville airfield. On another occasion Fee damaged a Messerschmitt 109 fighter as well as a German E-boat.

On July 19 he was given command of 412 Squadron RCAF, which was based at Merston in Sussex. This was just in time to take part in the raid on Dieppe on August 19. During this engagement he led his squadron on three different escort missions; for this he was awarded the DFC.

In November 412 Squadron became part of a new Canadian wing based at Kenley; on the twenty-sixth Fee was made Wing Leader. In the following months he led the wing on offensive sweeps over France. They were frequently heavily engaged and almost always outnumbered. On January 17, 1943, Fee, flying top cover, led his wing on the second sortie of the day: a strafing attack on trains near St Valery. He and his wingman were attacked by Focke-Wulf 190s and, in the fierce battle that followed, both were shot down and killed.

DFC & Bar   W/C   KIA Jan 17 1943
RefScs: CWC 119–26   DHist bf   RCTFFY f48 67 73 75–76 355
RS&A 76 100

FLEMING Mervyn Mathew

"First Capital City Flier to Win DFC"

W hen Merv Fleming received the DFC in January 1941 following his first tour — flying twin-engine Whitley bombers with the 58 Squadron RAF at Linton-on-Ouse against targets in both Germany and Italy — he became the first Ottawa, Ont., aviator to win the decoration.

During that tour he had flown in the first RAF raid on Berlin: the night of August 25/26, 1940.

Fleming had learned to fly at the Ottawa Flying Club and had enlisted in the British flying service in 1937. After his first tour of operations he was made navigation officer of No 4 Group. He then returned to Canada for a specialists' navigation course, after which he piloted a Hudson to England for Ferry Command. He was then made navigation officer at RAF Bomber Command HQ following which he was given command of 419 Squadron RCAF at Topcliffe, part of the newly formed Canadian 6th Bomber Group. He served in that capacity from September 1942 to October 1943. In all he had completed fifty operations.

Following WW2 Fleming joined the Department of Transport, where he was largely responsible for Canadian standards for licensing personnel and the operation of commercial air services. In 1951 he became Executive Assistant to the Director of Air Services and in 1958 was appointed Controller, Civil Air Operations and Regulations.

DSO DFC W/C Born 1915
RefScs: CITR DHist bf RA&S 112 RCTFFY 232

FLOODY Clarke Wallace

"The Tunnel King"

W hen Wally Floody was shot down over France on October 8, 1942, he could no longer fight the Germans with his Spitfire, but his determination to make life difficult and distressing for them took him a long way. Imprisoned at the notorious POW camp Stalag Luft III at Sagan, he immediately became a key member of a group planning a mass escape with the objective of diverting as much of the Wehrmacht as possible from essential war duties to hunting down escapers. The medium was a series of three underground passages out of the camp; here Floody's expertise came into play. Based on his prewar experience as a miner at Kirkland Lake, Ont., he supervised and personally led the digging of the tunnels as well as designing the lighting, ventilation and electrical systems. Several times he became trapped by cave-ins and had to be pulled out by his heels. When one of the tunnels was discovered by the German guards they became suspicious of Floody and several others and moved them to another camp before the breakout, which took place on March 24, 1944, without them. For that Floody and his comrades could thank their lucky stars. They, Floody most certainly, would surely have been on the Germans' hit list. Of the seventy-six who got out of

Wally Floody. Photo courtesy of Don Morrison.

the tunnel only three made good their escape. On Hitler's orders fifty of the rest were brutally murdered by the Gestapo.

Floody, who was born in Chatham, Ont., joined the RCAF in 1940. Posted overseas, he joined 401 Squadron RCAF at Biggin Hill, Kent, Britain's most famous fighter base. Following WW2 he became a public relations consultant and held interests in a scrap iron business. He died in Toronto in 1989 of a chronic lung disease, partially attributed to his tunneling as a POW. He was 71 years old.

MBE F/L Born Apr 28 1918 Died Sept 25 1989
RefScs: DHist bf RAW 430 SY 439 TGE

When Betty Floody learned that her husband had been shot down and made a prisoner she was sad — but far from despondent. "With his experience in mining, construction and riding the rails, I knew there was no one who had a better chance of escaping," she recalls.

Even in his last uncomfortable days, when he had to lug around a portable oxygen bottle, Wally remained humorously philosophical. When I needled that it must be a bit of a bind tied to all that equipment, he replied in his usual deep voice, which no amount of affliction could ever drown out, "Well it's a damn sight better than being dead!"

FORD Leslie Sydney

"First BCATP Graduate to Become Wing Commander"

Syd Ford of Halifax, N.S., was the first graduate of the BCATP to lead an RCAF wing. Joining the air force in June 1940 he completed his pilot's training in April 1941 and was posted overseas. He joined 403 Squadron RCAF, with which he was to serve most of his operational career. However in August Ford joined another Canadian squadron, 402 based at Debden. On September 27, flying a Hurricane, he fired his guns in anger for the first time and ended up sharing a Messerschmitt 109 fighter damaged with another pilot. In February 1942 Ford was transferred to 175 Squadron RAF, which was equipped with Hurricane fighter-bombers. By early summer he had been so successful in attacks on enemy shipping that he was promoted to flight commander and awarded the DFC.

In July he returned to his old unit, 403 Squadron. A month later he was made CO. Here he served for the next eight months and ran up a score of 6 German aircraft destroyed and 2½ damaged. For his leadership during the Dieppe raid on August 19, in which he destroyed two German aircraft, he was awarded a Bar to his DFC. In April 1943 he was given command of the Canadian Digby Wing. On June 4, while leading a low-level shipping strike against German E-boats, his Spitfire was hit by return fire and plunged into the sea off the Dutch coast.

At the time Ford was the youngest Wing Commander Flying in the British Commonwealth at just twenty-three years of age. In Liverpool, N.S., where Ford went to school, there is a stained-glass window erected in his honour at the Trinity Anglican Church.

DFC & Bar   W/C   Born Dec 30 1919   KIA June 4 1943
RefScs: CWC 127–40   DHist bf   OMAP(2) 112   RCTFFY 46 55–56 68
79 80 82–84 86–87   RS&A 86 215   TSBW 198

FULTON John

"Moose Squadron Named After First CO"

N o 419 Squadron RCAF was affectionately named "the Moose Squadron" after the nickname of its first CO, John Fulton. A native of Kamloops, B.C., Fulton was described as "one of the most popular squadron commanders." This squadron unwittingly set a pattern for the official christening of Canadian squadrons after beasts and birds of prey with related crests and mottos, i.e., crest: a moose attacking; motto: *Moosa Aswayeta*, "Beware of the Moose."

Fulton began flying at Oakland, Calif., in 1931; the following year he received his commercial licence from the Aero Club of B.C. in Vancouver. In 1934 he joined the RAF, was commissioned in 1935 and posted to a bomber squadron in Egypt. In January 1938 he was transferred to Mildenhall, Suffolk, where he served his first tour as a bomber pilot. During this tour Fulton made thirty sorties and was awarded the DFC. In 1941 he flew as a test pilot at the RAF Experimental Section at Farnborough, an assignment that earned him the AFC.

In December Fulton became CO of 419, then equipped with twin-engine Wellingtons, which was the third Canadian bomber squadron to be formed. As squadron CO he served for six months and made over twenty sorties. Returning from a raid on Kiel on April 28, 1942, Fulton's aircraft was badly crippled from an attack by a Messerschmitt 110 night-fighter: the rear gunner was wounded, and the instruments and one engine were put out of action. Yet miraculously he was able to land the plane safely back at base, a feat for which he received the DSO. Fulton failed to return from a sortie on the night of July 28, 1942. He was last seen crossing the coast after being attacked by German fighters.

DSO DFC AFC   W/C   Born 1918   KIA July 28 1942
RefScs: BB 176   DHist bf   RAW 272 309   RCTFFY 155 f160 166–67
171   RS&A 112 127

FUMERTON Robert Carl

"Leading Canadian Night-Fighter Pilot"

As a night-fighter, ace "Moose" Fumerton destroyed fourteen German planes and damaged another, making him the Canadian leader in the field. Born in Fort-Coulonge, P.Q., he learned to fly at the Sudbury Flying Club in Ontario; there he acquired his private pilot's licence. When WW2 broke out he enlisted in the RCAF, graduated in May 1940 and received posting overseas to 112 Squadron RCAF flying Lysanders. In October he transferred to 2 Squadron RCAF, which was equipped with Hurricanes. He was then posted to 1 Squadron RCAF (later 401) based in Scotland, where he flew defensive patrols. But it was not until he joined 406 Squadron RCAF at Acklington — the first Canadian night-fighter unit — that Fumerton had his first combat. On the night of September 1/2, flying one of the new Beaufighters over Bedlington, Fumerton shot down a Junkers 88 twin-engine bomber (see OdCWM). A week later he damaged a Heinkel 111 bomber.

Fumerton's greatest triumphs, however, were achieved in Egypt and the Mediterranean with 89 Squadron RAF, to which he was transferred in October. Based at Abu Suier, the unit's job was to protect the Suez Canal. Early in the morning of March 3, 1942, Fumerton and his observer tangled with an He 111 over the canal. He shot it down, but not before the German bomber's gunner had riddled the Beaufighter. Fumerton's gunsight was blasted, flying debris slashed him over the right eye and cheek, and a bullet struck his leg; both engines packed up, the undercarriage was damaged and the flaps were rendered inoperative. Then suddenly one of the engines came to life and Fumerton was able to land on the Edku Salt Flats. For that effort he received the DFC.

After a three-day stay in hospital Fumerton moved with his squadron to Edku to defend the port of Alexandria against air attack. On the night of April 7/8 Fumerton and his observer shot down two 111s in flames. In June the unit was again moved, this time to Luqa on Malta. During the next two months Fumerton shot down nine more German planes and won a Bar to his DFC. At the end of the year Fumerton was taken off operations and sent to Canada for six months' instructional duty.

In August he returned to England and took over command of 406 Squadron RCAF, which was re-equipped with Mosquitos in April 1944. Fumerton's final victory came on the night of May 14/15 when he shot down a Ju 188. In July 1944 he became CO of 7 Operational Training Unit at Debert, N.S. He performed so capably he was awarded the AFC. He retired form the air force in 1945 then in 1948 was hired for a short

PMR 77-555

period by de Havilland of Canada to train Nationalist Chinese pilots to fly the Mosquitos the company had sold to them.

DFC & Bar AFC   W/C   Born March 21 1913
RefScs: CA 216   CCMA 58   DHist bf   OMAP(2) 112   RAW 254–55
RCTFFY f112 123 126 353   RCTFY 148 152–54 f159 277 281–82
SY 141   TDS 40–42   TSBW 149   TTS 95–102
OdCWM: A portion of metal from the Ju 88, which bears a black cross and small swastikas denoting 406 Squadron victories, is on display at the Canadian War Museum in Ottawa, Ont.

GANDERTON Vaughan Francis

"Bomber Leader Held Key Administrative Posts"

Vaughan Ganderton, who flew two tours of operations as a bomber pilot over Europe in WW2, held several key administrative posts with the postwar RCAF, including that of Directorate of Air Intelligence. A native of Heath, Alta., "Gandy" joined the air force in 1941 and after graduation served as a staff pilot at a wireless school before being posted overseas. In 1943 he joined 427 Squadron RCAF first flying twin-engine Wellingtons and later four-motor Halifaxes from Croft in Yorkshire.

On the night of June 28/29 during a raid on Cologne, Ganderton's Halifax was so badly riddled by cannon fire from a German night-fighter that he had to turn back. After jettisoning his bomb load he nursed the crippled bomber back to England where, because of severe damage to the controls, the entire crew had to bail out. His actions won him his first decoration: the DFC.

Ganderton completed his first tour in December and was made Operations Controller at 6 Group RCAF Bomber Command. He served in that capacity until the following August in 1944 when he took command of his old squadron, 427, which was then stationed at Leamington in Yorkshire. On November 16 Ganderton led his unit on a daylight raid on the fortified German towns of Duren, Julich and Heinsburg, situated on the Roer. This was part of the support effort for the U.S. Army in which 1,200 aircraft took part and dropped 5,689 tons of explosives. The attack was so effective that no further raids were needed: the targets were completely obliterated. Shortly afterward Ganderton received the DSO.

Following the war he served in various staff positions, including Chief Administrative Officer of the Canadian Joint Air Training Centre at Rivers, Man. In 1953 he became a member of the Directing Staff of the Canadian Army Staff College in Kingston, Ont.

DSO DFC CD W/C Born Oct 26 1914
RefScs: DHist bf RCTFFY 228 355 RCTFY f79 RCTSY 60–61
RS&A 124

GARLAND John Wilburn

"Canadian Pioneer of Tactical Air Power"

A mong those who pioneered the use of tactical air power was a Canadian who helped perfect the art from beginning to end. John Garland began his operational career in Africa with 80 Squadron RAF, a division of Montgomery's 8th Army, at a time when Montgomery's Desert Rats were preparing to break through the German lines at El 'Alamain in the fall of 1942. It was there that the transition from aerial army co-operation — photographing and artillery spotting — to active participation in the land battle — attacking ground targets — took place.

Born in Carleton, Ont., Garland enlisted in the RCAF in 1940 and, after completing his pilot's training, sailed for the Middle East. There 80 Squadron's Hurricanes were being armed with four 20-millimeter cannons for use against troops, trucks and, when needed, enemy aircraft. On one of Garland's first sorties his unit tangled with Junkers 87 Stuka dive-bombers and Messerschmitt 109 fighters while attacking troop columns and truck convoys. That entire fall the squadron was busy pursuing the retreating Afrika Korps. In April 1943 the unit was re-equipped with Spitfires. Then, following the German surrender in Tunisia and the Allied conquest of Sicily, Garland's squadron moved to Italy. In addition to low-flying attacks on the German army the pilots also engaged in shipping strikes; on one occasion Garland set fire to a tanker in the Adriatic.

By March his first tour had ended and Garland did not return to operational duty until August 1944. When he rejoined 80 Squadron at Detling in England they had already converted to the powerful Tempests. In September the unit moved to Antwerp in Holland, and now a new target presented itself: trains. This was to have an ironic twist for Garland.

During his second tour he was successful against ground targets as well as flying targets: four German aircraft destroyed in the air, one of them a Messerschmitt 262 jet, and a share in the destruction of another on the ground. At this time he was awarded the DFC.

On January 29, 1945, Garland was posted to 3 Squadron RAF as a flight commander. But the appointment was short-lived. On February 8, after attacking a train, Garland's aircraft was hit by ground fire and he took to his parachute. Taken prisoner along with others, he was being transported by train to a POW camp deep inside Germany when a Mustang attacked. Fortunately the pilot's aim was accurate: he had damaged the engine but the rest of the train was untouched. The train eventually continued its journey. In April thousands of prisoners were taken from the camps and marched east; Garland was among them. Along with another prisoner, he escaped from the column and made it safely to the American lines.

Following the war he stayed in the service. Garland rose to the rank of Colonel by the time the Canadian Forces came into being.

DFC F/L Col(CF)   Born 1922
RefScs: DHist bf   RAW 181–82   TDS 158–65

GILCHRIST Peter Alexander

"POW, Escaper, Bomber, Ferry, Long-Range Command Veteran"

Peter Gilchrist had one of the most diversified careers in the service. A native of Weyburn, Sask., he joined the RAF in 1935 and, after training as a pilot, saw service in Iraq before returning to England to join 51 Squadron RAF. Flying twin-engine Whitley bombers, the unit's initial missions were to drop leaflets over Germany until the phoney war ended. Later Gilchrist served with 35 Squadron RAF.

In May 1941 he formed and commanded 405 Squadron RCAF, based at Driffield in Yorkshire. Equipped with twin-engine Wellingtons at the time, the new squadron was part of 4 Bomber Group RAF. On July 24, during the largest RAF raid to date (against the German battleships *Gneisenau* and *Prinz Eugen* berthed at Brest), the formations were heavily attacked by Messerschmitt 109 fighters and Gilchrist was shot down. Made a POW, he later escaped from the prison camp and made his way back to England via Switzerland. He was then assigned to RAF Ferry Command and later became CO of 59 VLR (Very-Long-Range) Liberator Squadron RAF. In 1945 he attended the RAF Staff College and transferred to the RCAF. He held several senior posts before retiring from the RCAF in 1964. His last position was as Deputy for Operations at Northern NORAD Region Headquarters, St Hubert, P.Q.

DFC CD A/C   Born Aug 1910
RefScs: DHist bf   RAW 272 275   RCTFFY 155 159   RS&A 89

GOBIEL Fowler Morgan

"First to Draw Blood for the RCAF"

As CO of 242 (Canadian) Squadron RAF, part of an exchange arrangement with the RAF, Fowler Gobiel shot down a German

Messerschmitt 110 twin-engine fighter over Menen in Belgium on May 36, 1940. Thus he became the first member of the RCAF to destroy an enemy aircraft. A native of Ottawa, Ont., Gobiel attended RMC and joined the Canadian air service in 1929. In 1930 he became a member of the Siskin aerobatic team. In 1939 he was sent to England as one of several RCAF officers seconded to the RAF to establish an early Canadian presence when WW2 broke out.

In October 1940 he formed 242 Squadron — equipped with Hurricanes — which was served mostly by Canadians in the RAF. Part of the British Advanced Air Striking Force stationed in France, the squadron was later commanded by the legendary legless ace Douglas Bader. Gobiel was also the first in the RCAF to come to grips with the enemy when, three days before his victory, he fought an ME 109 single-engine fighter near Berck in France.

Following his overseas service Gobiel returned to Canada to command No 4 Bombing and Gunnery School at Fingal, Ont. In 1942 he was transferred to Ferry Command at Dorval, P.Q. One of his most notable exploits was copiloting a Hadrian glider as it was towed by a Dakota across the Atlantic from Montreal, P.Q., to Scotland via Newfoundland, Greenland and Iceland between June 23 and July 1, 1943. A purely experimental flight, it covered 3,500 miles in twenty-eight hours flying time.

By war's end Gobiel commanded the Instrument and Flying School at Desoronto, Ont. After the cessation of hostilities he was transferred to Trenton Air Station, Ont., serving as staff officer, personnel administration. Then in 1953 he took over as CO of RCAF Station, Toronto, Ont. Gobiel retained this command until his retirement from the service in March 1958.

AFC W/C Born July 30 1906
RefScs: CA 209 229 CCMA 54 65 DHist bf RCTFFY 7–8 SY 46
TDS 20 174–76 TSBW 26–27

GODEFROY Hugh Constant

"Aerobatic Prowess Saved His Hide"

W hen RAF Fighter Command first went on the offensive over France — usually against overwhelming odds — it was quite common for a fledgling fighter pilot such as Hughie Godefroy to become separated from his squadron and find himself in the cockpit of his Spitfire surrounded by German Messerschmitt 109 single-engine fighters. In this type of situation a novice flier was frequently outnumbered by as many as fifteen to one. Godefroy's initiation came on October 27, 1941, when his squadron, 401 RCAF, was bounced from above by a gaggle of 109s during a sweep. They lost seven planes and five pilots in half that many minutes. Luck and consummate flying skill — an aerobatic ability for which he became famous — pulled Godefroy through on that occasion, as it would on many others.

A naturalized Canadian, Godefroy was born in Java (Indonesia), and brought up in Toronto, Ont. When WW2 broke out he enlisted in the RCAF. On April 22, 1941, he joined 401 Squadron at Digby in Yorkshire, which was equipped with Hurricanes at that time. On July 27 he made his first sweep over France. But it was not until two weeks later that he had his first dogfight.

By April 1942 he ended his first tour, having flown seventy-seven sorties. Although on several occasions he had mixed it up with enemy fighters who often outnumbered him, he had failed to score a victory. Nevertheless his aerial expertise did not go unrecognized: he was sent to an Air Fighting Development Unit at Duxbury and made a test pilot.

Godefroy rejoined 401 Squadron at the end of the year. On January 7, 1943, he and another pilot flew on a low-level Rhubarb. Godefroy scored for the first time, sharing the damage of two ME 109s. Three days later he made his first kill when he and a squadron mate attacked thirty Focke-Wulf 190s over the southeast British coast. Godefroy sent one of the enemy planes crashing into the sea.

Shortly afterward he was transferred to 403 Squadron and in March 1943 was made a flight commander. By June, with five aircraft destroyed and three damaged to his credit, he was appointed CO of the squadron. At the end of July, with 200 sorties under his belt, he took a month's leave. On his return to operations in September he was given command of 127 RCAF Wing at Kenley. On the twenty-fourth of that month he scored his last victory, bringing his total tally to seven planes destroyed and three damaged.

His second tour ended on April 15, 1944, and he was made a Staff Officer with the 2nd Tactical Air Force. Ironically it was in this capacity that the wing leader who had survived 289 missions without suffering a scratch experienced his closest brush with death. Shortly after D-Day Godefroy was flying a Spitfire over the English Channel to Normandy when his engine failed and he had to bail out. But he came down so fast he had no time to release his parachute and nearly drowned when he was dragged through a heavy swell. By the time he finished cutting the parachute loose and inflated his dinghy, he passed out from exhaustion. Though he had been unable to radio his position because the instrument was unserviceable, he was picked up some hours later by a trawler.

In 1945 he left the RCAF, graduated from McGill University as a doctor and moved to the U.S. to set up practice.

PL 15950

DSO DFC & Bar   W/C   Born Oct 28 1919   Author of *Lucky Thirteen*
RefScs: CWC 141–54   DHist bf   RAW 172 180   RCTFFY 75–76 83
85–86 94 f96 RCTFY   104–106 109–10 124 f126   RS&A 86 222   TTS
app

GODFREY John Morrow

"Parachute Saved His Skin — Literally"

On August 19, 1942, flying thousands of feet above the beach of Dieppe where the Canadian army was being slaughtered, Jack Godfrey had his own problems. His Spitfire had been hit by heavy flak. He was able to nurse it home to Tangmere in Sussex, however. Back at home base he discovered that, in addition to the damage to his aircraft, he had literally come within an inch of having a badly battered rump: a piece of schrapnel had pierced the metal seat and lodged itself in the silk of the packed parachute on which he sat.

John Godfrey. Photo courtesy John Godfrey.

Godfrey hailed from Port Credit, Ont., and attended RMC. After graduating he enlisted in the RCAF and in January 1940 he enrolled in the last Provisional Pilot Officers course. Upon his graduation Godfrey was assigned instructional duties for eighteen months. Then in April 1942 he was posted overseas. At his own request he flew a Hudson bomber to England rather than what he considered the riskier route by surface-vessel convoy. It also saved the country the $3,000 that American civilian pilots were paid to do the same job.

After OTU Godfrey was posted to 412 Squadron RCAF in August; he served part of his first tour with this unit. In June 1943 he was posted to 414 Squadron RCAF, a Mustang-equipped fighter-reconnaissance unit. He later became CO of this unit. Then Godfrey was made Airfield Commander in July 1943 of 128 RCAF Airfield — later designated 128 (New) Wing — a post he held until just before the invasion of Normandy in June 1944 when his tour ended.

Officially Godfrey should not have been flying at all on D-Day. But he had stayed on strength as Wing Commander Flying to take the wing to Normandy to hand the unit over to his successor. That afternoon Godfrey experienced his closest call since Dieppe. He and two others were reconnoitering the area between Evreux and Montfort when they were bounced by six Focke-Wulf 190 single-engine German fighters. The wing man was shot down, but Godfrey and the other pilot escaped.

Following WW2 Godfrey resigned from the RCAF and went into law practice in Toronto, Ont. In 1973 he was summoned to the Senate.

W/C   Born June 28 1912
RefScs: DHist bf   RCTFY 243   RS&A 104 220 222

I first met Jack Godfrey in July 1944 at Ewston railway station in London. We were both on our way back from Normandy to an RCAF repatriation centre at Warrington before shipping home to Canada. The gregarious wing leader made the journey a very pleasant one. But it very nearly hadn't turned out that way. We learned later that the platform from which we had boarded the train had been blasted by a V-1 flying bomb half an hour after our departure.

GORDON Donald Cameron

"Mind Over Mishap"

During his career as a fighter pilot in North Africa and Western Europe, "Chunky" Gordon had four aircraft accidents, was shot down three times, made three forced landings, had a car accident and was twice hospitalized. But none of these mishaps deterred him from destroying at least eleven enemy aircraft or rising from Sergeant-Pilot to Squadron Leader or winning the DFC and Bar.

Born in Edmonton, Alta., Gordon joined the RCAF in 1940. During his elementary training he suffered his first calamity when he ground-looped a Tiger Moth. However by November 1941 he was a member of 65 Squadron RAF flying Spitfires. And it was with one of these precious fighters that he had his next prang: he wrote off the undercarriage in a misjudged landing.

On December 26 on a Rhubarb over Cherbourg, Gordon was hit by flak and shot down for the first time; he had to be fished out of the English Channel by an Air Sea Rescue Service launch. In January he was posted to the Far East; while he was enroute, however, Singapore fell to the Japanese and he was redirected to the Western Desert, to 247 Squadron RAF, a unit that flew Hurricanes. There he began to run up a score: May 22 he was credited with a Junkers 87 Stuka probably destroyed; June 21 he shot down a Messerschmitt 109 and probably destroyed an Italian Macchi 202. He experienced the first of three forced

Donald Gordon surveys a German Tiger tank disabled in the ruins of Aachen, Germany, 1945. Photo courtesy D.C. Gordon.

landings on July 6 when his engine seized and he barely made it back to Debheala airfield. By year's end his tally totalled two aircraft destroyed, three probables and three damaged. Then he was posted to a Spitfire squadron, 601 RAF. With this unit he added a Messerschmitt 109 destroyed, an Italian Macchi probably shot down and two other aircraft damaged to his total between February 27 and April 1, 1943. On March 26 during that period he was shot down for the second time, but he crashed without injury. He had his third airplane accident on April 2 when he collided with another Spitfire on the runway. Then on May 2 he was knocked unconscious in a car accident and hospitalized.

He returned to operations in August with 417 Squadron RCAF with which he served until October before being assigned instructional duty. After completing this assignment in the summer of 1944 Gordon returned to Canada on leave.

On November 22 he reported to 422 Squadron RCAF, then stationed at Warmwell in England. Three days later the unit moved to Heesch in Holland. On the twenty-eighth Gordon had his fourth aircraft accident: he buckled the undercarriage of his Spitfire on landing. But he more than redeemed himself on New Year's Day 1945 when the Germans launched Operation *Bodenplatte*, a mass aerial attack on Allied fighter fields. While Gordon was on patrol he developed engine trouble and turned back. Suddenly he spotted a gaggle of Focke-Wulf 190s, he shot down two before another riddled his own aircraft. He was forced to land in a farmer's field, the third time he had been shot out of the air. This time he ended up in the hospital where seventeen pieces of shrapnel were removed from his body.

When he returned to duty in February he was made a flight commander. Before the end of the month he had shot down three more planes and shared another. In March 1945 he was transferred to 411 Squadron RCAF; with this unit Gordon scored another victory before he took over as CO of 402 Squadron RCAF.

Before the war ended he destroyed two more aircraft. Then on June 9 he had yet another forced landing when, flying an Auster touring plane, he got lost and ran out of fuel.

Gordon elected to stay with the RCAF after the war ended. Before his flying career ended Gordon had still one more forced landing when one of the engines of an Anson he was flying at Rockcliffe Park, Ont., seized up.

After a stint in Washington, D.C., Gordon was stationed at AFHQ, Ottawa, Ont. In 1948 he suffered from deafness, a neurological condition that required surgery a year later. Ironically, after all his hair-raising adversities and escapades in the air, he never recovered from this condition.

DFC & Bar   S/L   Born Feb 25 1920   Died June 26 1949
RefScs: DHist bf   OMAP(2) 112   RAW 199   RS&A 84   TTS 103–107

GORDON Ralph Alan

"Devised Burma 'Watchbird' Weather Patrol System"

As CO of 436 Transport Squadron RCAF based at Mawnubyin in Burma, Ralph Gordon was agonizingly aware of how quickly squalls and storms could blow up over the northern area where his unit was delivering supplies to the British 14th Army, along with another RCAF and two RAF squadrons. In one month alone the squadron had flown 1,238 sorties entailing 3,808 hours; they had carried seven million pounds of freight, and had transported 1,308 passengers and 204 casualties. In May 1945 the weather situation had become critical: monsoon season was approaching and rainfall in one day would soon reach 5½ inches.

At this point in the war the American transport units had been withdrawn to China; along with them went their weather station facilities. Gordon thereupon inaugurated the "Watchbird" meteorological service: an hour before the rest of the squadrons were to fly out on a mission one Dakota was sent out to keep watch on conditions over the delivery area until all had returned. The technique called for bi-hourly broadcast reports and answers to advice when requested. The scheme paid off as expected but provided additional information also. It was discovered that flying conditions in the monsoons were generally good. And by flying at 8,000 to 9,000 feet, turbulent cores of cloud masses could be observed and avoided. Another outgrowth was a recommendation that low flying be abandoned over a country so notoriously hilly.

A native of Bobcaygeon, Ont., Gordon joined the RCAF in January, 1940 as a pilot. His first operational duties were with 415 Squadron RCAF in Coastal Command, flying Albacores. On one occasion shortly after D-Day in June 1944, while investigating German shipping off Cap Gris Nez on the coast of France, his biplane was overturned by a close burst of flak. He took over 436 Squadron RCAF in October and remained as its CO until July 1945. For his efforts he was awarded the DSO and DFC as well as a mention in dispatches.

Following WW2 Gordon resigned from the RCAF but re-enlisted in May 1946. He was given a number of senior commands, including that of commander of Maritime Air Command from September 1965 to January 1966.

DSO DFC CD MID   A/C   Born 1917
RefScs: DHist bf   RCTFY 341   RCTSY 407 421 424–25   RS&A 133
210 SY 158

GRANT Duncan Marshall

"Train-Buster Extraordinaire"

"Bitsy" Grant pioneered the art of attacking trains by night at low altitude. Born in High River, Alta., he joined the RCAF in September 1940 and in July of 1941 reported to 400 Squadron RCAF at Odiham, Hamp. As the first Canadian squadron to go overseas (as No 110), it was equipped with Lysanders and assigned to an Army Co-operation role in 1941. Later the unit switched to Tomahawks; but it was not until 1942 when the unit received Mustangs that its mission changed from reconnaissance to seeking out ground targets. Essentially the Mustang was a low-level aircraft highly suited for this purpose and Grant wielded it with finesse as well as ferocity.

On January 9, 1943, he and another pilot set a new record when, between them, they destroyed and damaged twelve locomotives between

PL 7524

Ault and St Valery-en-Caux in northern France. On April 13, in the Paris area, Grant destroyed a Dornier 217, the squadron's first confirmed kill, though far from Grant's last. But his real métier was train-busting; at this he became an expert. He was also the first to attack locomotives at night. On the night of May 9 he destroyed seven trains as well as four German Messerschmitt 109 and Focke-Wulf 190 fighters on the ground. Five days later he and a wing mate battered six locomotives and nine transport cars. Ten days later he was awarded the DFC.

As Grant continued to destroy engines his luck also held with enemy aircraft. On May 12 he shot down a Do 217 and at the same time damaged two more locomotives. On August 9 he was attacked by a Junkers 88 night-fighter. Turning into the attack he fired head-on then got on the enemy's tail. Grant saw strikes all over the 88's fuselage, but rain began to blot it from sight and he only claimed a probable. On August 28 Grant's career came to an end when his aircraft was hit by heavy flak near Ault. He pulled up into the clouds but it was too late. Moments later the Mustang plunged down into a clump of trees and exploded.

DFC F/L Born Apr 8 1922 KIA Aug 28 1943
RefScs: DHist bf RAW 142 RCTFFY 307–309 311 314–15 317 355
TDS 149–51

One evening in the summer of 1943 I flew over from Redhill, where I was based, to Dunsfold, where Bitsy was stationed, to have dinner with my uncle Hank Burden (see Burden WW1), the airfield commander.

After dinner, with Hank's permission, Bitsy and I staged a practise dogfight to test the merits of the Mustang versus the Spitfire. It turned out just as we predicted: I could out-turn him and he could out-zoom me. And of course I had the advantage of being able to fly at higher altitude. All this changed later when the Americans replaced the Mustang's Allison engine with a Merlin and used it as a high-altitude, long-range fighter, the most successful in the piston-driven class of the war.

GRANT Frank George

"Canada's Most Decorated Typhoon Pilot"

Frank Grant was one of the outstanding Typhoon pilots in the 2nd Tactical Air Force whose job was close support with the ground forces by launching bombing, strafing and rocket attacks against targets along the lines and behind them. A native of North Sydney, N.S., Grant enlisted in the RCAF in October 1940 and joined 504 Squadron RAF in May 1941; he served with this unit until March 1942. He was then transferred to the Aleutians to join 118 Squadron RCAF, which was equipped with Kittyhawks; he became squadron CO in February of the following year.

When the Japanese withdrew from the Aleutians in September the squadron, renumbered 438, became the first of six home defence units released for overseas service. They began training with rocket-firing, bomb-equipped Hurricanes in preparation for the softening up campaign prior to the Normandy invasion. On March 10, 1944, after converting to Typhoons, Grant led the squadron on its first mission from Hurn, Hamps., against targets near Cherbourg. On April 24, carrying 1,000-pound bombs for the first time (the equal to what Canadian bomber crews carried aboard twin-engine Hampdens in 1941), Grant led his squadron on a raid against a bridge at St-Sauveur.

On D-Day his pilots bombed concrete emplacements overlooking the beach. Time and again throughout the Normandy campaign Grant led his "Bomphoons" against enemy bridges and other targets. The pilots dived from 6,000 to 3,000 feet, frequently in the face of heavy flak and with the ever-present danger of enemy fighters. The effectiveness of such bombing attacks was demonstrated on June 28 when Grant and his pilot left the German-occupied village of Verson in flames.

At the end of July, stricken with appendicitis, Grant had to be pulled out of battle. But not for long. In October he was given command of 143 RCAF Wing based at Eindhoven, which he led until the end of the war. This squadron took part in all major actions: the Ardennes battles, the Rhine crossings and the subsequent drive across Germany.

Following the end of WW2 Grant retired from the RCAF and went into business in Montreal, P.Q. However he remained active with the reserve and commanded 401 Squadron from October 1947 to April 1948.

DSO DFC NFC CdeGwSS(Fr)
RefScs: DHist bf   RCTFY 122–23 125 227–28 232 236 240 254 f255
RS&A 52 135 152 225   TDS 133–39

GRAY Roderick Borden

"Drowned While Saving Three of His Crew"

On the night of August 27/28, 1944, "Cy" Gray of Sault Ste. Marie, Ont., a navigator serving with RAF Coastal Command, gave his life to save three members of his crew when their twin-engine Wellington bomber was shot down into the bitterly cold North Sea while attacking a German U-boat. Gray joined the Canadian Army in July 1940 then transferred to the RCAF in October 1941 and trained as an observer. He graduated in September 1942 and, after advanced training, he reported to 172 Squadron RAF on June 2, 1943. He served with this unit for thirteen months, until the time of his death.

By August 1944 the Germans had developed snorkel breathing devices for their submarines, thus allowing them to stay submerged for extended periods. The one that Gray's crew attacked on the night of August 27, the U-534, had not been refitted with the new device, but as compensation for having to surface regularly it had been particularly well armed. Its platform carried four 20-mm cannons and two 37-mm guns. This was the awesome firepower the Wellington crew faced when they attacked after tracking it by radar.

One mile from the target the pilot switched on the Leigh light to illuminate the U-boat against the sea. But the German gunners were ready: they opened up with everything they had. Cannon shells set the Wellington's port engine on fire, then the starboard motor burst into flames. Trailing a fiery wake, the pilot doggedly continued to pursue his quarry. Gray bent over his gunsight, checked the settings then released his cluster of depth charges. After a short distance the Wellington plunged into the sea. Two of the crew were killed on impact. The other four managed to extricate themselves from the aircraft. Gray was the only survivor with a dinghy. The pilot was badly wounded and one of the air gunners had a broken arm and couldn't swim. With the help of the other airman Gray, although suffering from a broken leg, helped the pilot and the air gunner into the one-man life raft. Gray's companions begged him to climb aboard as well because he was in such pain. But Gray knew his weight would only capsize the dinghy. Instead he and the other crew member tied themselves to the sides. By morning Gray was dead. The three survivors were rescued by a Sunderland flying boat that afternoon. For his heroism Gray was awarded a posthumous George Cross.

GC   F/O   Born Oct 2 1917   KIA Aug 28 1944
RefScs: CCMA 72   TDS 98–101   VM 219

GRAY Ross Garstang

"Destroyed Ten Planes, Damaged Twelve in Three Sorties"

During daylight raids on September 21, September 30 and October 21, 1944, Mosquito intruder pilot Ross Gray of Edmonton, Alta, destroyed ten German aircraft and damaged twelve more. One of the raids extended as far into enemy territory as Czechoslovakia.

After joining the RCAF in January 1941 Gray spent most of the war as an instructor; in fact after getting his wings he held that position for the next two years, until he was posted overseas in December 1943. After OTU training he reported to 418 Squadron RCAF, based at Holmesly South in Hampshire, on April 12, 1944.

That summer Gray was engaged in hunting down V-1 flying bombs, one of which he destroyed. His initial combat against the Luftwaffe came some weeks later when he attacked a Focke-Wulf 190 over France. But his prey eluded him this time. In July he was appointed a flight commander. However his real successes were not until two months later. The first occurred on September 21 when, accompanied by another Mosquito over Bad Aibling airfield in Germany, Gray forced one enemy aircraft to crash in flames and damaged two others. But his Mosquito was so badly shot up that it looked like Swiss cheese. He barely made it back to base. Nine days later, in tandem with another intruder, Gray set off on a Day Ranger into southern Germany; he eluded enemy fighters en route by weaving through steep mountain passes. He then proceeded to beat up

Erding, Eferding and Horshing airfields. In the process Gray destroyed two German aircraft and damaged four.

But Gray's most eventful foray was on October 12 when, once again accompanied by another Mosquito, he took off into the darkness of the early morning to penetrate into Ceské Budejovice airfield in Czechoslovakia. He destroyed two Junkers W34 transports and damaged another. Gray's next objective was Nemecky Brod where twenty Ju 87 dive-bombers were parked on the field; Gray destroyed four of them and left five others damaged. By this time the protective cloud cover had disappeared so the two Mosquito crews went on to Italy. After lunch they flew directly back to England through the protection of thunderstorms.

That was Gray's final operational flight.

In October he was posted to Canada as CFI of No 7 OTU at Debert, N.S. Late in May he returned to England as CO of 406 Squadron RCAF, then based at Manston, Kent, a wind-down job. At the end of October Gray resigned from the RCAF to study law, after which he went into practice in Toronto, Ont.

DFC & Bar   W/C   Born Dec 15 1915
RefScs: DHist bf   OMAP(2) 113   RCTFY f174 188 191   RS&A 91
TTS 109–15

GRIFFITHS John Francis

"One of First Canadians Decorated for Aerial Combat in WW2, Looped Under and Over London Tower Bridge"

John Griffiths, who joined the RAF in 1926, was one of the first of two Canadian airmen decorated in WW2. Born in Niagara Falls, Ont., he took his pilot's training with the RCAF at Camp Borden, Ont., during the summers of 1924 and 1925 while still a cadet at RMC. In November 1926 he joined 24 Squadron RAF at Kenley. That Christmas he celebrated his commission by looping a Bristol fighter under and over the Tower Bridge of London. He subsequently received various postings, including India, Abyssinia, Estonia and Malta.

At war's outbreak Griffiths commanded 99 Squadron RAF, a bomber unit flying twin-engine Wellingtons, and was one of the first to participate in the leaflet raids over Germany. He was awarded the DFC for leading the search for the German fleet near the enemy coast on December 14, 1939. The fleet had been headed for an attack on a British convoy carrying the First Canadian Division. When the bombers intercepted the Germans they were attacked by twenty-five Messerschmitt 109 single-engine and 110 twin-engine fighters. It was the first time that the British had encountered cannon fire. In the ensuing melee Griffiths' squadron shot down one enemy aircraft but lost five Wellingtons. Griffiths also led his bombers on attacks on Stavenger during the invasion of Norway. His unit later served in France where he handed over his command to take over a Hurricane fighter squadron made up of Czechoslovakian pilots.

In 1941 Griffiths was assigned to the United States as a test pilot for the British Mission. He also made one trip across the Atlantic with RAF Ferry Command. Griffiths was killed in a car accident in May 1945.

DFC MC(Cz) W/C Born July 21 1905 KA May 1945
RefScs: AIC 200 CCMA 53 DHist bf RAW 272 SY 465

HAYWARD Robert Kingston

"The Relentless Hunter"

B ob Hayward became known for his aggressiveness in seeking enemy targets both in the air and on the ground. On fighter sweeps over France, Belgium and Holland in 1943 and early 1944, under the protective cover of his squadron, he and a wingmate would scour the countryside at low level looking for aircraft, transports, trains and other likely prey. Hayward was born in St John's, Nfld. In 1940, at age 17, he exhibited his ingrained bravery even before enlisting in the RCAF by saving from drowning an unconscious man who had fallen off a motor-boat; his action won him three medals for heroism. After graduating as a pilot Hayward became an instructor until 1942, when he was posted overseas. He joined 401 Squadron RCAF in March 1943 at Catterick in Yorkshire.

Hayward's first combat took place on July 19, 1943, when he shared in the probable destruction of a Focke-Wulf 190 fighter with three others. Then in February 1944 he scored his first positive kill: a twin-engine Messerschmitt 210. On March 15 he destroyed an FW 190, damaged another, shared in the destruction of one more and damaged an ME 410. On the evening of April 24 Hayward scored his most astonishing victory when the enemy pilot of a twin-engine ME 110 — which he eventually destroyed — tried to lead him into a chimney stack. Hayward opened fire at the German plane. His shells struck the building and it exploded — one confirmed factory destroyed!

In May Hayward was posted to 411 Squadron RCAF as a flight commander. On D-Day plus one Hayward reported naval vessels moored

PL 28539

off Le Havre. This was significant because these ships were set to attack the landing craft off the Normandy beaches. His report resulted in their total destruction by RAF rocket-firing Typhoons. Throughout that summer Hayward added to his aerial score along with destroying countless German vehicles. On August 5 he took command of 411 Squadron and a month later received the DFC. As the Allied armies swept toward Germany Hayward led his unit in support — on August 18 he destroyed twenty-four vehicles and damaged ten others — and was particularly active during the Arnhem campaign. In November, after making 195 sorties, his tour ended and he was awarded the DSO.

Leaving the RCAF in November 1945 he joined Molson Breweries where he became a sales executive. But Hayward remained active with the reserve and was responsible for the formation of the Canadian Fighter Pilots' Association. He retired in 1980.

DSO DFC S/L   Born Nov 12 1915
RefScs: DHist bf   OMAP(2) 113   RAW 173 197–201   RCTFFY 180
RCTFY 118 120 127 f143 239   RS&A 95

To Bob the Spitfire was not only a marvellous fighting machine — "you didn't fly it, you wore it like a glove and waved it around" — but it served an important tactical purpose also. "Take the Falaise Gap," he recalled, "where we decimated thousands of German troops and armour in a matter of hours. *That* no army could have achieved in a week. Think of the number of Allied lives we saved."

HENDERSON Selby Roger

"First Canadian to Participate in an Operational Sortie in WW2"

On September 4, 1939, the day after Britain and France declared war on Germany, Blenheim-bomber pilot Roger Henderson became the first Canadian to take part in an operational sortie in WW2 as Lead Navigator in a raid on enemy warships at Wilhelmshaven. A native of Winnipeg, Man., Henderson was awarded the DFC for the action, thus making him the first Canadian to earn that decoration in the second world conflict as well as one of the first two to officially receive it (see Griffiths). Henderson further distinguished himself on November 7 as a member of 206 Squadron RAF. While piloting a twin-engine Anson — later used as a training plane — on patrol off Terschilling Island near the Dutch coast, he shot down a German Dornier 18 flying boat and sent another packing before he ran out of ammunition.

Taken off combat duty in the spring of 1940, Henderson was attached to a navigation school for advanced training as an instructor. Returning to operations that summer he was killed in action on July 4.

DFC P/O KIA July 4 1940
RefScs: AIC 200 203   CCMA 51 53   CITR 159   SY 131 465

HILL George Urquhart

"Battling Bantam Bluenoser Won DFC Three Times"

George Hill, a high school featherweight boxing champion, was one of four Canadians to hold the rare distinction of having received the DFC and two Bars. Born in Antigonish, N.S., Hill joined the RCAF in 1939 when WW2 broke out; he was one of the last to train as a Provisional Pilot Officer and graduated in February 1940. He then became an instructor until he was posted overseas at the beginning of 1942. He reported to 421 Squadron RCAF, a Spitfire unit based at Digby, the following April. In June he was transferred to 453 Squadron, an Australian outfit, as a flight commander. In August he joined 403 Squadron RCAF in the same capacity. Only days later he shot down his first enemy aircraft, a German Focke-Wulf 190 single-engine fighter, and damaged another during the battle of Dieppe.

On February 2, 1943, Hill reported to 111 Squadron RAF, based at Souk-el-Kemis in northern Tunisia. Next day he damaged two Messerschmitt 109 single-engine fighters. On February 23 he shot an ME 109 down in flames and the following day shared in shooting down an FW 190. On March 4 he destroyed two Junkers 87 Stuka dive-bombers. On April 27, three days before he became CO of "Treble One," he was awarded his first DFC.

The squadron, when not on long-range strafing sweeps, patrolled over German airfields trying to pick off aircraft landing or taking off. To entice the enemy into the air Hill devised a scheme of having his pilots pass phoney information to each other over the radio; for example, that they were going home or were out of fuel. May 1 marked a banner day for Hill: he shot down a Heinkel 111 twin-engine bomber, which he attacked head-on; sent a twin-engine ME 110 down in flames; and shared in the destruction of two others. Five days later he shot down his last plane fighting in the African campaign, an ME 109. On May 13 he was awarded a Bar to his DFC.

In June the squadron moved to Malta; there Hill shot down three more enemy aircraft and received a second Bar to his DFC. He returned to Canada in September to a hero's welcome.

In March 1944 he went back to England to take over command of 441 Squadron RCAF at Digby. Then on April 25, over France in a scrap with an FW 190 that he and another pilot eventually destroyed, flying debris from the enemy fighter struck his Spitfire and forced him to land. For a month he evaded capture but eventually was taken prisoner. After being repatriated he left the RCAF to attend medical school and

PL 21682

later established a practice in Orangeville, Ont. He also ran twice as a candidate for the NDP. He was killed in a car accident outside his house in 1969.

DFC & 2 Bars   S/L   Born Oct 19 1939   KA Nov 12 1969
RefScs: DHist bf   OMAP(2) 113–14   RAW 179   RCTFFY 56 f97 353
RCTFY 123 128–29 f142   RS&A 139   SY 136   TTS 121–29

HODSON Keith Louis Bate

"Royal Canadian Air Force Exemplar"

The memory of Keith Hodson stands as a monument to everything the RCAF stood for. Fighter ace, brilliant strategist and tactician, and one of the ablest administrators to serve any air force, Hodson was first, foremost, and above all, a leader.

Born in the British Channel Island of Jersey, he inherited his inbred sense of discipline from his father, a senior officer in the Canadian Army. Educated in London, Ont., he joined the RCAF in 1937. After graduating as a pilot he spent his initial period of service as an instructor. After the outbreak of war he became one of the artisans of the BCATP. By 1941 he was Chief Flying Instructor at the SFTS at Moncton, N.B. That November he was attached to RAF Ferry Command and assigned as second pilot of a Liberator, which he helped fly overseas. Once in England he attended OTU and was then posted to 602 Squadron RAF, a Spitfire outfit commanded by the famous Irish ace Paddy Finucane.

All that winter and spring Hodson gained valuable operational experience; and in June of 1942 he was made CO of 401 Squadron RCAF stationed at Gravesend in Kent. Over the summer he led his unit on low-level attacks against ground targets, on bomber escort missions and on fighter sweeps aimed at luring German fighters up to fight. One of the squadron's most spectacular successes occurred on August 19 during the Canadian ground assault on Dieppe. Three times Hodson led his squadron over the blood-soaked beaches, enabling them to destroy one Focke-Wulf 190 single-engine fighter, probably destroy three others and damage five more; Hodson himself accounted for one of them. Late in September he was awarded the DFC for "exceptional leadership."

During his tenure as CO he flew eighty-five sorties with the squadron, which had run up a record of twelve aircraft destroyed, eleven probables and twenty-eight damaged. Hodson's tenure as CO ended in January 1943 when he took over as leader of the Kenley Wing, made up of four RCAF squadrons. Here he exhibited his qualities as a master strategist. He would position the wing for attack, then cover the squadron he had assigned to the target. Such precision enabled the wing to operate as

PL 110645

a superbly coordinated, well-trained team. Teamwork was Hodson's métier, a discipline he demanded of everyone who served with him. On March 1, 1943, he gave up command to become CO of 126 RCAF Airfield (later Wing) of the 2nd Tactical Air Force. In July 1944 he was transferred for duties with the 9th U.S. Air Force.

Following the war Hodson held a variety of senior posts, including

Commandant of the RCAF College in Toronto, Ont. When NORAD was formed in 1958 he was made Deputy Chief of Staff. On July 5, 1960, he was being checked out in a T33 jet aircraft when the engine flamed out. Hodson managed to bail out but became entangled in the shroud of his parachute, which strangled him.

OBE DFC & Bar DFC(Am) CdeGwGC(Fr) A/V/M Born 1915
KA Jul 5 1960
RefScs: CWC DHist bf RCTFFY 55–56 70–71 90 f96 RCTFY 100
126 RS&A 82 215 221

My own tribute to Keith, under whom I had the honour to serve, is to quote in part from the Wing Routine Orders he issued in Normandy on July 1, 1944, which I pasted in my log book:

Today is Dominion Day. Some of us have been away from home so long we forget momentarily what it means . . . Canada is a good place to live where a man of limited means can enjoy life and independence. Today, all over the [Commonwealth], men will be paying tribute to Canada. While here in France you and I will be working to keep Canada the way we want it . . . If we doubt the urgency of our work, think what will happen if the Army between us and the Hun is pushed back in our laps . . . There will be no letup this summer . . . But with our resources and our good heart, we will one day send aircraft which will have no target so that next Dominion Day we can walk down our own main street and say "I am one of the Canadians who really worked to finish that War."

HORNELL David Ernest

"Ordeal by Fire and Water"

First RCAF recipient of the VC, "Bud" Hornell earned the Commonwealth's highest award for valour by his heroism under fire and duress as captain of an anti-submarine Catalina amphibian in action over and in the cruel North Sea on a summer's day and night in 1944. Born in Mimico, Ont., Hornell joined the air force in January 1941 and, after receiving his wings, served for a short while as a test pilot. On

January 2, 1944, he was posted to 162 Squadron RAF Coastal Command at Reykjavik in Iceland to guard the northern flank of the route used by German U-boats to reach the Atlantic. In May he became part of a detachment sent to Wick in the Shetland Islands to cover both sides of the enemy's sea course.

When he and his crew set out for his fatal flight of June 24, in effect a routine patrol, Hornell had already logged sixty operational trips. On this occasion, after ten tedious hours during which they had not even spotted a sea gull, Hornell had just set course to return to base some 1,000 miles away when a surfaced submarine travelling at high speed suddenly appeared off the port beam. Hornell signalled "action stations" and immediately prepared to attack. But the U-boat, swinging at right angles to its assailant, opened fire first. Despite a jammed machine gun Hornell's forward gunner responded with a volley that raked the conning tower and killed most of the crew on deck.

Too late. Cannon shells had already ripped into the Catalina, torn two gaping holes in the starboard wing, and set the engine and main plane on fire. Vibrating violently, the aircraft became increasingly difficult to control as enemy fire struck it again and again. Despite the threat of fire to the fuel tanks Hornell pressed home his attack. Sweeping down low he dropped his depth charges in a perfect straddle on either side of the U-boat. In seconds the bow of the submarine, in an almost majestic gesture, lifted out of the water then slowly sank under the surface into the deep.

With the Catalina's weight alleviated by the release of the bombs Hornell was able to climb to 250 feet, but only with superhuman effort. Fire in the starboard wing had become so intense that the flaming engine dropped off, which made further stability impossible. Hornell had no choice but to ditch.

Turning the aircraft into the wind and levelling out with the utmost skill Hornell bounced the Catalina once, twice, before settling it on a heavy, rolling, seven-foot swell. The shattered hull started to sink immediately but all eight of the crew managed to abandon ship and take the two 4-man dinghies with them before it went under. However only one dinghy inflated properly; the other exploded. This left the shipwrecked airmen with a life raft that would uncomfortably hold seven; one man, on an alternating regimen, had to stay in the water clinging to the side. The sea turned so rough the men were bailing constantly.

At this point the crew was perhaps fortunate that they did not realize the hopelessness of their situation or, paradoxically, the luck they were about to experience. They were blissfully, maybe blessfully, unaware that their wireless transmission reporting their position at the time of the attack was never received; the radio had been knocked out of commission when the Catalina was first hit. That knowledge would only have added despair

PL 25355

to distress. Therefore it was purely by chance that, four hours after they had ditched, another Catalina spotted them. Otherwise they might never have been rescued. The flying boat signalled to the life raft by Very light that it had called for help and that a high-speed rescue launch was on its way.

But the ordeal was far from over. The waves had risen to twenty-five feet and the wind was blowing at some thirty knots. Overcome with the cold Hornell became seasick. Then the waves increased to a height of fifty feet and the wind increased to fifty knots. To ride out the waves the crew had to shift weight in unison. After fourteen hours in the sea the dinghy capsized. But with what strength they still had left, the airmen righted it and got back in. As conditions worsened one of the crew died of delirium. His body was lowered overboard with the sobering if somewhat morbid realization that they no longer had to take turns in the water.

Suffering from extreme exposure Hornell began to go blind. Two hours after the Catalina had spotted them a Warwick transport aircraft dropped an airborne lifeboat, which drifted away due to high winds; Hornell, in spite of his increasing weakness, insisted on swimming after it. However, before he could do so, his copilot forcibly restrained him.

After nineteen hours in the sea and with no further sign of rescue the crew became increasingly discouraged. Another one had died of exposure. But Hornell, by now totally blind and only semi-conscious, continued to exhort his crew in an effort to cheer them. Then, after they had endured twenty hours and thirty-five minutes in the North Sea, the launch finally arrived. All six of the survivors were taken aboard. And although Hornell, who had lost complete consciousness, was given intense medical treatment for over three hours, he never revived. His grave lies in the military plot in the Shetland Islands, a bleak though symbolic monument to the memory of his bravery under the most sombre of conditions.

VC F/L Born Jan 20 1910 KIA June 24 1944 Ind CAHF 1973
RefScs: CA 239 CAHF 36 CCMA 71 DHist bf RCTFY 290 f302
307–12 VM 185

In March 1991, as this book was being written, David Hornell's Victoria Cross was placed on permanent display in the Bishop Building, Canadian Forces Air Command Headquarters in Westwin, Man. Several of his crew and his brother were on hand for the ceremony.

HOULE Albert Ulrich

"Wrestling Champ RCAF Mediterranean Ace"

Bert Houle of Massey, Ont., was the only RCAF ace whose entire operations were confined solely to the Mediterranean Theatre. A born scrapper — he won the 1936 Canadian Intercollegiate Wrestling Championship — Houle joined the RCAF in 1940. On graduating as a pilot he was immediately posted overseas. After attending OTU in July 1941 he boarded the aircraft carrier *Furious*. Using the carrier as a base in the middle of the Mediterranean, he and a host of others flew long-range, tank-carrying Hurricanes, first to Malta, then to Egypt and next to Cyprus, where Houle reported to 213 Squadron RAF. At the end of the year the unit moved to Edku near Alexandria.

In February 1942 Houle had his first brush with the enemy, a Junkers 88 twin-engine bomber, before being grounded for having crash-landed after failing to check his fuel tanks. Reinstated, he flew fighter sweeps over the El 'Alamain line, which Rommel attacked on August 31. The following day Houle scored his first victory by shooting down a Ju 88. Two days later he downed a single-engine Messerschmitt 109 fighter. At sunset on October 29 Houle and another pilot waded into a gaggle of Ju 87 Stuka dive-bombers; Houle shot down two enemy planes, probably destroyed another and damaged two more, a feat that earned him the DFC.

After the Battle of El 'Alamain Houle's squadron and another unit landed 100 miles behind the German lines and blasted everything in sight: airfields, cars, trucks, anything to harass the retreating Afrika Korps.

Later in November Houle was made a flight commander of 145 Squadron RAF, which was equipped with Spitfires and based at Gazela. On January 9, 1943, he chalked up his first victory in his new role when he shot

RE 74-216

down a Messerschmitt 109. In June he became a flight commander with 417 Squadron, the only RCAF fighter unit in the Middle East. Flying from Luga, Malta, the squadron took part in the Sicilian landings and eventually moved to that island. Touring the battle area in a Jeep with his CO, Houle was wounded when the vehicle struck a land mine and blew him through the roof. Both of his eardrums shattered so he did not return to combat until mid-September. For a brief period he took over a flight with his old unit, 145 Squadron, before being promoted to CO of 417.

His final string of victories began on December 5 when he shot down two ME 109s. Then on January 22 he shot down his first Focke-Wulf 190 over the Anzio beachhead. On February 7 he destroyed an ME 109, but a week later he was shot down and wounded. On February 21, after receiving a Bar to his DFC, he turned over his command to his successor.

Following the war Houle remained with the RCAF and retired to Manitock, Ont., in 1965, surrendering his post as CO of the Central Experimental and Proving Establishment. After retiring from the military Houle joined an Ottawa stockbroking firm.

DFC & Bar G/C   Born March 24 1914
RefScs: DHist bf   OMAP(2) 114   RCTFFY f337 356   RCTFY 172
174–75 f175   RS&A 109   TTS 131–38

HYNDMAN Robert Stuart

"Put Combat to Canvas"

B ob Hyndman's painting "Above Falaise," which hangs in the Canadian War Museum in Ottawa, Ont., shows Spitfires and Messerschmitts at close quarters in a dogfight. This painting depicts the action no photographer, and few artists, could ever have hoped to convey. But Hyndman, who served as a flight commander with 411 Squadron RCAF, was no ordinary virtuoso with the brush when it came to recording aerial combat on canvas. His paintings captured the mood exactly, the excitement perfectly, the dash graphically, the detail authentically. In the same way an alert photographer focusses his lens on a subject he wants to film Hyndman would grab his pad and capture his subject with pencil or charcoal on the spot. In the air he had a cinemagraphic memory he could bring to bear later with his oils.

Hyndman, who was born in Edmonton, Alta., joined the RCAF in 1940. After graduating as a pilot he spent the next twenty-one months as an instructor at Uplands Service Flying Training School in Ottawa,

Ont. On July 20, 1943, he was posted overseas to join 411 Squadron, equipped with Spitfires, at Redhill in Surrey. On completion of his operational tour in September 1944 he was appointed an official War Artist before returning to Canada in 1945. Hyndman was then attached to RCAF HQ, where he portrayed many of the senior officers of the service. In March 1946 he was transferred to the reserve. In 1954 he was called back to full-service for a period to paint pictures of the RCAF in Europe.

F/L   Born June 28 1915
RefScs: DHist bf   RAW 331 335   RCTFY f230

A radio transmission by Bob on one of our fighter sweeps over northern France during the winter of 1943/44 persists in my memory: "Look at that beautiful cloud formation over there on the left." A moment of silence broken by another voice: "And look at that beautiful formation of Huns on your right!"

INGALLS Ross Baxter

"One of First Observers to Graduate from BCATP"

A native of Danville, P.Q., Ross Ingalls was one of the first observers to train and graduate from the BCATP. Joining the RCAF in 1940 he was posted overseas to join 405 Pathfinder Squadron RCAF. He served two tours and earned the DSO and the DFC with this unit. Following WW2 Ingalls remained with the RCAF and served in a number of capacities, including staff officer at Northern NORAD Headquarters in North Bay, Ont.

DSO DFC CD   G/C   Born July 1914
RefScs: DHist bf   RCTFY f335 348

KEEFER George Clinton

"Most Highly Decorated RCAF Fighter Pilot"

During three operational tours of combat George Keefer flew over 400 operational hours, shot down 18 enemy planes, probably destroyed two more and damaged at least seven others. He became the most highly decorated fighter pilot in the RCAF and only one of four to be awarded a Bar to the DSO. In all that time he never received so much as a scratch.

Born in New York City, N.Y., and raised in Charlottetown, P.E.I., Keefer joined the RCAF in 1940 and went overseas in 1941. He reached 274 Squadron RAF — known as the Desert Squadron — in North Africa via aircraft carrier and long-range Hurricane, with a stop at Malta just prior to the British advance into the Cyrenaica region in November.

Keefer shot down his first enemy aircraft, an Italian Macchi 200, on December 7. During his first tour he accounted for another three destroyed, one probable and six damaged in the air battles surrounding the British advance, and the spring and summer German counter-offensives of 1942.

Returning from one sortie Keefer spotted a downed Allied pilot near Tobruk, deep inside enemy territory. He promptly landed in the desert and picked him up.

In August he was taken off operations, awarded the DFC and completed a stint as an instructor at an OTU in Egypt. He was then posted to England in April 1943 as a flight commander with 416 Squadron RCAF, a Spitfire unit stationed at Digby. On June 25 he was given command of 412 Squadron RCAF after the CO was shot down. A month later, heading home from a sweep over France, his engine packed up. He barely made it to the coast and, with his altitude down to 1,000 feet, was able to bail out over the English Channel. From his dinghy he could easily make out people and houses along the French shore. Fortunately no Germans saw him and he was eventually rescued by flying boat.

In April 1944 Keefer was given command of 126 RCAF Wing, of which his own squadron was a member, and awarded a Bar to his DFC. On D-Day he led his wing over the invasion beaches and the following day shot down a Focke-Wulf 190. From that date to the expiry of his tour on July 9 the wing under his leadership shot down 56 planes and destroyed over 400 vehicles.

Keefer returned to Canada that summer but became restless. By the fall he had wangled his way back overseas and on arrival was presented with the DSO. In November he was given command of 125 RAF Wing stationed at Eindhoven in the Netherlands. Between March 9 and April 2, 1945, he destroyed five enemy aircraft in the air and another nine of the ground. At war's end he was awarded a Bar to his DSO.

Keefer remained with the RCAF until 1947, serving at the Air Force Staff College in Toronto, Ont., and the Canadian Joint Staff in Washington, D.C. After several positions with the aircraft industry he bought a plastics factory in Granby, P.Q.

DSO & Bar DFC & Bar CdeGwGC(Fr) DFC(N)   W/C   Born July 11 1921
RefScs: CWC 166–82   DHist bf   OMAP(2) 115   RAW 189 200 370
RCTFFY 98 108 110–11 356   RCTFY 100 103 113 124–25 f126 129–30 227–30 232 235 237 247 249   RS&A 100 221   TTS 141–48

KEILLOR Hubert George

"Expert E-boat Eliminator"

W hen it came to shipping strikes "Cub" Keillor was a real tiger. His specialty: German E-boats. Twice in one week he attacked eight of the speedy torpedo-carrying vessels, sinking two on the first sortie and blowing another apart on the second. When WW2 broke out Keillor, a native of Mitchell, Ont., was a member of the Canadian Army Militia. In 1941 he transferred to the RCAF and, after advanced training, graduated as a pilot. He joined 415 Squadron, RCAF, serving in the Coastal Command in October 1943. Based at Bircham Newton in Norfolk, the unit was equipped with Albacore biplanes and twin-engine Wellington bombers. It was with the latter that Keillor made his name and became one of the most highly decorated anti-shipping pilots.

On the night of May 10, 1944, off the Dutch coast, he made his first score when, despite the fact his bombsight wouldr.'t work, he dropped a stick of explosives on the stern of a 3,000-ton merchant vessel, scoring a direct hit. On June 9 Keillor's crew attacked two minesweepers and, although they couldn't be absolutely sure of their success, their bombs caused such a tremendous explosion amidships on one of them that they claimed it as probably sunk. Four nights later Keillor won his first decoration when he and his mates bombed five E-boats off the coast of Holland, one of which they destroyed and three others they probably sunk. For the night's work Keillor and his navigator each received a DFC. On July 3 Keillor saw his last action with 415 Squadron, which transferred to Bomber Command, when he destroyed another German vessel.

He was next posted to a 524 Squadron RAF Coastal Command, where his successes continued to mount. On July 23 he attacked three ships off Terschelling. During August and September Keillor and his crewmates made six separate night attacks on German torpedo boats.

Then came the night of November 30. Patrolling off Ijmuidin Keillor and his crew spotted a long wake heading west. As they got closer they identified several E-boats in line astern, the formation used for hit-and-run strikes against Allied shipping. From 5,000 feet Keillor attacked the leader, dropping two 250-pound bombs, the first pair of which scored a direct hit, and caused a large flash of flame and a shower of debris. As Keillor circled for a second attack the bomb-release mechanism failed just as the Wellington came under severe anti-aircraft fire. He made four more bomb runs and finally completed the attack by using the jettison bar. The last six bombs dropped in a salvo and explosions could be seen among the torpedo boats, which scattered in all directions. For the action Keillor received the DSO.

He remained in the RCAF after the war and with 3,000 hours on 60 different types of aircraft became one of its most experienced pilots. On May 17, 1949, Keillor and another pilot were flying an Auster trainer out of Trenton Air Station, Ont., when the engine suddenly cut out. The aircraft rolled over and dived into the ground, killing both occupants.

DSO DFC & Bar   W/C   KA May 17 1949
RefScs: RAW 360   RCTFY f319 338 340 342   TDS 101–103

KENNEDY Irving Farmer

"Spared Luftwaffe Pilot He Forced Down"

On July 2, 1944, south of Caen, "Hap" Kennedy had a German Messerschmitt 109 in the gunsight of his Spitfire when he ran out of ammunition. He pulled up to try and knock the enemy fighter's tailpin off with his wingtip. Suddenly he had to throttle back as if the German pilot had put on brakes. As Kennedy pulled up alongside the reason became obvious: the ME 109's propeller was windmilling; its engine had stopped. The German glided down into a field with Kennedy following. He then made several passes to record the event on his cine-camera as the enemy pilot climbed out of his wrecked machine and waved back to the Spitfire. That was but one unorthodox incident in the career of Kennedy, who flew two tours and was credited with over twelve planes shot down and another probably destroyed.

Born and raised in Cumberland, Ont., Kennedy joined the RCAF in October 1940 and arrived overseas the following year. Early in 1942 he joined 263 Squadron RAF, flying twin-engine Whirlwinds, a poor match for the German ME 109s. To his relief Kennedy was transferred to a Spitfire unit in June — 421 Squadron RCAF based at Fairwood Common in Wales. However he soon tired of endless convoy patrols and the odd sweep over France and he put in for a posting to Malta. He was transferred and arrived there in December; he was assigned to 249 Squadron RAF. On February 7, 1943, he shared in the destruction of a Junkers 52 transport over Sicily. By mid-April he had added three Ju 88 bombers to his score; then on April 22 he shot down two Ju 52s. On June 10 he destroyed an ME 109 and an Italian Macchi 202 fighter. At the end of July he was awarded the DFC and sent to 111 Squadron RAF based in Sicily. There he continued to add to his score and in mid-October was transferred to 93 Squadron RAF as a flight commander; by that time the Allies had invaded Italy.

Kennedy's first tour ended in December. He had flown 365 operational hours and had ten aircraft to his credit. Kennedy was an obvious candidate for the job of gunnery officer and was now consigned to that position in England.

In mid-June, only a week after the Normandy invasion, he joined 401 Squadron RCAF at Tangmere. Three days later he was flying his Spitfire from an airstrip in France at Beny-sur-Mer as his unit now flew from the other side of the English Channel. On the twenty-fifth the unit lost a flight commander and Kennedy filled his shoes. On July 2 the CO also went missing and Kennedy took his place. The casualties had given Kennedy fast promotion but as it turned out it worked both ways. July 26 he was himself brought down by ground fire over Dreux airfield. With the help of the French maquis underground he managed to evade capture for nearly a month, when he was liberated by the Americans. Later he learned he had been awarded a Bar to his DFC.

Following WW2 Kennedy studied medicine at the University of Toronto, Ont. Graduating in 1956 he set up practice in his home town.

DFC & Bar   S/L   Born Feb 4 1922
RefScs: DHist bf   OMAP(2) 115   RAW 282 230   RCTFFY 356
RCTFY 23–29 246 253   RS&A 82   TTS 149–50

KENT John Alexander

"Fought Forty Messerschmitts Single-Handedly"

O n October 1, 1940, 20,000 feet over the English Channel, Johnnie Kent of Winnipeg, Man., became separated from his squadron. Suddenly he found himself embroiled with forty Messerschmitt 109s. Twisting and turning his Hurricane he somehow escaped being shot down or even hit. By the time the melee ended he had sent one of the German fighters down pouring smoke, sent another down in flames and damaged still another. Kent was one of the most brilliant of the Canadian WW2 fighter pilots.

Born in 1914, at 17 years old he became the youngest licensed pilot in Canada; two years later he became the country's youngest commercial pilot. In 1935 he enlisted in the RAF and joined 19 Squadron; with this unit he learned air-gunnery. In 1937 he was posted to the Royal Air Establishment at Farnborough where his main job was testing aircraft balloon cable-cutting devices, an exercise he conducted with such skill he was awarded the AFC. In May 1940 he was assigned to the Photographic Development Unit at Heston, where he engaged in high-speed, photographic reconnaissance aircraft experiments. On one test, in a Spitfire over the Rhine, he had his first taste of enemy fire when an anti-aircraft battery opened up on him.

At the time of the German assault on the West a detachment of Kent's unit was sent to France. On one occasion Kent tangled with an ME 109, which high-tailed it to the east when the pilot realized he was in a scrap with a Spitfire.

After the fall of France Kent was assigned as a flight commander to 303 Squadron RAF at Northolt. Equipped with Hurricanes, the unit was made up of Polish pilots who had escaped from their homeland, and it was here the Canadian became known as "Kentowski." On September 9 Kent gained his first victories, damaging a Junkers 88 twin-engine bomber and destroying an ME 110 twin-engine fighter. On the twenty-seventh, after bringing down an ME 109 the day before, he destroyed a Ju 88. But in the process the enemy gunner put two bullets in Kent's Hurricane, the only time his aircraft was ever hit.

In mid-October, with four planes destroyed to his credit, Kent was awarded the DFC and given command of 92 Squadron RAF, a Spitfire unit based at Biggin Hill. For the remainder of the year the unit was occupied with defending against ME 109 fighter-bomber nuisance raids. But Kent added three aircraft destroyed and one probable to his score. In January 1941 the squadron moved to Manston — on the southeast coast of England — and began carrying out the first offensive flights over France.

Kent was taken off operations in March and posted to an OTU as Chief Flying Instructor. Meanwhile he had been awarded the Polish Virtuti Militari. In June he was given command of a wing at Northolt and before the end of August had run his score up to thirteen. Early in October he was posted to nonoperational duties and given a Bar to his DFC.

Following the war, among other appointments, he acted as Personal Staff Officer to the Military Governor of British Occupied Germany. In 1956 he retired from the RAF to take up a position in the aviation electronics industry.

DFC & Bar AFC CD VM(P)   G/C   Born June 23 1914   Author of *One of the Few*
RefScs: CA 213   CWC 183–93   DHist bf   OMAP(2) 144   OTF(biog)
RAW 165–66   RCTFFY 20   TDS 5 17   TSBW 144   TTS 157–63

KIPP Robert Allen

"First in RCAF to Destroy Four Planes in One Night"

On May 2, 1944, Bob Kipp, piloting a Mosquito deep into southern Germany, shot down four Focke-Wulf 190 fighters to become the first in the RCAF to destroy that many enemy aircraft in a single night; at the same time he boosted his squadron's total to over 100 destroyed.

A native of Kamloops, B.C., Kipp joined the RCAF in June 1940 and after receiving his wings served as an instructor until 1943, when he was posted overseas. After advanced training he reported to 418 Squadron RCAF, then stationed at Ford in Surrey, in November.

Kipp joined the squadron at a time when they were changing tactics from night intruder sweeps over airfields in France, which had become nonproductive, to day and night Rangers. Flying in pairs, the Mosquito crews at times penetrated right into Germany and ranged as far as Denmark and Norway. Kipp flew the second such sortie undertaken by the squadron on December 2. He showed his mettle early by sharing in the destruction of a Heinkel 111 bomber and the probable destruction of another. Then on the night of February 18/19, 1944, he destroyed two Messerschmitt 410 fighter-bombers trying to return to their base following a 200-plane raid on London. On April 14 Kipp and the crew of another Mosquito destroyed four Junkers 52 transports engaged in minesweeping off the coast of Denmark. To lower his speed during the attack Kipp dropped his wheels, which actually touched the water. On the same sortie Kipp destroyed two Dornier 217 bombers and damaged a third on an airfield near Copenhagen. Following his four-in-one-night foray, Kipp scored two more victories, bringing his total tally to 12½ destroyed, one-half probably destroyed and three damaged before his tour of thirty-five sorties ended.

Taken off operations, Kipp was assigned to various staff duties until the end of the war when he resigned from the RCAF. In 1946, however, he re-enlisted. On January 4, 1949, Kipp was given command of 410 Squadron at St Hubert, P.Q., the first regular force unit to be formed since WW2 and the first to be equipped with Vampire jet fighters. Kipp was killed in a plane crash in July of that year while practising low-level aerobatics for the Canadian International Air Show.

DSO DFC S/L   Born Oct 12 1919   KA July 25 1949
RefScs: DHist bf   OMAP(2) 116   RAW 261 389   RCTFY 158–59
160–61 164–66 170 174 351 355   SY 214   TTS 165–71

KLERSY William Thomas

"Top Gun of the Top Squadron"

B ill Klersy emerged as the premier ace of the highest scoring Canadian fighter outfit of WW2. Between the Battle of Britain and V-E Day 401 (nee No 1) Squadron RCAF destroyed 195½ enemy aircraft, probably destroyed 35 and damaged 104, ranking it first among all Canadian fighter units. With 16½ German planes destroyed and 3½ damaged, Klersy not only became the squadron's top gun but also its last war-time CO and its most highly decorated pilot.

Born in Brantford, Ont., Klersy enlisted in the RCAF in June 1941. After receiving his wings he was posted to 130 Squadron at Bagotville, P.Q., an Eastern Air Command unit flying Kittyhawks and Hurricanes. There Klersy established himself as a crack marksman, sharing top target shooting honours with another pilot.

In July 1943 he joined 401 Squadron at Redhill, Surrey. Flying clipped-wing Spitfire VBs for medium-altitude bomber escort duty Klersy and his comrades had little chance to engage the enemy. It was not until the following March in 1944 when the squadron was re-equipped with the formidable Spitfire Mark IX Bs that he made his first kill. On the seventh of that month he shot a Focke-Wulf 190 fighter down in flames over northern France. On June 7, D-Day plus one, he scored his second victory. Then on June 28, by which time the squadron had moved to an airstrip at Beny-sur-Mer in Normandy, Klersy posted a double-kill south of Caen against two 190s. By then he was on a roll. At the end of July his tally stood at seven enemy aircraft downed, he had been made a flight commander and he was awarded the DFC.

In September his first tour ended with a staff duty assignment at Group Headquarters, a hiatus that didn't last the customary six months. When the CO of 401 Squadron was shot down on Christmas Day Klersy was given command of his old unit, then based at Heesch in the Netherlands. His initial victory on his second tour, like his first, took place on a March day. On the first of that month in 1945 he scored a triple-kill, destroying two Messerschmitt 109s and an FW 190. He bettered that performance on April 20 — Hitler's birthday — shooting down three enemy machines and sharing in the destruction of another. He scored his last two victories

Bill Klersy (l.) with Jack Sheppard. Photo courtesy Bill Klersy.

on May 3 while leading a strafing mission on a German airfield northeast of Kiel. Next day he flew his final operational sortie — number 321.

Klersy had lived out the war only to die on May 22 when his Spitfire crashed into a hill near Wesel in Germany while on a flight to London for a reunion with a group of his former 401 buddies at the Savoy.

DSO DFC & Bar   S/L   Born July 30 1922   KFA May 22 1945
RefScs: DHist bf   HBB 15 24 174–76   OMAP(2) 116   RAW 199
RCTFY 119 229 238 246   RS&A 82–83   SY 135   TTS 173–78

The circumstances surrounding Grissle's (my own nickname for him from a popular cartoon character in the English comics) death have never been satisfactorily explained. He was reported to have flown into a cloud layer with two others who somehow managed to climb out of it. I flew with Bill long enough to know he was sufficiently expert on instruments to control his aircraft even in the thickest cumulus. Something must have gone wrong.

But what?

My theory, and it is no more than that, is that his Spitfire failed him. On May 6 the squadron had surrendered its Mark IXs for XIVs, treacherous beasts with a record of catching fire. My guess is that that is exactly what happened. I support this supposition with the fact that when Bill's body and aircraft were found both had been severely burned.

LAMBERT Frederick Frank

"Star-Studded Career Stretched From Frontier Wars to Intruder Missions, Through Navy, Army, Air Force"

Born in Wilkie, Sask., Fred Lambert began his military career by enlisting in the RCNVR in 1933, then switching to the local militia and finally transferring, in 1936, to the RAF. On completing his pilot's training he was posted to 27 Squadron RAF in India. Flying de Havillands and Wapitis, he took part in the tribal wars. When WW2 broke out he was sent back to England. In 1942 he became a member of 141 Squadron RAF, at that time flying Beaufighters on intruder missions over the occupied European countries. The following year the unit was re-equipped with Mosquitos. On the night of December 16, just east of Berlin, Lambert became embroiled in a running aerobatic dogfight with a Messerschmitt 110 twin-engine night-fighter until he finally scared off the enemy attacker.

In January 1944 Lambert was given command of 515 Squadron RAF stationed at Little Snoring in Norfolk, where he quickly made a name for himself: in nine operations he destroyed three enemy aircraft and countless ground targets. In August the squadron's operations were extended from Ranger raids to long-range bomber escort. After flying fifty-six operations he was assigned to a staff job.

Toward the end of the war Lambert transferred to the RCAF, with which he held a number of senior posts, including Assistant Chief of Intelligence, Allied Air Forces Central Europe and Director of Intelligence, North region, North American Air Defence. He retired in 1962.

DSO DFC CD MID CdeG(Fr) W/C Born June 18 1914
RefScs: CITR 159 CWC 195–201

LANE Reginald John

"Bomber-Pilot, Pathfinder Survived Three Tours"

Reg Lane of Victoria, B.C., flew three tours — one as a bomber pilot, two as a pathfinder — against virtually every vital enemy target in Europe. Lane enlisted in the RCAF in 1940 and flew his first operational sortie on November 7, 1941, as a Halifax copilot in a raid on Berlin. He flew with 35 Squadron RAF, commanded by the famous Leonard Cheshire VC. On December 18 and 30 of that year he also participated in two notable raids against the German warships *Gneisenau* and *Scharnhorst* berthed at Brest in France.

On one sortie to bomb the battle-cruiser *Tirpitz*, anchored in a fjord in Norway, Lane had a close call when his aircraft was hit by cannon shells that cracked the main spar in the starboard wing and just missed the fuel tank. By March 3, 1942, Lane was made bomber captain and flew sorties against the Ruhr and targets in France. In August the squadron switched to pathfinder duties and on October 15 his first assignment in this new capacity was a raid on Kiel.

In May 1943 Lane was temporarily taken off operations to become an instructor. In September that year he flew the first Canadian-built Lancaster bomber, the "Ruhr Express" (KB700), from Montreal, P.Q., to England.

One month later he was back in action as a flight commander with 405 Squadron RCAF based at Gransden Lodge; and in January 1944 Lane took over as CO. In August he was again taken off operations, this time permanently, and assigned to an administrative post with 6 Group RCAF Bomber Command.

Following WW2 Lane stayed in the RCAF holding many senior positions, including Commander 1 Air Division HQ at Metz, France.

DSO DFC & Bar CD MID   A/V/M (RCAF)   M/G(CF)
Born Jan 4 1920
RefScs: DHist bf   P 107–108   RAW 316–17   RCTFFY 225 353 356
RCTFY 66 f78   RS&A 89 209 211 221   TDS 69–71

LARDEN Alan

"Bomb-Aimer Took Over Controls from Crippled Pilot"

On the night of August 12/13, 1943, over Turin, the last Italian city to be bombed before that country's surrender, a nervous Allied air gunner let fly with everything he had. But the target he had mistaken for an enemy fighter turned out to be a British Stirling four-engine bomber of 218 Squadron RAF. The damage was frightful: the windscreen had been shattered; the front and rear gun turrets were put out of action; three engines were hit, one of them rendered useless. Worse still, the navigator had been killed, three other members of the crew were wounded and the pilot wounded critically with a crippled arm, a bullet in one

196 TRUE CANADIAN HEROES IN THE AIR

lung, a broken jaw and his face partially shot away. After being removed from the cockpit and given a shot of morphine the pilot twice tried valiantly to take over the controls. But this proved impossible, he was too weak to hold the bomber on course.

The bomb-aimer, Alan Larden of North Bay, Ont., though he had never flown an aircraft, seated himself in the pilot's cockpit determined to somehow rescue the situation. The captain, who could not even speak, had to give Larden written instructions on how to handle the machine. He also ordered him in writing to head for Africa instead of England because the plane, with one engine out, could never make enough height to climb over the Alps. By the time they finally reached Bone field in Tunisia the pilot made a vain attempt to take over the controls again to land the bomber. After four unsuccessful tries he turned the controls back to Larden with written orders of how to put the aircraft down. Miraculously the bomb-aimer managed to land the Stirling — wheels-up — without further injury to the crew. An indication of the pilot's critical condition lay in the fact that he died nine hours later. For his bravery Larden, who had enlisted in the RCAF in 1942 and joined his squadron in the spring of 1943, was awarded the CGM.

CGM   F/O
RefScs: RAW 309   TDS 61

LARICHELIERE Joseph Emile Paul

"Canadian Battle of Britain Ace Downed Six Planes in Two Days"

At the height of the Battle of Britain Joe Laricheliere destroyed six German aircraft in two days. Flying from Tangmere with 213 Squadron RAF on August 13, 1940, Laricheliere shot down two Bf110s and a Bf 109. Two days later, on August 15, he duplicated the hat-trick by destroying two Bf 110s and a Ju 87 Stuka dive-bomber. Next day he was killed in a dogfight over the Isle of Wight.

Born in Montreal, P.Q., Laricheliere joined the RAF in 1939 and was formally commissioned in May 1940.

F/O   Born Dec 3 1912   KIA Aug 16 1940
RefScs: CITR 159   DHist bf   NM app   TSBW 144

LAUBMAN Donald Currie

"Destroyed Eight Enemy Planes in Three Days"

B etween September 25 and 27, 1944, over the Allied Arnhem pocket, Don Laubman destroyed eight German fighters, four of them on the last day. A native of Provost, Alta., Laubman joined the RCAF in

1940. His flying career got off to an inauspicious start when, during his elementary training, he attempted to get into a practice dogfight (against regulations) with another Tiger Moth trainer, which happened to be piloted by the Chief Flying Instructor. Luckily the infraction was overlooked and Laubman eventually graduated as a pilot. He served with 133 Squadron at Boundary Bay, B.C., before being posted overseas in 1943 to join 412 Squadron RCAF; that unit flew Spitfires from Staplehurst in Kent.

Laubman's first encounter with enemy aircraft occurred on December 30 when he attacked three Messerschmitt 109 fighters over France — but he forgot to put the gun button on. On March 23, 1944, he scored his first victory when he shared in the destruction of a Junkers 88 bomber with another pilot.

By July Laubman's squadron had moved to Beny-sur-Mer, an airstrip in Normandy. Now his score began to mount. Between July 2 and August 10 he shot down four more German planes and shared in destroying another. On September 25, the start of his great shooting spree, he was awarded the DFC. A month later he was given a Bar to the decoration. Laubman went off operations in November but before it ended he shot down two Focke-Wulf 190 fighters bringing his score to fifteen destroyed.

He returned to Canada but on March 25, 1945, he was back overseas as CO of 402 Squadron RCAF based at Rheine in Germany. He had flown only twelve sorties before being forced to bail out when his Spitfire was damaged in an attack on a half-track vehicle. On landing he was confronted by angry German civilians and members of the Hitler Youth. But he was rescued by soldiers who packed him off to a POW camp.

Laubman retired from the RCAF right after the war with the intention of becoming a bush pilot. However he re-enlisted in 1946 and, after several flying assignments, he was given a number of senior posts as a staff officer, including CO of Canadian Forces No 1 Air Division at Lahr, Germany, and Chief of Personnel at CF HQ in Ottawa, Ont. He retired from the service in 1972.

DFC & Bar CD   A/C (RCAF)   L/G(CF)
RefScs: DHist bf   OMAP(2) 117   RAW 48   RCTFY 120 f239 245 247
261   RS&A 84 101 173 217   SY 60 136 216 342 336 357–58   TTS 179–86

LAYTON Michael Shakespeare

"Master Sub-Hunter"

As a navigator Mike Layton became such an authority on submarine hunting — and sinking — that when the defeat of the U-boat was placed at the top of Allied priorities for 1943, due to the appalling losses to convoys which threatened the supply of men and material to England for the invasion of Europe, he was one of two in RCAF Eastern Air Command to be summoned to evaluate the role of anti-submarine sweeps and make recommendations. His pilot, an RAF officer, was the other. Both were highly qualified: together they had sunk at least two submarines and Layton had been in on half a dozen attacks that had earned him the DSO.

A native of Montreal, P.Q., Layton enlisted in the RCAF in 1940 and in July 1941 joined 120 Squadron RAF Coastal Command at Nutt's Corner in Ireland. Equipped with Liberators, it had only recently been formed for patrol duty in the North Atlantic. That winter the sorties were mainly unsuccessful. On one occasion Layton's aircraft was hit by a German Arado's aircraft fire, which punctured the fuel tank.

The first attack on a U-boat that Layton was involved in took place on June 15, 1942, 600 miles from Land's End. Although the crew could see oily scum on the surface of the sea, it was not claimed as a kill. In September a detachment of the squadron flew to a new base at Reykjavik, Iceland, to cover territory out of range of aircraft from Canada or Great Britain. On October 12 Layton's crew, while on their way to meet a convoy, attacked a U-boat. It was a masterpiece of bombing on the navigator's part: one depth-charge exploded on the stern and two others amidships. The submarine shuddered, lifted up then sank. On October 16 they scored again. This time the stern of the U-boat seemed to hang in mid-air at a 20-degree angle before the sea finally swallowed it up. Before returning to base they attacked another submarine but were unsuccessful. November 5 marked one more banner day for Layton's crew. Ordered to escort a convoy that had been badly battered — it had lost sixteen ships since leaving port — they sighted a submarine at the same time they found the convoy. But it was too late; the U-boat quickly submerged. Then they sighted a second one. This time they were luckier. Layton's depth-charges completely enveloped the submarine. As the bombs exploded the stern rose in the air — almost at a right angle to the horizon — then sank. However a third submarine sighted also managed to elude them.

On December 8 Layton's crew took part in the most remarkable incident in convoy protection of the war. On that date they spotted thirteen submarines. Three Liberators from 120 Squadron attacked twelve of them. One of the U-boats was destroyed by Layton's crew; the accuracy of the hit was such that a six-foot piece of metal from the U-boat was sent flying up into the air. His crew probably destroyed another because following their bomb's detonation a solid column of water shot up thirty feet from the surface.

Layton's contribution to U-boat warfare in 1942 was officially described as "unmatched in the annals of Coastal Command." His most significant criticism in 1943 was that Eastern Air Command placed too much emphasis on distant anti-submarine sweeps and not enough on searches near the convoys. He and his pilot also emphasized the need for VLR (Very-Long-Range) bombers to ensure the convoys were covered from the air at all times.

DSO W/C
RefScs: DHist bf TCNAF 530–49 587

MacFADYEN Donald Aikins

"Night-Intruding Perfectionist"

L ong before he became a hot-shot Mosquito night-intruder ace, Don MacFadyen of Montreal, P.Q., was willing to risk disciplinary action for insubordination to make his point. And why not? Few pilots in RCAF Training Command could match his credentials. Before he put on the blue uniform in July 1940 he had already logged forty-five hours as a pilot and was the first to solo in his class at elementary school, where he also led his classmates in ground marks and flying. Likewise at service flying training school he took top honours. As an instructor he was the first BCATP graduate to be awarded the coveted A2 rating and before long he was raised to A1 category. He argued that the training system needed improving. (In fact he ended up as one of those who rewrote the manual.) Then he began to run afoul of authority. While lecturing a class at the Central Flying School the Station Commander took issue with him. MacFadyen suggested that the CO might like to take over the proceedings and promptly stomped out of the room.

A speedy posting followed — a lateral one — to Ferry Command in Dorval, P.Q. However MacFadyen considered it a bonanza: it lifted him out of instructing and propelled him overseas. On May 9, 1943, he was on his way to England at the controls of a Boston medium-bomber. He trained on Mosquitos at OTU, where his grading was marked "exceptional" because he had accustomed himself to a night vision on a par with normal day sight.

On December 17 MacFadyen joined 418 Squadron RCAF based at Ford in Sussex. On the night of December 22, while flying over France, he fired his guns in anger for the first time — without result. Then on February 24, 1944, he had better luck when he shot down his first enemy plane, a Messerschmitt 410 fighter-bomber near Schweinfurt. On March 1 — the only time he flew a day ranger — while in company with

PL 26049

another Mosquito he demolished a line of gliders at Hagen airfield then shot down a Messerschmitt 109 fighter trying to get airborne from a field at Luxeuil. On May 2 he was awarded the DFC. The next night he celebrated the event by destroying a Heinkel 111 bomber. But in the process his own aircraft was hit and he had to fly home on one engine. On the night of the Normandy invasion, June 6/7, he shot down a Junkers 52 transport in flames. On June 12 he spotted one of the first V-1 flying bombs launched against London and for the next few weeks the squadron busied itself chasing the Doodlebugs. MacFadyen accounted for five of them. Later in the month he was posted to an OTU as an instructor; there he distinguished himself as, in the words of the CO, "possibly the best pilot this OTU has ever had."

In November he joined 406 Squadron RCAF at Manston on the Kentish coast. With improved Mosquitos MacFadyen was able to make deep night penetrations, using radar to pick out German aircraft. By this method he soon began adding to his score. On March 3, 1945, he flew to Ceské Budejovice in Czechoslovakia where he blew one Focke-Wulf 190 fighter out of the sky and trashed three others on the ground. Then on April 9 he shot down two Junkers 88 fighter-bombers at Flensburg. He flew his last operational sortie on April 24, by which time his score stood at twenty-one aircraft destroyed (counting those on the ground), two probables and sixteen damaged.

MacFadyen left the RCAF after WW2, although for some time he was a member of 411 Auxiliary Squadron in Toronto. He joined an aerial survey group with which his efforts led to the development of major mineral and hydrological resources in South America.

DSO DFC & Bar   S/L   Born Dec 18 1920
RefScs: DHist bf   OMAP(2) 118   RAW 48 78 262–69   RCTFY 158 161
163 167 187 190 192 f271 275   TTS 193–202

MacKAY John

"Caused Destruction of Three Enemy Planes Without Firing a Shot"

On two occasions Johnny MacKay of Arbakka, Man., brought about the destruction of German fighters without firing a shot from his Spitfire's machine guns and cannon. The first took place on New Year's Day morning of 1945 when Luftwaffe fighter-bombers attacked Allied tactical fields in Belgium and Holland. MacKay and his fellow pilots were barely able to scramble their aircraft from Heesch when the Germans appeared. But MacKay quickly got on the tail of a Focke-Wulf 190, which he exploded with his gunfire. He next followed another FW 190 into enemy territory and lost it. Then two others appeared. MacKay attacked one on the deck, while an RAF Tempest pilot tackled the other.

MacKay fired several bursts, which exhausted his ammunition. But as he continued to close in on the FW 190, the enemy aircraft attempted to make a sharp turn to port and struck its wing on the ice of a lake below. It blew apart. On pulling up MacKay saw a Messerschmitt 109 headed east and gave chase; he forced it down on the deck where it struck some trees and broke into pieces (see below). Three days later, after shooting down two FW 190s in flames, MacKay was attacked by another Focke-Wulf and broke viciously to port. The German pilot tried to follow; but he lost control, went into a spin and crashed into the ground — another phenomenal logbook entry.

MacKay, who joined the RCAF in 1941, spent a year as an instructor before being posted overseas in 1943. After OTU training he joined 401 Squadron RCAF at Beny-sur-Mer in Normandy in August 1944. He made his first score on September 21 when he damaged an ME 109. On October 5, flying from Rips in Holland, MacKay was one of five who brought down an ME 262, the first jet plane destroyed by Commonwealth pilots. By the time his tour ended in April 1945, his score stood at 10½ destroyed and 6½ damaged.

Following WW2 MacKay stayed in the RCAF. In 1953 he served in Korea where, flying F86 Sabres, he added a MiG to his tally from WW2 and won the U.S. Air Medal; this kill was the last by a Canadian in the Korean War. In 1969, after logging 3,000 hours in the air during his 27-year service career, MacKay retired to live in Surrey, B.C.

DFC & Bar CD AM(Am) W/C Born Feb 15 1920
RefScs: DHist bf OMAP(2) 118 RAW 181 184 SY 261 TSBW 221
TTS 203–208

MacKay's combat report seemed so incredible that the 401 Intelligence Officer at first refused to accept it. But MacKay's squadron mates found the wreckages exactly where he had left them and Army observers confirmed the kills. Mackay was awarded an immediate DFC.

MAGWOOD Charles McLaughlin

"Sharpshooter"

Though his score of five German Focke-Wulf 190s destroyed and three damaged gave him ace status, it was for his marksmanship that Charlie Magwood was most noted. As a shot he had few equals. His method

Charlie Magwood (l.) being awarded his pilot's wings by General Hutchinson. Photo courtesy J.M. Magwood.

was to get in close and let go with short, rapid bursts of cannon and machine-gun fire that inevitably disintegrated his target. Such talent did not go unnoticed or unrecognized. In between tours he was made gunnery officer at Kenley in Surrey, where he served as CO of two RCAF fighter squadrons.

A native Torontonian, Magwood joined the air force in 1940 as a pilot. He went overseas the following year where, in November 1941, he joined 403 Squadron RCAF, then based at Martlesham Heath; the unit was flying Spitfires. His first year with the unit was uneventful. In fact the unit spent the last six months of 1942 at Catterick in Yorkshire for a respite from combat. In December Magwood was appointed a flight commander and shortly afterward, when the squadron moved south to Kenley, he made his first score. On February 15, 1943, during a fighter sweep over France, he attacked an FW 190 from the quarter beam. He saw strikes along the fuselage and grey smoke trailing behind as the enemy aircraft dived out of range. Magwood was credited with a damaged. On March 8 he shared a damaged with another pilot. On April 3 he destroyed an FW 190 and the next day brought down two more. On one of the attacks he got in close and fired, watching his bullets and cannon shells strike the centre section of the fuselage and wings. Chunks flew off the aircraft; then it completely disintegrated, leaving only a black cloud hanging in the air. By the time his first tour ended in June Magwood had destroyed one more aircraft, damaged another and had been awarded the DFC.

After his stint as gunnery officer Magwood took over as CO of 421 Squadron RCAF. With this squadron he damaged one FW 190 and destroyed another.

When his second tour ended he was assigned to No 3 Personal Reception Centre in Bournemouth as an administrator. The unit was attached to RCAF Overseas HQ in London. His RCAF career concluded when he was placed on the reserve list in October 1945. Following WW2 Magwood became chief buyer for one of Canada's largest retail stores and made his home in Toronto, Ont.

DFC W/C Born Nov 27 1913
RefScs: DHist bf OMAP(2) 119 RCTFFY 79 82–83 86–88 91 94
RCTFY 109–11 f114 RS&A 86 115

MANNING Ralph Viril

"Air-War Historian Made Air-War History"

L ong before he became the RCAF Historian Ralph Manning of Vancouver, B.C., made some pretty memorable air-war history of his own. Enlisting in the RCAF as a pilot he was posted overseas in the summer of 1941. He immediately joined 42 Squadron RAF Coastal Command. Equipped with twin-engine Beaufort torpedo-bombers, the squadron was engaged in the highly dangerous role of attacking enemy shipping off the Dutch, Danish and Norwegian coasts. In reporting to the unit Manning was told that only 50 percent of new crews completed their first mission. But Manning survived his first mission and many more, becoming one of the most deft and experienced practitioners of his trade.

A sortie on May 17, 1942, marked one of his most spectacular flights. The objective was the German battleship *Prinz Eugen*, which was being readied for a run from Trondheim, Norway, to Kiel, Germany. Manning's Beaufort was one of two sections of six to bore in on the heavily escorted vessel while twelve Hudson bombers acted as a diversion from above. As Manning started his bomb-run right at the deck the battleship began evasive action. Meanwhile four destroyers laid a smoke screen. In addition the *Prinz Eugen* used her big guns to churn up a wall of water to obscure the view; at the same time other batteries fired point blank at the incoming aircraft. Three Beauforts accompanying Manning on his run were shot

PL 104989

down, so as he zeroed in on the target, dropping his torpedo at 800-yards range, he was all alone. Suddenly his aircraft was hit! He half-rolled as he passed right between the ship and one of the destroyers, sustaining more damage to his aircraft. Then three Messerschmitt 109 fighters attacked but were driven off by other Beauforts. Manning was lucky to make it back to base, where he crash-landed. The *Prinz Eugen* had escaped but valuable lessons had been learned.

Manning applied his newly acquired knowledge with skill in North Africa, where he joined the Beaufighter-equipped (a step up from the

Beaufort) 47 Squadron RAF in August. Its role was to prevent ships from supplying Rommel's Afrika Korps. On October 26 the German tanker *Porserina* arrived within sight of its destination, Tobruk. After a long search Manning, along with two Bisley aircraft, attacked. On his first run the enemy tanker took sharp evasive action and Manning had to come around again. On this run his torpedo found the target: it exploded amidships.

In November Manning was transferred again — this time to India, where he rejoined his old squadron, 42, carrying out army cooperation duties. In the spring of 1943 the unit moved to Burma in support of Wingate's expedition against the Japanese. Later Manning joined 217 Squadron RAF in Ceylon, where he was engaged in convoy patrols, converting pilots to Beauforts and instructing on air-sea rescue procedures. In the latter case he was able to give his pupils a first-hand lesson when he was forced to ditch in the sea while on convoy patrol. The aircraft's dinghy failed and Manning and his two crew members — neither of whom could swim — had to rely on their Mae-West life-preservers to keep them afloat in shark-infested waters. Nevertheless Manning successfully kept their spirits up until all three were rescued by one of the ships they had been escorting.

Following WW2 Manning remained in the air force, serving at the RCAF Staff College in Toronto, Ont., and NORAD Headquarters, Colorado, before being appointed RCAF Historian in 1980. In that capacity he was instrumental in securing the hangars at Rockcliffe Air Station, Ont., to display the National Aviation Museum aircraft collection. Manning retired from the RCAF in 1965 and joined the Canadian War Museum in Ottawa, Ont., of which he became curator.

DFC CD MID(2)   Born 1916
RefScs: DHist bf   SY 155   TDS 106–11

McCARTHY Joseph Charles

"Dam Buster Survived Three Death-Defying Tours"

Hand-picked to lead one of the raids on the Ruhr dams, for which he was awarded the DSO, Joe McCarthy treated that historic mission as just one more sortie in his record of sixty-nine trips during three tours of operations.

A native of New York City, N.Y., McCarthy came to Canada to enlist in the RCAF early in 1941. After receiving his pilot's wings he was posted overseas in January 1942 and made his first three trips on operations while still at OTU on twin-engine Hampden bombers. He was posted to 97 Squadron RAF, which was stationed at Woodhall Spa, Lincolnshire. He flew Lancasters on thirty-four night raids against virtually every major target in Germany, including Berlin, Cologne, Duisburg, Hamburg and Munich, as well as several points in Italy.

Some of his sorties were hair-raising. On December 9, over Turin, the hydraulic system of his bomber failed and he had to fly the machine home with the landing gear extended and execute a flapless landing. On another trip his aircraft was attacked by a Junkers 88 night-fighter, which set a port engine on fire. McCarthy dropped his bombs, feathered the prop and headed home. During this first tour many of his sorties were against the heavily defended Ruhr industrial area.

When his tour ended on March 22, 1943, he was invited to join a new squadron being formed. It was a squadron of crack bomber crews preparing for a special mission. Based at Scampton in Yorkshire, this was 617 Squadron RAF eventually known as the Dam Busters. On the night of May 16/17 McCarthy was late getting off due to a coolant leak. By the time he reached the target area of the other four Lancasters that made up his formation two had been shot down and the others so severely damaged by enemy flak they were forced to return to base. That left only McCarthy and his crew to attack the Scorpe Dam, accompanied by a single reserve aircraft. But although both planes dropped their bombs they failed to breach it.

Afterward, due to a compass failure, McCarthy and his crew found themselves over Hamm in Germany instead of the English Channel and the navigator had to map-read his way home.

McCarthy continued on a tour that lasted into March 1944, by which time he had flown fifty-two operational sorties. Some targets were Italian centres and entailed him continuing on to Africa. He also flew occasional Pathfinder missions on Mosquitos.

McCarthy began his third tour in April. One notable sortie took place on the night of June 5/6 prior to the Normandy landings when the squadron flew at low-level off the Pas de Calais to simulate a sea convoy and deceive the Germans into thinking it was the landing force.

McCarthy flew his last operational trip on July 4; it was his sixty-seventh. He was then posted as CO of a fighter-affiliation practice unit in Yorkshire, a position he held until the war in Europe ended. Following the cessation of hostilities he stayed in the RCAF and retired from the Canadian Forces in 1968.

DSO DFC & Bar CD W/C
RefScs: RAW 295–97   RCTFFY 353 357   TDS 55 57–61

McELROY John Frederick

"Brought Crippled Spitfires Home Four Times"

"**M**ac" McElroy had an affinity for attracting enemy bullets. Shot-up four times, he managed to bring his riddled aircraft back home on each of them. However on most occasions his Spitfire was a write-off. Yet he walked away from every one of the crashes and was wounded only once — and then not too severely.

Born in Port Arthur, Ont., McElroy enlisted in the RCAF in June 1940 and was commissioned as a pilot in November 1941. Posted overseas, he completed operational training and joined 54 Squadron RAF at Castletown, Scotland, in March 1942. That May McElroy had his first brush with danger: on a practice low-level Rhubarb over the sea his propeller struck the water. Despite a violently vibrating engine he managed to land the Spitfire safely at Wick. Though unhurt he was badly shaken. It was an omen of things to come.

Posted to Malta in June, McElroy reported to 249 Squadron RAF. He quickly established himself as one of the leading aces on the island — and the most shot-up. On July 2 he damaged a Messerschmitt 109 fighter, the first of a string of victories that, before the end of the month, totalled five enemy aircraft destroyed, one shared and four damaged. In September he added one more to his tally. Then during October he shot down five more, probably destroyed another and damaged three others. But he paid a heavy price. Three times that month his Spitfire was riddled with enemy bullets. On October 12, in a 50-minute bout with six ME 109s, his aircraft was so badly shot-up it looked like a sieve. Three days later he was wounded slightly in the leg and his aircraft set on fire. When black smoke filled the cockpit he decided to bail out but the canopy jammed. Then the plane dived down out of control. However McElroy managed to level out just in time to make a crash-landing. Next day an ME 109 got the better of him and he was forced to crash-land again. At the end of the month his tour was over and McElroy was awarded the DFC. He was also sent back to England for a stint as an instructor.

In January 1944 he returned to operations as a flight commander with 421 Squadron RCAF based at Kenley, Surrey. Engaged in dive-bombing and strafing missions, McElroy had little chance to add to his score until after D-Day. On June 15 he damaged an ME 109 but another German fighter shot his port aileron off, depriving him of any lateral control. With a shudder the Spitfire stalled. Luckily McElroy had 15,000 feet of altitude to play with; by skillfully manipulating the elevators and rudders he pulled out of the spin and reached a temporary airfield where he could land his ailing aircraft. The aircraft was a write-off but McElroy once again walked away from it none the worse for wear. On June 29, when the CO of 416 Squadron RCAF was wounded, McElroy took his place. In that capacity he shot down three ME 109s and shared in the destruction of another. By the time his tour ended at the end of October his tally stood at 13½ destroyed, three probables and nine damaged.

McElroy resigned from the RCAF in 1945 but re-enlisted three years later serving as an instructor and, for a time, flying Sabre jets with 421 Squadron in Europe. He retired from the service in November 1964 to live in London, Ont.

DFC & Bar S/L   Born Nov 3 1920
RefScs: DHist bf OMAP(2) 119 RAW 375 RCTFFY 357
RCTFY 232 235 239 252 RS&A 107 TTS 187–91

McGREGOR Roy Gordon

"Webster Trophy Winner — Battle of Britain Ace Wing Leader — Airline Chief"

At age 38 Gordie McGregor was the oldest Canadian pilot to fly in the Battle of Britain; and with the award of the DFC he was also one of the first three in the RCAF to be decorated in WW2. A native of Montreal, P.Q., McGregor learned to fly in 1932 at Kingston, Ont., while working for the Bell Telephone Company. Three times between 1935 and 1938 he won the Webster Trophy, awarded annually to the outstanding Canadian amateur pilot. In 1938 he joined 115 Auxiliary Squadron RCAF in Montreal and was mobilized when war started. He went overseas in June 1940 as a flight commander with No 1 Fighter Squadron. The unit, which was stationed at Middle Wallop, was equipped with Hurricanes; to gain experience, McGregor and the CO were temporarily attached to 111 Squadron RAF before taking their outfit into combat from Northolt.

On August 28, over Biggin Hill in Kent, McGregor shot down his first German plane: a twin-engine Dornier 215 bomber. This was the third victory by an RCAF pilot and the first by a Canadian Squadron. As the battle wore on his tally began to mount. On September 15, "Battle of Britain Day," he scored a probable. Then on September 27 he claimed two Messerschmitt 109 fighters damaged and one Junkers 88 bomber probably destroyed. By the time McGregor took command of the squadron on November 2 (renumbered 401 Squadron on March 1, 1941) his score

PL 5863

had reached four enemy aircraft destroyed (see page 211), three probables and five damaged.

In January 1941 he was transferred to 402 Squadron RCAF (nee No 2) as CO. Then in April he took over as Wing Commander Flying at the Canadian Digby wing in Lincolnshire, which was made up of two

RCAF fighter squadrons. On the fifteenth of the month he led twelve Hurricanes of 402 Squadron, escorted by RAF Spitfires, across the English Channel to the Boulogne area on the French coast; this marked the first RCAF sweep over enemy territory.

After a stint as Director of Air Staff at RCAF Overseas HQ in London, McGregor returned to Canada to take command of X Wing RCAF at Anchorage, Alaska, in July 1942. During that tenure the wing conducted the first all-Canadian offensive mission against the Japanese in a raid on Kiska in the Aleutians from Adak Island. For this operation McGregor received the OBE. In July 1944 he went back overseas as Station Commander of 126 RCAF Wing of the 2nd Tactical Air Force based in Normandy. He held this post until September 1945, by which time the wing was based at Utersen in Germany.

After retiring from the RCAF McGregor joined Trans Canada Airlines as general traffic manager. In 1948 he became TCA's first full-time president, a position he held for twenty years. He also served as president of the International Aviation Transport Association and as a member of the advisory council of the RCAF Association. He died in Montreal in 1971.

OBE DFC CdeG(Fr) OONK(Dch) G/C Born Sept 26 1901 Died Mar 3 1971 Ind CAHF 1973 WTw3
RefScs: AIC 120 CAHF 46 CWC 203–17 CWM DHist bf
RAW 116 121 167–68 200 RCTFFY 11 14–16 18–19 23–25 27–28 31 37 357 RCTFY 249–55 262 265–67 270 RS&A 21 215 225 226 SY 149 TSBW 138–41 147 202 204 219

In 1977 the Sussex and Surrey Aviation Historical Society recovered the wreckage of a Ju 88 Gordie had claimed on September 27, 1940, as a probable. This brought his number of German aircraft destroyed to five ranking him, posthumously, as an ace — thirty-seven years after the event!

McINTOSH David

"Overcame Terror to Complete Hair-Raising Mosquito Tour"

Dave McIntosh of Stanstead, P.Q., a navigator with 418 Squadron RCAF, admitted he was frightened out of his wits most of the time he was on operational sorties. Yet he suppressed his fear sufficiently

Dave McIntosh (l.) with pilot Sid Seid.

to steer his dare-devil Mosquito pilot to and from the target on forty-one different missions. These were hair-raising, often mind-boggling, ventures that included day and night strafing attacks on airfields, transports and trains, shipping and rocket sites. These ventures even included occasional bomb raids that ranged across Germany, Czechoslovakia, Denmark and Norway, as well as downing V-1 flying bombs over England.

McIntosh joined the RCAF in 1942 and after graduation went overseas in 1943. On D-Day June 6, 1944, after OTU, he joined 418 Squadron, then based at Holmsley South; this was Canada's only night-intruder squadron. Three days after reporting for duty he and his pilot made their first sortie: a "flower" patrol over German airfields. They made a second one a few days later. Then on June 13 the first V-1s fell on England and the squadron was assigned patrols to prevent these flying bombs from reaching London. McIntosh and his pilot accounted for half a dozen of them, flying so close to them that one explosion blackened their Mosquito.

In July McIntosh's terror was put to the supreme test when he and his teammate joined the circuit over Argelsried airfield in Germany and shot up a passenger train. On the way home they ended up in the middle of flak and searchlights over Wiesbaden, which was the RAF Bomber Command's target for the night. One engine caught fire, which McIntosh managed to extinguish; however it was completely burned out and the pilot had to make the rest of the flight on only one motor.

After a series of moves at the end of July and the beginning of August the squadron settled at Hundson, thirty miles north of London. Flying out of the new base on a sortie shortly afterward, McIntosh and his pilot experienced more engine trouble. This time one motor began to vibrate uncontrollably and the other caught fire. McIntosh extinguished the flame and the plane made it back on the faulty running engine. McIntosh and his pilot's crowning achievement occurred in October when on a single mission they destroyed eight enemy aircraft on the ground. It was on their forty-first and final sortie that the pair encountered a German plane in the air for the first and only time.

His tour completed, McIntosh returned to Canada as an instructor at 31 OTU at Debert, N.S. Retiring from the RCAF at the end of WW2 McIntosh joined Canadian Press and became a foreign, defense and political correspondent for thirty years. In 1972 he began writing and producing films for federal agencies and made his home in Ottawa, Ont. He is an honorary member of the Parliamentary Press Gallery, in which he has been an active member for many years.

DFC F/L Born 1921 Author of: *Terror in the Starboard Seat*
High Blue Battle
RefScs: RCTFY 188 191–92 f271 285–86 TISS(biog)

To appreciate the full horror of war read Dave's description of a crashed Mosquito that caught fire and burned before its occupants could escape: pp 118–23 *Terror in the Starboard Seat*. It is as chilling an account as I have ever read.

McKNIGHT William Lidstone

"The Fighter Jock"

To no one could the sobriquet "Fighter Jock" have been more aptly applied than to Willie McKnight. It fit so well it might have originated with him. Short, nimble and wiry, he resembled the racehorse jockey in every respect whether on a firm (clear) or cuppy (cloudy, wet weather) track. At the reins of his aerial steed he had complete control. And regardless of the odds for or against him, he always went all-out to win.

Born in Edmonton, Alta., McKnight enlisted in the RAF early in 1939 and, by the time WW2 broke out, had almost completed his pilot's training. In November he was posted to 242 Squadron RAF, a unit largely made up of Canadians and that was equipped with Hurricanes at the turn of the year. In April 1940, after the Germans invaded Norway, the squadron moved to France in anticipation of a German assault on the West. The assault began on May 10. On the nineteenth, while attached to another unit at Abbeville, McKnight first drew blood when his flight was attacked by Messerschmitt 109s near Cambrai. Four bursts from his eight Browning machine guns sent one of the German fighters diving into the ground. That was his last action on the continent.

McKnight's squadron flew back to England, ostensibly for a rest. However, R&R was cancelled when the evacuation of Dunkirk began on May 27 and the unit was promptly ordered to Manston to cover the withdrawal. During that period, McKnight's success was spectacular. In five days he destroyed seven aircraft, scoring a hat-trick of two ME 109s and a Dornier 17 bomber in one battle. A week later he received the DFC. When the evacuation ended there were still troops in France and 242 Squadron was sent back to the continent to cover their retreat through Le Havre. Following this duty the squadron moved to Coltishall to regroup. The unit was given a new CO, the legendary legless ace Douglas Bader. By mid-July Bader had the squadron back on an operational basis and ready for the Battle of Britain.

After moving south to Duxford the unit saw its first action since Dunkirk on August 30. McKnight performed his second hat-trick by shooting down three ME 110 twin-engine fighters. On September 9 he scored again, adding two more aircraft — ME 109s — to his tally. But in the process he had an aileron shot off. Then on September 18, when the squadron attacked thirty unescorted German bombers, McKnight shot down a Do 17 and shared in the destruction of a Junkers 88 twin-engine bomber. His final victory took place on November 5 over an ME 109 low-level nuisance raider, which he sent spinning into the ground. The award of a Bar to his DFC followed swiftly.

Later in the month the squadron moved to Martelsham Heath on the coast to take part in offensive sorties over France. It was on a low-level Rhubarb strike against ground targets early in the new year that McKnight went missing. He and his wingman were attacking a battalion of German soldiers over Gravelines when they were bounced by a dozen ME 109s. Both pilots took refuge in the clouds. But McKnight was never seen again and the death of the epitome of the "Fighter Jock" was never determined. His score at the time stood at 16½ aircraft destroyed (see page 216) and one damaged.

In 1971 a boulevard in Calgary (a route to the airport) was named after him, as was a hall in the Chapelhow Branch of the Royal Canadian Legion in September 1991.

> DFC & Bar   F/L   Born Nov 18 1918   KIA Jan 12 1941
> RefScs: CA 246   DHist bf   OMAP(2) 119   RAW 165   RCTFFY 8
> RFTS 195 198 205 206 211 213 223 227 232 236 244 TTS 209–16

Possibly his score was eighteen enemy aircraft destroyed; this is according to no less an authority than historian Hugh Halliday of the Canadian War Museum.

McLEOD Henry Wallace

"Highest Scoring RCAF Ace"

W ith 19 enemy aircraft shot down, one probably destroyed and 9¼ damaged, Wally McLeod was the RCAF's leading ace. A native of Regina, Sask., McLeod joined the air force in 1940. He went overseas the following year and served short stints with 132, 485 and 602 RAF fighter squadrons. He was eventually posted to 411 Squadron RCAF, a Spitfire unit stationed at Hornchurch, Essex, in December 1941. During his five months with the squadron he racked up two German aircraft damaged before being transferred in June 1942 to Malta to join 603 Squadron RAF. On his first flight with the squadron McLeod was shot-up by an enemy fighter, which riddled his Spitfire and nearly ripped off his tailplane. However shortly afterward he shot down an Italian Macchi 202 fighter, sending it crashing into the sea.

Though few pilots were as aggressive (the score meant everything) or would take such enormous risks to ensure a victory, with McLeod's killer streak went a sense of chivalry also. When he shot down his second plane from Malta — a Messerschmitt 109 fighter — the German pilot parachuted into the sea. McLeod dropped his dinghy to the downed flier. That the enemy pilot did not respond to this generous gesture by inflating it was explained later when the Air Sea Rescue Service launch crew reported the pilot had been so badly wounded that he died en route to hospital. Six days later McLeod again demonstrated his determination when, with seven others, he waded into a gaggle of sixty enemy aircraft and, although his wings were badly shot-up, bored right in to bring down a Junkers 88 bomber.

In October he was made a flight commander of 1435 Flight, to which he had transferred earlier, and awarded the DFC. During that month,

PL 11993

from the eleventh to the thirteenth, McLeod destroyed five aircraft, damaged four others and was himself shot down. Over the next eight days he added two more destroyed to his tally as well as one damaged. Thus he became the second-ranking Canadian Malta ace, behind George Beurling, but still the top RCAF ace (Beurling was RAF) on the island. His last sortie in that theatre occurred on October 22 when he destroyed a Macchi 202, bringing his total to thirteen destroyed and four damaged, and earning him a Bar to his DFC.

However the incessant action, nightly air raids and poor food had taken their toll; in the four months he had been on the island McLeod lost twenty-five pounds. He was sent back to England then Canada to recuperate. In March 1943 he was made a gunnery officer at No 1 OTU RCAF, Bagotville, P.Q. Then in January 1944 he was transferred to Eastern Air Command as CO of 127 Squadron RCAF based at Dartmouth N.S., which he took overseas. At Digby, Lincolnshire, the unit was equipped with Spitfire IXs, renumbered 443 Squadron and became part of the wing commanded by the famous Johnnie Johnson, who ended WW2 as the top Allied ace in the Western Theatre.

McLeod's burning ambition was to surpass Beurling's score of twenty-nine destroyed. He had a long way to go but he wasted no time getting back into stride. His squadron became operational on April 13 and six days later he recorded the first victory of his second tour by shooting down an Dornier 215 bomber over Belgium. Then on May 5 he destroyed a Focke-Wulf 190 fighter. In the melee he lost his wingman and his long-range belly tank refused to jettison. Under the circumstances he should have broken off the engagement. But in his determination to increase his score he ignored the risk and closed to seventy-five yards range, crashing the enemy plane into the ground where it exploded.

Following the invasion of Europe the wing moved to an airstrip at St-Croix-sur-Mer in Normandy. During June McLeod added three more to his score: an ME 109 and two FW 190s, which he shot down for the incredibly low expenditure of thirteen rounds from each of two cannon, establishing a record never equalled. On July 20 he had the unusual experience of seeing the pilot of an FW 190 he was chasing bail out before he even fired a shot. Ten days later he claimed his last victim, an ME 109, which he destroyed after a long chase on the deck. On August 17 he was shot down for the third time when, while attacking enemy transports, ground fire punctured his glycol cooling tank. Early in September he received his third decoration, the DSO.

Then on September 27, while patrolling between Nijmegen and Velno in Holland, McLeod was killed in a melee with nine ME 109s. He was last seen streaking after a looping Messerschmitt by his wingman, who blacked out pulling up from a dive and lost sight of him. Later his body was found in the wreckage of his Spitfire, which had crashed near the scene of the fight.

DSO DFC & Bar   S/L   Born Dec 17 1915   KIA Sept 27 1944
RefScs: CA 246   DHist bf   OMAP(2) 119   RAW 180 375
RCTFFY 354   RCTFY 123 127–29 131 232 235 250–51 f254 261 266
RS&A 60 142 224   TDS 11–13   TSBW 200–201 204 207–208   TTS
217–22   WL 184 216 218 245 251–56

Johnnie Johnson's first impression of Wally was enlightening — and right on target: "A killer if there ever was one I thought . . . he might be inclined to stick his neck out too far. . . . "

McNAB Ernest Archibald

"First to Lead the RCAF into Battle"

As CO of No 1 Canadian Fighter Squadron Ernie McNab was the first to take an RCAF unit into combat and the second in the service to destroy an enemy aircraft. Born in Rosthern, Sask., McNab became a member of the air force while attending university. In 1928, after graduating as a civil engineer, he joined the RCAF and received his wings in August. In the years before WW2 he was assigned a number of duties, including reconnaissance, transport, instruction and carrying air-mail. In addition he became an exchange officer with the RAF and was also a member of the Siskin Flight, the RCAF's first aerobatic team that, in 1930 and 1931, toured Canada and the U.S.

On November 1, 1939, McNab, who had been a flight commander with No 1 Squadron and one of the first to fly a Hurricane in Canada, became CO of the unit; he was the third since its formation in 1937. As the unit's first wartime commander McNab's first duty was to move the squadron from St Hubert, P.Q., to Dartmouth, N.S., for preliminary training before shipping overseas in June 1940. On arrival in England the squadron was first based at Middle Wallop then Croydon, where it underwent battle training.

To gain first-hand combat experience McNab and one of his flight commanders were attached to 111 Squadron RAF. On August 11, while still serving with that unit, McNab shot down a Dornier 17 bomber over Westgate-on-Sea to become the second member of the RCAF to destroy an enemy aircraft. On August 17 No 1 Squadron moved to Northolt, where it was stationed for the duration of the Battle of Britain. On August 26 the squadron went into action against the Germans for the first time, destroying three twin-engine Dornier 215 bombers and damaging three others; McNab accounted for one of them. September 27 saw the squadron's most successful day in the battle: it flew three sorties, shooting down eight enemy aircraft, probably destroying one and damaging another. McNab himself destroyed a Messerschmitt 110 fighter and shared in the destruction of a Junkers 88 bomber. In October, with a score of five

PL 905

destroyed, one probable and three damaged, McNab became the first RCAF ace and, with the award of the DFC, the first in the service to win a war decoration.

On November 1 he relinquished his command and was transferred to RCAF Overseas HQ in London. In February 1942 he was posted to Canada to command No 4 SFTS Saskatoon, Sask. He returned to England in July 1942 as Station Commander of Digby fighter station in Lincolnshire.

Following the war he held a number of staff positions, including that of Chief Staff Officer, No 5 Air Division, Vancouver, B.C., from August 1954 until his retirement in February 1957. He died in Vancouver at age 73.

OBE DFC CD CzWC   G/C   Born Mar 7 1906   Died Jan 10 1977
RefScs: CA 211 213   CCMA 27 54–56   DHist bf   HBB 5–6 19 23–24 29
32 34–35 37–39 46   OMAP(2) 120   RAW 17 166–68 180   RCTFFY 9–12
14 f16 17–19 21–22 f32 357   RS&A 21 52 219   SY 41   TDS 14–16
TSBW 108 118 137 141

McNAIR Robert Wendell

"Wartime Bravery, Leadership Extended into Peacetime"

T wice forced down into the English Channel in flames, "Buck" McNair survived three years of combat in Europe and Malta to become one of Canada's leading fighter pilots — and one of the most aggressive of any nation. He was also the only RCAF ace to hold a senior command during WW2.

Born in Springfield, N.S., McNair joined the RCAF in July 1940. His first operational posting was in the summer of 1941 to 411 Squadron RCAF, a Spitfire unit at Digby, Lincolnshire. Shortly after joining it he saw his first combat on September 27 during a bomber-escort sortie over northern France when he damaged a Messerschmitt 109.

Several weeks later, while returning from a fighter sweep, McNair spotted seven ME 109s circling low over a shot-down British pilot in the English Channel. Ignoring the odds he plunged into the middle of them, one German fighter falling quickly to his guns as he calmly radioed for Air Sea Rescue Service help. Then the ME 109s ganged up on him. Smoke filled his cockpit as his aircraft was hit from all sides. But he managed to shoot down another one before his aircraft caught fire. Down at 400 feet he bailed out, his parachute opening just as he hit the water.

In March 1942 McNair was posted to Malta and was one of the first to fly into the besieged island from an aircraft carrier. In Malta he joined 249 Squadron RAF. He flew his first combat sortie on March 19 and damaged an ME 109. A week later he shot down a Junkers 88 twin-engine bomber and damaged two others. As the blitz against the island wore on McNair's successes continued to mount. On one occasion, while leading a small section of four Spitfires, he attacked a gaggle of ME 109s escorting a formation of Ju 87 Stuka and Ju 88 bombers. In short order he shot down one of the fighters then damaged a Ju 88. Several days later, in a head-on attack, McNair damaged two ME 109s, one Ju 87 and a Ju 88. On May 22 he was awarded the DFC. By then he had destroyed seven aircraft and damaged an equal number. On June 1 he was made a flight commander of his squadron before being posted back to England three weeks later — but not before shooting down an ME 109 on June 10.

In Britain he rejoined his old squadron, 411, this time as head of a flight. And he continued to add to his tally. During the Dieppe raid on August 19 he shot down a Focke-Wulf 190

In September McNair was sent to Canada for a War Bond drive then returned to England in 1943, first with 403 Squadron RCAF then, in May, taking command of 416 Squadron RCAF at Kenley. The following month he transferred to 421 Squadron RCAF as CO of that unit.

On the afternoon of July 28, while escorting Flying Fortresses, McNair's engine began to vibrate uncontrollably. Ten miles off the French coast his Spitfire caught fire, forcing him to parachute into the Channel. Badly burnt about one eye and with his dinghy in shreds, he could only bobble about in the sea and rely on his Mae West lifejacket to keep him afloat. Rescued by a Walrus flying boat, he knew from the pain that he had suffered permanent damage. But despite severe migraine headaches and some loss of sight. McNair kept on shooting, bringing his list of kills up to sixteen and receiving two Bars to his DFC.

Then in October of 1943 he became Wing Commander Flying of 126 RCAF Wing at Biggin Hill. After six months, however, he was taken off operations and given an administrative job. He ended the war as Deputy Commander of a Tactical Air Force Wing with responsibility for five airfields and overseeing fifteen squadrons.

Following the war McNair stayed in the RCAF where he further distinguished himself by holding a number of senior positions, including that of Deputy Commander of NORAD in Duluth, Minn. In his peacetime career McNair also continued to display his inbred bravery. On December 30, 1953, a North Star transport, in which he was a crew member, crash-landed at Vancouver, B.C. McNair supervised the rescue of all passengers from the wreckage. Though soaked in gasoline and aware that fire could break out at any moment, he refused to leave the aircraft until everyone was accounted for. McNair died of leukemia in 1970.

DSO DFC & 2 Bars CdeG(Fr) Ld'H OONK(Dch) W/C Col(CF)
Born May 15 1919 Died Jan 15 1970 Ind CAHF 1990
RefScs: CAHF 138 CWC 219–28 DHist bf RAW 162 172 180 200 374
376 389 391 RCTFFY 47 95 f96 101 105 108–109 110–11 113 356
RCTFY 100 102–103 106–108 114 120–21 123–24 f126 RS&A 107 217
221 TSBW 148 200–201

PL 10-620

One day, while flying over the Channel, Buck ordered us to empty our guns. I didn't hear him. My radio was U/S (Unserviceable, not working). At the debriefing, in front of the rest of the wing, he asked me why I hadn't fired. I told him. He then asked whether I had reported it to the ground crew when I landed. My reply was negative. I'd forgotten to. "Bishop," Buck bellowed, "Some day there'll be a Hun up your tail and I'll yell 'Break!' But you won't hear me and you'll be shot down. Then what's old man Bishop going to say?"

McRAE Donald Farquhar

"Victor Over Three U-boats"

During his 460 operational hours with RAF Coastal Command, flying from bases as far flung as Gibraltar and North Africa as well as out of England, Don McRae emerged as conqueror over three German U-boats. Born in Stavely, Alta., McRae joined the RCAF in May 1941. After graduating as a pilot he was seconded to RAF Ferry Command in July 1942. At the beginning of the new year he was posted to 179 Coastal Command Squadron RAF, which operated with twin-engine Wellingtons from Chivenor in southwest England. In March 1943 an important development occurred when the bombers were equipped with Leigh Lights, powerful beacons with 120-million candlepower used for illuminating U-boat targets in the dark.

On the night of August 24, 1943, McRae put his new searchlight to full effect when his crew made contact with a submarine, which they had run down on their radar. At 900 yards range he switched on his Leigh Light, illuminating a stationary U-boat. Out of position to make an attack he switched off his light, banked away, then returned. When the submarine opened fire the Wellington replied with its own guns. McRae bracketed the conning tower with six depth-charges and the flak subsided but he could see no evidence that he had sunk the U-boat. However the Germans confirmed that the U-1346 had indeed been lost. On September 3 he attacked another submarine at an angle of 30 degrees to the vessel's wake and dropped six 250-pound bombs, but with inconclusive results. Three nights later, while flying over the Bay of Biscay, the radar picked up a U-boat. Once he spotted it McRae bored in to attack. As his navigator opened fire McRae dropped six depth-charges, which exploded between the conning tower and the stern. Yet the submarine still managed to stay afloat. However it was forced to seek refuge at Vega Harbour in Spain, where its crew and vessel were interned — a victory as decisive as if the U-boat had gone to the bottom.

That same night, when McRae reached the base at Port Lyautey in North Africa, to which he had been diverted, the field was covered with fog. Then both engines of the Wellington failed, making a forced landing imminent. Fortunately a farmer at Meknès in French Morocco was burning stubble in a wheat field; it acted as a beacon. McRae lowered his undercarriage and, from the aircraft's landing lights, saw that he was headed for a gully at the end of the field. He pulled up the wheels and the aircraft skidded to a stop just in time.

On November 18, flying from the Azores on a bright, moonlit night on convoy patrol, the radar picked up a U-boat 900 yards ahead, which

McRae quickly tracked down. To achieve surprise, and for fear it would light up the convoy he was trying to protect, McRae decided not to turn on his Leigh Light. As the submarine opened fire he dived down to fifty feet, straddling it with depth charges. With a flash it exploded amidships and the U-211 sank with all hands aboard. McRae was awarded the DFC.

On completing his tour McRae returned to Canada in January 1944. Following WW2 he resigned from the RCAF then re-enlisted in October 1946, serving until January 1961 when he retired.

DFC CD S/L   Born Mar 19 1913
RefScs: DHist bf   RAW 350   TDS 89-91

MEEK Richard John

"Wounded Navigator Steered Crippled Bomber and Crew Home"

Shot-up four times over Berlin by a night-fighter, the Lancaster bomber in which Richard Meek was riding as navigator on the night of January 30, 1943, became so riddled with enemy fire it resembled little more than a flying wreck. Yet, although badly wounded and with his navigational instruments shot out, Meek plotted a course so accurately his pilot was able to steer the bomber home to their base.

Born in Vancouver, B.C., Meek joined the RCAF in 1941. Arriving overseas in December 1942 he underwent operational training and joined 626 Squadron RAF at Wickenby in November that year.

On January 30, 1943, on his third mission, Meek's crew was part of a bomber force of 500 aircraft sent off to bomb Berlin. As they neared the target night-fighter opposition became heavy and Meek's Lancaster was attacked four times within eight minutes by one of the defenders. On the initial pass the wireless operator was killed and both gunners so severely wounded they lapsed into unconsciousness. All electrical circuits were destroyed, the hydraulic and communications systems shot out and the side and rear panels of the mid-upper gun-turret blown off. With the aircraft's communications gone the pilot had to take evasive action as best he could without instruction or warning from the crew. Nevertheless he successfully completed his bomb run. Then the night-fighter struck again, causing more damage to the bomber. On a third assault Meek was severely wounded, a bullet grazed the pilot's leg and the aircraft absorbed further gunfire. In the final attack Meek was again struck by a bullet and his instruments destroyed. Although desperately wounded in his chest, close to his heart and in the shoulder, he remained at his post. Though deprived of most of his navigational equipment Meek nonetheless managed to plot a course home to base with extraordinary determination and skill. On reaching Wickenby the pilot successfully crash-landed the bomber without further injury to the crew. For his heroism in the face of fire Meek was awarded the CGM.

After convalescing from his wounds Meek rejoined his squadron at the beginning of April and completed his tour of operations, which included bombing D-Day targets and flying-bomb sites. At the end of 1944 he was posted to an OTU as an instructor.

DFC CGM F/O Born 1908
RefScs: DHist bf RCTFY 348 TDS 63–64

MOLSON Hartland de Montarville

"One of the First of the Canadian Few to Hit the Silk"

On October 5, 1940, Hartland Molson of Montreal, P.Q., was one of a wing of twenty-four Hurricane and Spitfire pilots scrambled from Northolt fighter station in Middlesex to intercept sixty German Messerschmitt 109 single-engine fighters and fifteen ME 110 twin-engine fighter-bombers 20,000 feet over the south of England. During the furious fight that ensued, in which his squadron, No 1 RCAF, accounted for three of the fighters shot down and another three damaged, Molson's Hurricane was hit by enemy fire and he was forced to bail out. He thus became one of the first in the RCAF to take to his parachute in WW2. But Molson was badly wounded in the leg and for him the Battle of Britain, in which he had fought almost daily for a month and a half, was over.

A graduate of RMC, Molson learned to fly in the late 1930s with the Montreal Light Aeroplane Club at Cartierville, P.Q. At the same time he joined 115 Auxiliary Fighter Squadron RCAF, equipped with Fleet Fawns. When WW2 broke out in 1939 Molson enlisted in the RCAF, received his wings and in June 1940 went overseas with No 1 Squadron. As soon as it reached England the unit began battle-training. It became operational in mid-August and Molson went into combat for the first time on the twenty-sixth of the month. But it was not until September 4 that he tallied his first score by damaging two ME 110s. On September

PL 8363

11 he destroyed a Heinkel 111 bomber and, before he was shot down in October, damaged a Dornier 215 bomber.

After being released from the hospital at the end of 1940 Molson returned to Canada, where on July 23 he became CO of 118 Squadron, Eastern Air Command, stationed at Dartmouth, N.S. Initially equipped with Goblins, the unit later switched to Kittyhawks.

In June 1942 Molson relinquished that command to become CO of 126 Squadron, also based at Dartmouth. He then served at Eastern Air Command HQ in Halifax, N.S., and later became CO of two different Service Flying Training Schools, first at Moncton, N.B., and next at Weyburn, Sask. Following this he was given command of RCAF Station

St Hubert, P.Q. In July 1944 he was appointed Director of Personnel at RCAF HQ, Ottawa, Ont. He held this post until his retirement from the air force in 1945. Following the war Molson returned to the family brewery business, Molson Breweries. In July 1955 he was appointed to the Canadian Senate.

OBE G/C Born May 29 1907
RefScs: Dhist bf HBB 31–33 41   RAW 17   RCTFFY 14 16 18
RS&A 52 59 TSBW 17–18 141

MONCRIEFF Ernest Hutchison Glen

"Instrumental in Success of Fighter Reconnaissance Groups"

In January of 1943, at an airfield constructed by the Canadian Engineers at Dunsfold in Surrey a month earlier, Ernie Moncrieff organized the last of three RCAF Army Co-operation — later designated Fighter-Reconnaissance — squadrons to be formed overseas. Numbered 430 Squadron, it was equipped with Mustangs, and Moncrieff's post as CO was but a harbinger of the leadership and organizational role he would play in RCAF fighter-reconnaissance commands.

Born in Winnipeg, Man., he began his air force career with 112 Auxiliary Squadron RCAF of that city, flying Moths and Tutors. At the outbreak of WW2 he joined the air force, serving both as staff officer and instructor, for which he was awarded the AFC before being posted overseas in 1942.

In July 1943, having served as CO of 430 for six months, Moncrieff's administrative abilities were again called in to play to organize 129 Airfield RAF — later 129 (Fighter-Bomber) Wing — of the 2nd Tactical Air Force at Gatwick, Surrey. Then in February 1944 he was appointed commander of 39 Reconnaissance Wing, 2nd TAF, stationed at Redhill, Surrey. In June, following the Normandy invasion, the wing moved to France and, as the Allied armies advanced, to airfields in Holland and Germany. By the time Moncrieff relinquished his command in February 1945 the unit was based at Eindhoven.

Moncrieff retired from the RCAF later in the year and joined Trans Canada Air Lines in an administrative capacity.

OBE AFC MID(2) G/C Born 1909
RefScs: DHist bf RCTFFY 305 310–13 316   RTCFY 139 145 272
RS&A 127 220 223   TSBW 204

MOORE Kenneth Owen

"Sank Two Subs in Twenty-Two Minutes"

In the early hours of D-Day plus two, flying a Liberator bomber on an anti-submarine patrol over the Atlantic west of Brittany and preventing German U-boats from hampering the Normandy invasion fleet, Ken Moore succeeded in sinking two submarines in twenty-two minutes — an unheard of feat in the annals of anti-U-boat warfare and one that has never been repeated.

Born in Rockham, Sask., Moore joined the RCAF in 1941. After completing his training as a pilot he was posted to 224 Squadron RAF Coastal Command on July 27, 1943; with this squadron he made his first attack on a submarine on the night of March 31, 1944, over the Bay of Biscay. The crew spotted the U-boat after picking it up on radar. Moore dived down to 50 feet and unloaded six 250-pound depth-charges onto his target. They appeared to damage the rudder, but the submarine quickly submerged and made its escape.

With the Normandy invasion of June 6, the U-boats from Biscay came out in force. At 2:11 a.m. on June 8 Moore's radar registered a blip

PL 32005

12 miles ahead. Making his approach, he eased the Liberator down from 500 to 100 feet at a right angle to the U-boat. As Moore closed in the nose gunner opened fire, killing several of the crew on the conning tower and platform. The Germans fired back. But it was too late. Moore's depth-charges landed on either side of the vessel: a perfect straddle! Spouts of water shot into the air, the bow of the submarine lifted out of the sea then broke apart and sank.

At 2:40 a.m. the crew made a second radar contact six miles away. From 2½ miles the navigator sighted a submarine floating on the surface. Moore wheeled the Liberator around to approach the target from the starboard beam at a height of 50 feet. The U-boat opened fire. But the Liberator's nose gunner quickly silenced it. Depth-charges erupted around the submarine, knocking out the conning tower. As Moore circled to begin another attack the vessel listed to starboard, the bow rising out of the water until it was nearly vertical, then the U-boat sank from sight. Moore turned on his Leigh Light and saw dinghies containing survivors surrounded by oil and wreckage.

A few days later at Plymouth, Moore had the unique experience of talking to the skippers of the U-629 and U-373 who admitted they had been taken completely by surprise.

For his exploit Moore received the DSO and the American Silver Star. After WW2 he resigned from the RCAF then rejoined. In July 1948 he was awarded the King's Commendation for Valuable Service in the Air for his part in an Arctic rescue mission.

DSO SS(Am) S/L Lt/Col(CF)
RefScs: CCMA 70 DHist bf RAW 356 RCTFY f335 349
TCNAF 587 TDS 92–95 TSBW 233

MORRISON Donald Robert

"Shot Down into the Sea, Rescued Man from Drowning"

It was 10:00 a.m., on the sunny morning of April 19, 1942 — the day the Canadian Army assaulted Dieppe. Flying 1,000 feet over the English Channel the engine of Don Morrison's Spitfire suddenly konked out. It had been damaged by flying debris from a German Focke-Wulf 190 fighter he had shot down only moments earlier. Morrison managed to climb to 2,000 feet before bailing out. Then his parachute snagged on the tail of his aircraft. Before he could yank it loose he had dropped

Donald Morrison on rescue ship at Dieppe, August 1942. Photo courtesy Don Morrison.

to 200 feet. Too close for comfort. The canopy only billowed out the second he hit the water. Picked up by a British rescue launch, he spent the rest of the day off the invasion beach watching the air battle raging above and helping the crew pull downed airmen out of the sea. At one point he dived overboard to save a badly wounded airman from drowning. All the while the boat came under incessant attack from enemy fighters. Morrison took it all cheerfully in stride and often seemed oblivious to personal danger.

A native of Toronto, Ont., Don Morrison joined the RCAF in October 1940. Posted overseas in the summer of the following year and after operational training he joined 122 Squadron RAF, which was flying Spitfires at Scorton, Yorkshire. Finally he was posted to 401 Squadron RCAF, stationed at Biggin Hill in Kent, in October 1941. On November 18 he was credited with probably destroying a Messerschmitt 109 over Le Touquet, France. Four days later, near Desvres, he destroyed one FW 190 and damaged another. On December 8 he repeated the performance west of Cap Gris Nez against a pair of ME 109s. During the Channel dash, from Brest through the Strait of Dover to Helgoland, by the German battleships *Gneisenau, Prinz Eugen* and *Scharnhorst* Morrison shared in the destruction of an ME 109 with two others off Calais on

February 28, 1942. Morrison's successes continued to mount and at the end of June he was awarded the DFM and appointed a flight commander.

From the time of his Dieppe adventure up to November 8 his score rose to six planes shot down, five probables and four damaged, making him the leading RCAF ace in RAF Fighter Command. But on that date his career as a fighter pilot came to an end. While escorting Flying Fortresses over Lille he and his wing man attacked two FW 190s below them. Both were shot down by other German fighters from above. Morrison's oxygen tank was hit and he passed out. That is all he remembered when he regained consciousness in the hospital ten days later. Somehow he had managed to bail out minus his left leg which stayed in the Spitfire.

After a period of convalescence he was imprisoned at a POW camp in August 1943. But his stay was short. As an amputee he was repatriated on a prisoner-exchange basis. Though he never went into combat again, back in Canada he continued to fly as an instructor.

After the war he made his home in Toronto and joined TCA/Air Canada, rising to Customer Relations Manager before retiring in 1986. In 1982 he was elected president of the RCAF POW Association and was made vice-president of the National Council of Veterans Associations in Canada. He also served as a director of the Canadian Fighter Pilots Association.

DFC DFM S/L   Born June 20 1921
RefScs: DHist bf   HBB 84–86 94–95 99 101 104 105–108 110 113 114
OMAP(2) 120–21   RAW 45–46 205–11 222 248 348 444   RCTFFY f33
48 50 52–53 56 57–59 61 65–68 71 357 360   TSBW 197–98

MORRISON Howard

"WW2 Pathfinder Pilot Served on Transports in Korean Conflict"

Howie Morrison flew two tours as a Pathfinder pilot in Europe in WW2 then became an airlift pilot during the Korean War. Born in Winnipeg, Man., he joined the RCAF in 1940 and on completing his pilot's training served as an instructor until 1943, when he was transferred overseas. There he joined 405 Pathfinder Squadron RCAF based in Yorkshire; with this squadron he was awarded the DSO and DFC, the former for an action that took place on September 28, 1944, the day after he had been appointed CO. During an attack on Le Havre, which was still in German hands, he was flying at 2,000 feet as Master

Bomber over $^8/_{10}$ cloud when he noticed that the markers were off the aiming point. Ordering the main force to orbit Morrison tried to pinpoint the target. On his fourth run his Lancaster was hit by three bursts of flak, making the aircraft uncontrollable. Morrison ordered his crew to bail out and followed the last crewman. All except one of them landed safely behind their own lines.

In 1948, while still with the RCAF, Morrison joined 426 Transport Squadron and participated in flights to the Far East during the Korean campaign, for which he was awarded the AFC. After several senior posts at home and overseas Morrison was appointed Vice Commander of Central NORAD Region, Richard-Gebour Air Force Base, Kansas City, Miss., in 1968.

DSO DFC AFC CD   A/C   B/G(CF)   Born 1919
RefScs: DHist bf   RS&A 89 167   SY 310

MORROW Robert Ellis Evan

"Fighter-Bomber Leader Survived Ferrying Crash, Bail-Out into Arctic Waters"

T hat Bob Morrow ended WW2 with only an occasional nagging backache verged on the miraculous. Morrow was born in Crossfield, Alta.; when war broke out in 1939 he left law school in Montreal, P.Q., to enlist in the RCAF. A year later, after a prolonged period of training, he went overseas and joined 112 Army Co-operation Squadron RCAF in Salisbury. The squadron moved to Digby in November, was renumbered No 2 (later 402) Fighter Squadron and converted from Lysanders to Hurricanes.

On April 15, 1941, Morrow flew on the first RCAF offensive sortie over France. On May 13, east of Mabelthorpe, he damaged a Junkers 88 raider. Shortly afterward he was appointed a flight commander. Subsequently during his tour he shot down a Messerschmitt 109, damaged a Focke-Wulf 190 and shared with five others in the destruction of another.

But that was not his only forte. Morrow's real expertise lay in leading bombing raids. In October, 402 became the first RCAF fighter-bomber squadron, its Hurricanes armed with two 250-pound bombs and its armament increased from eight machine guns to twelve. A powerful arsenal, but the extra weight cut the aircraft's speed to 100 miles per hour slower than any German fighter. Morrow was the first to take a "Hurri-Bomber" off the ground.

In December he became the squadron's CO. Objectives were Luftwaffe airfields, shipping in the English Channel (the most hazardous of all, what with flak ships protecting the convoys) and static targets. Morrow's crowning achievement came on February 16, 1942, when, just as it was turning dark, he led his squadron on an attack against a fleet of German destroyers off the Ile de Batz, west of Brittany. Bombing at deck level the squadron sank one warship and damaged another. Shortly afterward the unit switched to Spitfires and reverted to the role of a fighter squadron. In August, after having flown 161 sorties, Morrow was taken off operations and returned to Canada, where he was attached to RAF Ferry Command.

In November he was posted back overseas to take command of a fighter wing and assigned to fly a Boston medium-bomber to England. Off Gander, Nfld., he encountered icing and was forced to fly through snowstorms and squalls, frequently losing control of the aircraft. After a hair-raising eight hours the Boston went into a spin and crashed on the Newfoundland coast.

In March 1943 Morrow was given command of X Wing RCAF at Anchorage, Alaska. The unit was to act as a deterrent against the Japanese presence in the Aleutian Islands. But Morrow persuaded his American counterparts to allow the RCAF, in addition to its defensive duties, to participate in offensive missions alongside the USAAF fighters. On May 6 he took off in a Kittyhawk and after climbing to 2,000 feet the engine caught fire. Morrow bailed out, striking the tailplane with his back and shoulder and temporarily knocking himself unconscious. He landed in the frigid 32-degree water and managed to inflate his dinghy before passing out again. He was finally rescued by American soldiers, who formed a rope line to haul him ashore. He spent some time in the hospital while a fracture to his vertebrae healed, then returned to his command.

In November he was appointed CO of RCAF Station, Boundary Bay, B.C. Morrow was then posted overseas, where he attended the RAF Staff College. His last two appointments were as CO of No 4 Bombing and Gunnery School, Fingal, Ont., and No 1 Wireless School, Mount Hope, Ont. Following the war he returned to law school and went into practice in Montreal.

DFC   W/C   Born Jan 20 1916
RefScs: CWC 229–47   DHist bf   RCTFFY f33 62–63 65 357
RCTFY 121   RS&A 84 225   TCNAF 4 19

Long after the war Bob still chaffed at the tactics used on fighter sweeps by Fighter Command; that is, staying under German radar range by flying at low level across the Channel until reaching the enemy coast, then climbing as fast as possible. Who was kidding whom? The German's own radar system got the Luftwaffe fighters off in plenty of time and they were always waiting . . . and always at a greater height.

MUSSELLS Campbell Haliburton

"Pathfinder Pilot in WW2, CO of Airlift Squadron in Korean Conflict"

C ampbell Mussells of Montreal, P.Q., completed two tours of operations as a member of 405 Pathfinder Squadron RCAF and during the war in Korea he commanded 426 Transport Squadron. As a Pathfinder pilot he won the DFC and DSO, the latter awarded for an action on a daylight raid on the Mockau marshalling yards in Leipzig, Germany, on April 10, 1945. Mussells had just completed his first run over the target when his Lancaster was attacked by a Messerschmitt 163 rocket-fighter, which shot away the gun turret and starboard rudder with one burst. Both rudders were smashed and both elevators badly damaged. The Lancaster began to dive steeply and with the trimming controls of no use Mussells had to struggle desperately before he could pull out. To keep the nose up he lashed the controls with wire to hold the aircraft steady. Escorted by Mustang fighters he managed to fly the crippled bomber back to England. When he crossed the coast he ordered the crew to bail out. But the mid-upper gunner was so seriously wounded he was unable to jump. Mussells remained at the controls, flew to the nearest airfield and, despite lack of flaps, landed the aircraft safely.

Mussells joined the RCAF in 1940 and served as an instructor in Canada before being transferred overseas in 1944 and posted to 405 Squadron, then based in Gransden Lodge, Beds. Remaining in the RCAF after WW2, he was assigned staff duties at RCAF HQ in Ottawa, Ont., from 1947 to 1949, when he took over command of 426 Transport Squadron. For his part in the Korean airlift he was awarded the OBE. In 1967 he was appointed Director of Exchange Services at Canadian Forces HQ in Ottawa.

OBE DSO DFC CD   A/C
RefScs: DHist bf   RCTSY 163–64

MYNARSKI Andrew Charles

"Clothes Aflame, Tried to Rescue Crew-Mate"

D uring a raid on the Cambrai railway yards in France on June 12, 1944 — a night in which 6 Group RCAF Bomber Command lost fifteen aircraft — Andy Mynarski made a heroic effort to pry his rear gunner from the turret of his burning Lancaster even though his own

PL 38261

parachute and clothing were on fire. Ironically Mynarski, who was able to bail out, died in the action while the gunner, who was trapped, survived to tell the tale.

Three-and-half years earlier Mynarski had joined the Winnipeg Rifles, a Manitoba militia unit in the city of his birth. But in September 1941 he enlisted in the RCAF and trained as an air gunner, going overseas at the end of 1942. Following operational training he served with 9 Squadron RAF until April 19, 1944, when he joined 419 Squadron RCAF at Middleton St George in Durham as a mid-upper gunner.

Mynarski had already completed twelve missions when he and his crew took off at 11:44 p.m. on that fateful night in June. The weather was clear and because visibility was excellent the bomber crews had been briefed to keep a sharp lookout for German night-fighters. But the only defenses they encountered on the way to the target were interceptor rockets, missiles that rose to the same altitude as the aircraft then exploded. On this occasion they proved harmless. As the pilot neared Cambrai he dived to 2,000 feet and levelled out.

Just then the rear gunner called for evasive action. But it was too late. A twin-engine Junkers 88 attacked from behind and below and the enemy's aim was deadly. Both port engines were shot out. Fire erupted between Mynarski's turret and the rear gunner's as well as along the right wing. The hydraulic system was so badly damaged the turrets wouldn't work. As flames enveloped the Lancaster the pilot ordered the crew to bail out. When Mynarski reached the escape hatch he saw the rear gunner struggling to get out of his turret. Climbing through the flames to reach his crew-mate, Mynarski ignored the danger as well as the fact that his own clothes and parachute had caught fire. But his efforts proved futile: the turret wouldn't budge. Finally the rear gunner told him to get out and save himself while he still could. Once more Mynarski had to fight his way through the flames to get back to the escape hatch. Just before he jumped Mynarski turned to face the gunner, came to attention and saluted. He then leapt from the flaming bomber.

French people on the ground watched Mynarski's descent, which resembled a Roman Candle with his clothing and parachute blazing. By the time they reached him he was beyond help. Shortly afterward he died from his burns and the injuries sustained when he struck the ground.

Mynarski's act of heroism went unheard of and unheralded until after the war. Miraculously, when the Lancaster crashed the rear gunner, whom Mynarski had tried to save, somehow survived. He served alongside the Free French Underground until September 1, 1944, when he was liberated by a British armoured regiment. At that time he reported the epic incident. In 1946 Mynarski was awarded the VC posthumously.

VC P/O Born Oct 14 1916 KIA June 13 1944 Ind CAHF 1973
RefScs: CAHF 54 CCMA 70 DHist bf RAW 286 432–33
RCTSY 423–30 TDS 84–85 TSBW 188–89 VM 183

Mynarski's VC is on display in the Bishop Building at Canadian Forces Air Command HQ in Westwin, Man. Among the many who attended the inaugural ceremonies was Pat Brophy, the surviving air gunner Mynarski tried to rescue.

NEAL Eugene Lawrence

"The Boss"

On most fighter squadrons the commanding officer was called "Boss." If it sounded familiar and disrespectful it nevertheless served a useful purpose. It stripped the rigid formality required by correct military procedure but at the same time retained the respect the highest rank in the unit merited. The result was a high degree of esprit de corps built on strong leadership. And no squadron fighter-leader fitted that mold so aptly or characterized the role so well as "Jeep" Neal did. Nicknamed after *Popeye*'s Eugene the Jeep comic character, Neal had a gift for picking the right men and inspiring them. He also had a talent for developing leaders. Four pilots under his command eventually led squadrons of their own, two of them winning the DSO, a rare distinction for RCAF squadron leaders in Fighter Command (see Hayward and Klersy entries).

A native of Quebec City, P.Q., Neal joined the RCAF at the outbreak of WW2. After graduating as a pilot he was posted overseas. Early in 1941 he joined No 1 Squadron RCAF, which was equipped with Hurricanes. The squadron was stationed in Scotland to enjoy a period of relative inactivity after a strenuous stint in the Battle of Britain. On April 16, by which time the squadron had returned south to Digby, Lincolnshire, and had been renumbered 401, Neal damaged a Messerschmitt 109 over France between Le Touquet and Sangatte. Then while flying off the British coast north of Skegness on August 8 he scored a probable against a Junkers 88, whose return fire hit an oil line and forced him to crash-land near Horncastle.

In September the squadron converted to Spitfires and on October 27 Neal added to his score by probably destroying a Messerschmitt 109 and damaging another. On November 22 in a ferocious fight over the Brest peninsula Neal was nailed by three Focke-Wulf 190s and forced to bail out over the English Channel. He was rescued two hours later.

In May Neal, by then a flight commander, was awarded the DFC. It was at this time he became famous for exhorting his fellow pilots and was regarded as the squadron morale-builder. On July 24, as his first tour drew to a close, Neal and another pilot shot down a monoplane

"Jeep" Neal (r.) with Ian Ormston. Photo courtesy G.L. Neal.

cabin-aircraft. They learned later that among those killed was a prominent German ace and a senior staff officer.

With eighty-eight operations under his belt Neal returned to Canada. He was made CO of 130 Squadron, a fighter squadron serving in Eastern Air Command, based at Bagotville, P.Q., for a brief spell in November and December. Then on January 22, 1943, he took over as CO of his old squadron, which he commanded until mid-December. It was during that tenure that he established himself as the epitome of the fighter-squadron "Boss." After the war Neal joined one of Canada's largest paper producers, where he rose to become a senior executive.

DFC S/L Born July 13 1917
RefScs: DHist bf HBB 74–76 78 80 85–87 98 101 125 128 RAW 171 198 209 211 RCTFFY f48 51–52 106 357 RCTFY 100 103 113 114 RS&A 61 82 SY 135

NESBITT Arthur Deane

"Father Figure Shot Down Twice"

A t first glance Deane Nesbitt resembled a father figure. But added to that image was a cheery personality, an exceptional ability as a pilot and a strong administrative acumen. In 1935 Nesbitt, who was born in Montreal, P.Q., began flying at the Montreal Light Aeroplane Club. He obtained his private pilot's licence that same year. In September 1939 he received a commission with 115 Auxiliary Squadron RCAF and took his pilot training at Camp Borden, Ont. On graduation in May he was posted to No 1 Squadron at Halifax, N.S., and proceeded overseas in June. By August the unit was based at Northolt and Nesbitt went into action on the twenty-fourth of the month. Just two days later Nesbitt damaged a Do 215.

On September 4 he drew blood for the first time by shooting down a twin-engine Messerschmitt 110. He destroyed a second German plane on September 15, a single-engine Messerschmitt 109 fighter; but in so doing Nesbitt was shot-up from behind. With his Hurricane on fire Nesbitt took to his parachute near Tunbridge Wells. He suffered head injuries from the jump but he was soon back in action. Then on October 7 he was shot down again. With a dead engine, he managed to force-land his aircraft at Biggin Hill.

A week later the squadron moved to Scotland, where it remained until February when it moved back south. Meanwhile Nesbitt had been made a flight commander. Then in March he became CO of what was now officially renumbered 401 Squadron RCAF. Flying from Digby, Lincolnshire, he led offensive missions over northern France. At the end of August, by which time he had been awarded the DFC, he relinquished his command.

Returning to Canada he was made CO of 111 Fighter Squadron based at Rockcliffe in Ottawa, Ont., flying Kittyhawks. When the Japanese attacked Dutch Harbor in the Aleutians in June 1942 Nesbitt was posted to Annette Island, the first RCAF base in Alaska, as CO of the Canadian squadrons stationed there. In October Nesbitt was transferred to RCAF HQ in Ottawa, Ont., as Wing Commander Fighter Operations; a year later he was placed in command of No 6 SFTS at Dunnville, Ont. In March 1944 he returned overseas to become Station Commander of 144 Airfield, one of three RCAF wings that were part of 83 Group in the 2nd Tactical Air Force.

Following D-Day the wing moved to the continent and in July Nesbitt was posted to 83 Group HQ as Wing Commander, Operations. On January 1, 1945, the day the Luftwaffe struck at Allied airfields in Belgium and the low countries, Nesbitt took command of 143 (Fighter-Bomber) Wing RCAF. The unit was made up of three Canadian Typhoon squadrons and based at Eindhoven in Holland. That morning the Germans destroyed fifty-six aircraft on the ground at his field alone, a fiery indoctrination into his new post.

When WW2 ended Nesbitt returned to Canada and received his discharge from the RCAF. He entered the family investment firm Nesbitt, Thomson and Co., and held the presidency for twenty-five years; during that time he handled the financing of Trans-Canada Pipelines. On February

Deane Nesbitt with ground crew. Photo courtesy A.D. Nesbitt.

4, 1978, Nesbitt had a skiing accident that left him almost totally paralyzed. He died in Montreal later in the month.

OBE DFC CdeG(Fr) OONK(Dch) G/C Born 1909 Died Feb 24 1978
RefScs: DHist bf   HBB 23 31 35 40–41 52 60 69 76–77 178   RAW 118
120 167 208   RCTFFY 14 16 18 f32 f48 357   RCTFY 129   RS&A 42 82
223–24   TSBW 137–39 153 202 216 219

Rod Smith (see Rod Smith) recalls: "One day in 1941, when I was on 412 Squadron, I had a very fierce practise fight with a Hurricane from 401 for twenty minutes. After I landed, I found out the 401 pilot was the commander, Deane Nesbitt. He was in his [early thirties] and getting bald. I remember marvelling that such an old man could put up such a great fight."

NEWSON William Francis Montgomery

"Last Canadian Pathfinder-Leader Amassed 6,000
Flying Hours on Twenty-Five Different Aircraft"

From the time he joined the RCAF in 1939 until his retirement from the Canadian Forces in 1972, Bill Newson accumulated over 6,000 flying hours on twenty-five different makes of aircraft. A veteran of two tours of operations, Newson was born in Calgary, Alta., attended RMC and, when war broke out, enlisted in the air force. He graduated as a pilot and, after a stint as an instructor, he was attached to Ferry Command. Newson finally joined 408 Bomber Squadron RCAF at Leeming, Yorkshire — which was equipped with four-engine Halifaxes — in the fall of 1942 as a flight commander. Twice on operations over Germany Newson's Halifax was badly damaged by enemy fire. But on both occasions he brought it safely back to base.

In June 1943 he was appointed CO of 431 Squadron RCAF, based at Tholthorpe, Yorkshire, at a time when the unit was converting from twin-engine Wellingtons to Halifaxes. By May 1944 he had completed his first tour, had been awarded the DFC and Bar and was made Station Commander of Leeming Bomber Station.

In November 1944 he became the last wartime CO of 405 Squadron RCAF. Flying Lancasters from Linton-on-Ouse in Yorkshire, the unit formed part of the elite Pathfinder Force. April 25, 1945, was the unit's last bombing sortie; they accomplished their mission, which was to obliterate Hitler's refuge at Berchtesgaden, erasing one of the last vestiges of Naziism. On May 7 the squadron's final Pathfinding mission was to mark the aiming point for dropping supplies to the people of Rotterdam.

Following WW2 Newson, who was awarded the DSO at the conclusion of his second tour, remained with the RCAF and later the Canadian Forces. He held many senior posts, including that of Assistant Chief of Air Operations, Central Europe. After he retired Newson served as president of the Wartime Aircrew Association and became executive vice-president of Canada's Aviation Hall of Fame.

DSO DFC & Bar CD   G/C   B/G(CF)   Born July 10 1917
Ind CAHF 1984
RefScs: CAHF 118   DHist bf   RAW 322   RCTFFY 357   RCTFY f62
f78 94 224   RS&A 89 128 216   TSBW 159

NORTHCOTT Geoffrey Wilson

"Took Ops, Score, All in Stride"

G eoff Northcott ended WW2 credited with nine German aircraft shot down, many probably destroyed and several damaged. He did this in three tours of operations in which he flew 328 missions and rose from Sergeant-Pilot to Wing Commander. An enviable record. But it failed to phase Northcott one way or another. He even shrugged off a crash-landing with twenty-two cannon shells in his engine, a result of being shot-up by an enemy fighter. Half the time he would only claim a probable, which would later turn out to be confirmed as a destroyed. To the stocky pilot from Rapid City, Man., it was all in a day's work.

Northcott enlisted in the RCAF in 1940 and in June 1941 joined 401 Squadron RCAF at Digby, Lincolnshire. It was during his eighth sortie, on July 23, that his Hurricane became the target of a Messerschmitt 109 over northern France. But on November 22 he got even by damaging an Me 109 near Mark, Eng. Then on February 12, 1942, during the Channel dash by the German battleships *Gneisenau*, *Prinz Eugen* and *Scharnhorst*, he shared in damaging two more. When his first tour ended on April 19 after ninety-five sorties, he was posted to Malta via aircraft carrier, where he joined 603 Squadron RAF at Ta Kali.

During this second tour he destroyed two Junkers 88 bombers and damaged several enemy fighters. He left the unit on August 15 after flying sixty-seven sorties over the island and being promoted to flight commander. Northcott was sent back to England to serve as an instructor. Then in June 1943 he was made CO of 402 Squadron RCAF at Digby. On the twenty-seventh of the month he destroyed his third enemy plane: an ME 109. Shortly afterward he was decorated with the DFC.

On August 2 Northcott scored a double kill against two 109s. That fall he continued to add to his tally. Then on November 3 he shot down his ninth victim, which he blew to pieces. This earned him a Bar to his DFC. On D-Day Northcott's squadron was the first RCAF fighter unit over the Normandy Beaches. Ten days later the squadron moved to an air strip at Crepon in France.

In July Northcott relinquished his command and returned to Canada on leave. In January 1945 he was appointed Wing Commander Flying of 126 RCAF Wing, which was made up of five Spitfire units based at Heesch in Holland. On the last sortie of his last tour Northcott fired his guns at an enemy plane for the last time — and claimed a Focke-Wulf 190.

Following WW2 Northcott joined Trans Canada Air Lines. Then in 1955 he was appointed General Manager of TransAir Limited. From 1948 to 1951 he served as CO of 442 City of Vancouver Auxiliary Squadron RCAF. (Photo: See Lloyd Chadburn)

DSO DFC & Bar OONK(Dch) W/C Born Nov 25 1920
RefScs: CWC 249–57 DHist bf OMAP(2) 122 RCTFFY 48 50 102
113 RCTFY 101–102 107–108 110–11 f126 134 226 RCTSY 241
RS&A 84 199 221 TSBW 215

O'BRIAN Peter Geoffrey St George

"Only Canadian Sword of Honour Winner/Battle of Britain Veteran"

Peter O'Brian, who joined the RAF in 1937, graduated from the RAF College at Cranwell as the only Canadian ever to receive the institute's Sword of Honour. By the time WW2 broke out O'Brian, who hailed from Toronto, Ont., was serving with 26 Squadron as adjutant; the unit flew Lysanders from Catterick in Yorkshire. In the summer of 1940 he flew Spitfires with 152 Squadron RAF, which was based at Warmwell. Even handicapped by the clumsy, outdated Gladiators, O'Brian still managed to down a Heinkel 111 twin-engine bomber and to share in the destruction of a Junkers 88 twin-engine bomber and another Heinkel.

In September he was posted to 257 Squadron RAF as CO. Stationed at Roborough in the southwest of England, the unit was equipped with Gladiator biplanes, which it traded for Hurricanes at the beginning of 1941. Its assignments were night operations, convoy patrols and day interceptions.

In May 1942 O'Brian turned over his command to a successor to become Wing Commander Training of No 10 Group. In September he was given command of the Portreath Sector (Cornwall and Devon) Wing of 10 Group, flying Spitfires. Operations consisted of fighter sweeps over Brest

P.G. O'Brian. Photo courtesy Peter O'Brian.

and strikes against German E-boats that were interfering with British shipping.

It was on one such sortie in April 1943 that O'Brian ended up in the drink. He was leading 412 Squadron RCAF in an attack on a trawler when two Focke-Wulf 190 fighters bounced the formation. As he zoomed in on his target O'Brian was shot down from behind. After parachuting into the sea he spent the next eight hours in his dinghy before being rescued at first light by two French-manned Motor Torpedo Boats.

In June 1943 he was again assigned to 10 Group, this time as Wing Commander Training, then was posted to the RAF Staff College. In April 1944 he was appointed to the Joint Planning Staff at the Cabinet Offices in London, where he served until the end of WW2.

Remaining with the RAF after the war, O'Brian became CO of 8 Squadron at Aden in the Middle East and also commanded 14 Squadron at Wahn near Cologne in Germany. He then held a number of posts, which included a posting to the U.S. on an exchange basis as well as that of RAF Fighter Command Group Captain of Operations. In 1958 he became the Aide-de-Camp to the Queen in London before retiring in 1959. Following that, he returned to Canada to live in Toronto.

OBE DFC & Bar   G/C   Born Dec 17 1917 ADC(HM)
RefScs: CITR 176   DHist bf

OGILVIE Alfred Keith

"Shot Down Raider that Bombed Buckingham Palace, Figured in The Great Escape"

On September 15, 1940, a day in which the RAF shot down more German planes than any other during the Battle of Britain, a twin-engine German Dornier 215 dropped bombs on Buckingham Palace. Moments later "Skeets" Ogilvie, flying a Hurricane with 609 Squadron RAF, shot down a Do 215 over London. It was generally conceded that his victim had been the one that had, accidentally or otherwise, unloaded its explosives on His Majesty's residence.

A little over eight months later, by which time his score stood at six enemy aircraft destroyed, three probables and three damaged, Ogilvie was shot down over France. He was made prisoner but later took part in The Great Escape.

Born in Ottawa, Ont., Ogilvie joined the RAF in August 1939 and by June of 1940 was training to be instructor. He applied for a transfer to fighters — over everybody's head — to no less a personage than Marshal of the RAF, Lord Trenchard. Whether His Lordship ever saw the request is not known; however it was accepted and on August 20 Ogilvie joined 609 Squadron RAF at Middle Wallop in Hampshire. By May of the following year the squadron had been re-equipped with Spitfires and Ogilvie had been awarded the DFC.

On July 4, 1941, as part of an escort of Stirlings bombing Lille, he was shot down and badly wounded in the left arm and shoulder. After nine months in hospital he was taken to Stalag III, where he became one of the prisoners engaged in tunnelling. On the night of March 24, 1944, Ogilvie was one of seventy-six who crawled out of the tunnel before it was discovered by a German sentry. However Ogilvie was picked up by a patrol two days later and imprisoned again. He was lucky: the Germans shot fifty of the seventy-three prisoners they recaptured. Following WW2 Ogilvie transferred to the RCAF. He stayed in the service until 1963, when he retired.

DFC S/L Born Sept 14 1915
RefScs: CITR 177 DHist bf NM 497 RAW 9

OLMSTED William Alfred

"On the Move — Covered Four Invasions"

During his operational career as a fighter pilot Bill Olmsted was witness to four of the major Allied landings and involved in five key battles. A native of Victoria, B.C., Olmsted joined the air force in August 1940 and on receiving his wings became an instructor. Before going overseas in September 1942 he had already logged 750 hours flying time. After a brief familiarization stint with 323 Norwegian Squadron in England, he was posted to North Africa. Flying his Spitfire from Gibraltar to Tingley airfield, ten miles south of the Mediterranean coast, he joined 81 Squadron RAF. The unit flew bomber-escort missions in support of the Allied forces driving into Tunisia from the West. On April 20 and 23, 1943, he damaged two German Messerschmitt 109s and later covered the British 8th Army attacking the Mareth Line, the last Afrika Korps stronghold in North Africa.

With the German Tunisian surrender in May, Olmsted, now a flight commander with 232 Squadron RAF, moved to Ta Kali airfield in Malta to take part in the invasion of Sicily. On June 29 he destroyed an ME 109 and by the end of July the squadron had moved to Lentini East in Sicily to participate in the invasion of Italy as well as the Salerno

Bill Olmsted in his Spitfire 'R'. Photo courtesy Joan Brown.

landings. On September 21 Olmsted damaged a Focke-Wulf 190 and on October 23, by which time the squadron was stationed at Gioia del Colle on the Italian east coast, he destroyed another ME 109.

In November he was hospitalized with malaria and then developed yellow jaundice. After recovering and returning to England he went to gunnery school; he was then made gunnery officer of the RAF Detling Wing.

On D-Day, June 6, 1944, he wangled a sortie with 274 Squadron RAF over the Normandy beachhead. At the beginning of July he was back on operations full time as a flight commander with 442 Squadron RCAF, part of a wing under the famous Johnnie Johnson, top Allied ace in Europe. He wasted no time adding to his score by destroying an FW 190 and damaging another on July 20, and a week later probably destroying an ME 109.

But the unit's main focus was on ground strafing and during the battle of Falaise Olmsted destroyed eighty-nine vehicles. As the Allied armies advanced the squadron moved to keep as close to the front line as possible. By September Olmsted had been awarded the DFC and been given command of the unit, now stationed at Vokel in Holland. From that base Olmsted had several frustrated encounters with the overwhelmingly fast German ME 262 jets. On October 29, while attacking a train, he had a bomb hang-up which suddenly dropped as he was strafing transport from low altitude. The blast damaged his Spitfire so seriously he was forced to bail out and landed on a rooftop. A few days later his aircraft was hit by flak. Again Olmsted took to his parachute when his engine cut out. That was Olmsted's final flight. On leave in London on his way back to Canada he learned he had been awarded the DSO and a Bar to his DFC. Following WW2 he operated a construction business in North Bay, Ont. In May 1986 he was killed in a car accident near Huntsville, Ont.

DSO DFC & Bar   S/L   Born July 1 1920   KA May 1986   Author of
Blue Skies
RefScs: BS   (biog)DHist bf   RCTFY 250   RS&A 141   TSBW 210

Bill was a student of anything and everything he did, forever practising — a perfectionist. He and I spent endless hours discussing the lack of gunnery schooling and practice on the part of average WW2 fighter pilots. The emphasis was on formation flying.

Following the Dieppe raid in August 1942, the most concentrated air battle up to that time, a scientific analysis was made from the yards of combat film available comparing it to the combat reports. The conclusion was that three-quarters of the pilots in RAF Fighter Command couldn't shoot straight. Also the pilots' estimate of the range at which they fired was out by as much as 300 percent. A pilot reported opening fire at 300 yards while the cine-film showed the range to be 1,000 yards.

The result of discovering these shortcomings was the development of the automatic gyro-gunsight, which computed the range and angle of deflection.

ORMSTON Ian Campbell

"Firebrand"

Ian Ormston was one of the most aggressive fighter leaders in the business, always looking and always on the attack. He enlisted in the RCAF in 1940 in Montreal, P.Q., the city of his birth. The following year he went overseas to join 401 Squadron RCAF at Digby, Lincolnshire, which was then flying Hurricanes but later switched to Spitfires. Ormston won his first victory on November 22 near St Omer when he shot down a Messerschmitt 109. During the Channel Dash on February 12, 1942, when the three German warships *Gneisenau, Prinz Eugen* and *Scharnhorst* broke out from Brest through the Strait of Dover, he nailed another 109. On March 29, by which time he had been made a flight commander, he scored a probable and on April 16 damaged a Focke-Wulf 190. In May he was awarded the DFC.

Ormston returned to Canada that summer and after a stint as an instructor at No 1 OTU at Bagotville, P.Q., was posted overseas to Redhill, Surrey, in June 1943 as a flight commander with his old unit, 401 Squadron. On July 19 he got back in stride by sharing an FW 190 destroyed with three others. In early August the squadron moved to Staplehurst in Kent.

Then on September 26 Ormston went for a swim. Flying at 11,000 feet over the English Channel off Dieppe, his engine packed up; because of a glycol leak, he lost his engine coolant. Gliding down to 2,500 feet Ormston bailed out. He was picked up by the Air Sea Rescue Service and was back in the mess in time for lunch.

Later that month Ormston was given command of 411 Squadron RCAF, which in October moved to Biggin Hill in Kent. However a near-fatal crash ended his operational career in Europe. On December 21 he was leading the wing with orders to fly under 500 feet to mid-Channel before climbing. He had reached 400 feet when his engine went limp. Below him another squadron was still taking off, which ruled out landing on the runway. Carrying a long-range belly tank he was unable to jettison meant that he couldn't risk a pancake either. He had to attempt a wheels-down landing on the grass. On his approach he hit the barbed-wire entanglement of a gun battery at the end of a runway. His Spitfire cartwheeled then cracked open in two. Ormston rolled out, still strapped to his seat. But the impact had broken his back and he spent the next six months in hospital.

He returned to Canada and in June 1944 was made CO of 133 Squadron at Sea Island, then at Patricia Bay, B.C., his last command of the war. After WW2 he moved to Kitchener, Ont., where he opened and operated his own welding supply business. (Photo: see "Jeep" Neal)

DFC S/L Born June 27 1921
RefScs: DHist bf   HBB 85 94–95 98–99 128–29   RAW 174 180 198 207
RCTFFY 48 50–51 108 357   RCTFY 109 115   RS&A 62 98

One of the most important practise exercises was tail-chasing: following the leader through any and every maneuver. Its purpose was two-fold: to cling to the leader in battle and to stay on the tail of an enemy. I had a lot of practice tail-chasing with many, many pilots, including (for fun) Beurling. But the toughest to follow, in my experience, was Ormy. He could practically bend a Spitfire in two.

PEPPER George

"Motorcycle Champion Became Night-Fighter Ace"

G eorge Pepper mastered motorcycles before becoming an expert on Beaufighters. A native of Belleville, Ont., where he was known as a champion motorcycle racer, Pepper joined the RAF in 1940, one of the last Canadians to do so. In December of 1941, having completed his pilot's training, he joined 29 Squadron RAF, then flying Beaufighter night-fighters.

On the night of June 27, 1942, he scored his first kill by destroying a German Heinkel 111 bomber northeast of Foreness. Over the Thames Estuary on the night of July 16 he damaged a Junkers 88 bomber then destroyed a Ju 88 south of Dungeness on August 8. On August 21, southeast of Beachy Head, he shot down an He 117 and in September was awarded the DFC.

On the night of October 31 Pepper scored his greatest triumph when fifty Dornier 217 bombers attacked Canterbury in two raids four hours apart. On the first assault, around 8:00 p.m. east of Foreness, Pepper shot down one of the raiders from 250-yards range, sending it plunging into the sea in flames. After refuelling he and his navigator took off shortly before midnight and, southwest of Folkestone, destroyed two Do 217s. Pepper was awarded a Bar to his DFC but he never wore it. On November 17 he and his navigator were killed in a crash near Detling.

DFC & Bar F/O Born 1915 KIA Nov 17 1942
RefScs: DHist bf RAW 254 SY 466

PITCHER Paul Brooks

"Battle of Britain Veteran First to Lead RCAF in the Desert"

P aul Pitcher fought in the Battle of Britain with the RCAF squadron he later commanded; became CO of a Canadian unit flying offensive sorties over the continent; and took another RCAF unit to Egypt to lead it on patrols and offensive sweeps. Therefore, by the time he was taken off operations at the end of 1942 he had commanded four Canadian squadrons within two years.

Born in Montreal, P.Q., Pitcher joined 115 Auxiliary Squadron RCAF in Montreal in 1935. When WW2 began he joined the RCAF and sailed overseas with No 1 Squadron RCAF in June of 1940, going into battle in August from Northolt on Hurricanes. On September 15, in one of his first encounters with the enemy, he damaged a German Heinkel 111 and twelve days later he damaged a Dornier 215. On October 5 Pitcher, by then a flight commander, destroyed an ME 109 and damaged an ME 110. A week later the squadron was pulled out of the front line and moved to Scotland; on December 14 Pitcher became the unit's CO. However he never led the squadron in combat. Triple trouble prevented it.

On January 31, 1941, he caught measles, then had a bout of pneumonia followed by a siege of scarlet fever. By that time the unit had moved south, first to Driffield in Yorkshire for a week, then to Digby in Lincolnshire. Along the way the squadron was renumbered 401 Squadron RCAF and Pitcher remained its CO until March 11, though he never flew with it under its new designation. Even so he had achieved some sort of RCAF first: theoretically serving as CO of two "different" units without changing command.

On June 16, 411 Squadron RCAF was formed at Digby and Pitcher, now fully recovered, was given command. Equipped with Hurricanes then Spitfires, it was the sixth RCAF squadron inaugurated overseas, the fourth fighter squadron. Pitcher led it on cross-Channel fighter sweeps and bomber-escort sorties over northern France, Belgium and Holland. Then in December he was made CO of 417 Squadron RCAF and in the spring of 1942 his unit was posted to the Middle East to defend the Nile Delta and the Suez Canal with Hurricanes.

Pitcher relinquished his command in November after the defeat of the Afrika Korps at El 'Alamain in October. His squadron, once re-equipped with Spitfires, had taken the offensive.

Back in Canada Pitcher was temporary CO of X Wing RCAF at Adak Island in the Aleutians from May 19 to June 27, 1943, when its CO was injured in a flying accident. Following the war Pitcher went into law practice in Montreal.

DFC W/C Born 1917
RefScs: DHist bf HBB 34 38 41 59 61 63 RCTFFY 25–29 f32 f33
326–29 RS&A 22 82 98 109 225n

POLLARD Michael Evelyn

"Youngest Wing Commander in the RAF"

W hen Michael Pollard transferred to the RCAF in 1944 he was the youngest Wing Commander in the RAF at only 22 years of

PL 22773

age. Born in Croydon, England, Pollard was brought up in Montreal, P.Q., and joined the RAF in 1938. Graduating as a pilot the following year, he flew twenty-two operational flights on Lysanders with No 22 Army Co-op Squadron and was decorated with the DSO, DFC and AFC. Next he served with 114 Squadron flying Blenheims on twenty-six operations. From October 1943 Pollard flew Boston IIIs on thirty-five operations with 107 Squadron. By August 1944 he was CO of 84 Group Control Centre in support of the 1st Canadian Army.

In November 1944 he was repatriated to Canada, his first posting with the RCAF being the Directorate of Postings and Careers at Air Force HQ in Ottawa, Ont. In 1952 he was given command of No 2 Fighter Wing at Grostenquin, France. The following year Pollard assumed duties as Senior Air Staff Officer at No 1 Air Division Headquarters at Metz. In 1966 he was appointed Commander of both Air Defence Command and Northern NORAD Region based in North Bay, Ont. Then at the beginning of 1969 he has made Comptroller General of the Canadian Forces in Ottawa.

DSO DFC AFC CD   A/C   L/G(CB)
RefScs: DHist bf   RS&A 191 208 217

RAPHAEL Gordon Learmouth

"First WW2 Canadian Airman to Be Mentioned in Dispatches"

Gordon Raphael, who flew as both a bomber pilot and night-fighter ace, became the first Canadian in WW2 to be mentioned in dispatches — awarded him for early operations in February 1940. Born in Brantford, Ont., Raphael enlisted in the RAF in 1935 and by war's outbreak was serving with 77 Squadron RAF at Driffield, which was flying twin-engine Whitley bombers.

He received the MID in February 1940. In May 1940, when the Germans invaded Norway, Raphael took part in raids on enemy airfields at Oslo and Trondheim. On one sortie his aircraft was so badly shot-up by a Messerschmitt 110 he was forced to ditch in the North Sea. Rescued, he was hospitalized and awarded the DFC.

In July he was transferred to 10 Squadron RAF at Leeming in Yorkshire, also a Whitley outfit. He flew with this unit until May 1941, when he was posted to 85 Squadron RAF at Debden, flying Havoc night-fighters. On the tenth of the month, during the last major blitz on London, he destroyed a Heinkel 111 bomber. Shortly afterward he received a Bar to his DFC. By the summer of 1944 he had destroyed seven enemy aircraft, probably destroyed one more and damaged another; he had also destroyed two V-1s. By that time he had become CO of the squadron, which by then was flying Mosquitos, and had been awarded the DSO. In April 1944, while flying with 605 Squadron, he was killed when the Spitfire he was piloting collided with a Dakota.

DSO DFC & Bar MID   W/C   Born Aug 25 1915   KA April 10 1945
RefScs: DHist bf   OMAP(2) 123   RAW 253–54

ROBILLARD Joseph Guillaume Laurent

"First RCAF Evader Who Had a Price on His Head"

During the summer of 1941, when Larry Robillard hid out with a farm family to avoid capture after being shot down near Lille in northern France, the Germans posted a reward of 100,000 francs for information as to his whereabouts. He was promptly turned over to the French Resistance, who facilitated his escape, making him the first RCAF evader and the first to have a price on his head.

Born in Ottawa, Ont., Robillard received his private pilot's licence before enlisting in the RCAF in July 1940. Going overseas in 1941 he joined 145 Squadron RAF, where he soon made his mark by shooting down two Messerschmitt 109s.

Then on July 1, in a melee with several German fighters, one of the ME 109s blew a wing off his Spitfire and knocked him unconscious. Robillard was blown free of the aircraft when it exploded. He came to just in time to pull the rip chord of his parachute, so he floated safely to earth. Immediately rescued by a French farmer, he was sheltered from the Germans until they put a price on his head. At that time and for the safety of all concerned, he was turned over to the underground.

Robillard's escape began on August 8; it was a journey that took him through Paris, Toulouse and Marseille to the Pyrenees, where he crossed the mountains into Spain. After reaching Gibraltar in October he returned home to Canada for a hero's welcome.

In 1943 he went back to England, where he returned to operations in 1944 and eventually became a flight commander with 443 Squadron RCAF. On June 28 he shot down a Focke-Wulf 190 and continued to add to his score. By August 23 his tally stood at eight enemy aircraft destroyed and one damaged.

Following WW2 Robillard went into the mining business then became a sales representative for several major aircraft manufacturers.

DFM   F/L   Born Nov 28 1920
RefScs: DHist bf   OMAP(2) 123   RAW 428   RCTFFY 361
RCTFY 239 250–51 f254 262   WL 239–43

ROHMER Richard

"Only Member of RCAF to Head Up Reserves"

R ichard Rohmer of Hamilton, Ont., served as a fighter-reconnaissance pilot during WW2. After lengthy service with the RCAF Auxiliary postwar, in 1967 he became the first — and only — member of the RCAF to become Chief of Reserves. Rohmer joined the RCAF in 1942 and, after graduating as a pilot, went overseas in March of 1943. Following OTU instruction Rohmer joined 430 Squadron RCAF stationed at Ashford in Kent flying reconnaissance missions on Mustangs. His tour ended in November 1944; at that time he was a flight commander of his unit, which was then based at Eindhoven in Holland.

Following the war Rohmer left the RCAF to go into law practice in Toronto, Ont., where he was CO of 400 and 411 Auxiliary Squadrons. He was also a director of the Canadian International Air Show.

DFC CD   F/L   M/G(Res)   Born Jan 24 1924   Author of *Patton's Gap*
Rommel and Patton
RefScs: DHist bf   RCTFY 270   RS&A 127 150 165

Refer to *Rommel and Patton* pp 302–306 for Rohmer's description of
spotting the car in which Rommel was riding and calling in Spitfires.
The fighters attacked and wounded the Desert Fox, who committed suicide
in the aftermath of the plot to kill Hitler.

ROSS Arthur Dwight

"Lost a Hand Rescuing Crew from Blazing Bomber"

On the night of June 27/28, 1944, Arthur Ross lost his right hand
when, with the help of three airmen and despite fire and bomb
explosions, he made repeated attempts to rescue the crew of a burning
bomber of 425 Squadron RCAF. Ross, who was born in Winnipeg, Man.,
attended RMC and joined the RCAF as a pilot in 1928, receiving his
wings the following year. At the outbreak of WW2 he commanded No 5
Squadron at Sydney, N.S., assigned to anti-submarine duties. Between
1940 and 1942 he was CO of No 3 SFTS at Calgary, Alta. After a
tour at Eastern Air Command HQ he was posted overseas, where he
became CO of No 62 "Beaver" Base at Linton-on-Ouse; he controlled
Linton-on-Ouse, East Moor and Tholthorpe Bomber Stations.

It was at this last station that Ross watched his bomb crews return
from a raid on the Foret d'Eweay; he was about to enter the debriefing
room when he saw a yellow flash on the field. Ross dashed toward it.
He found a Halifax bomber had landed on three engines and had crashed
into a parked aircraft, which was fully bombed-up although no one was
aboard. By the time he reached the scene both planes were burning fiercely
with imminent danger of the gas tanks and bombs exploding.

With the assistance of several airmen Ross helped the bomb-aimer
out of the aircraft and had just extricated the pilot when ten 500-pound
bombs exploded, throwing the rescue party to the ground. Undeterred
by the flames Ross and the bomb-aimer rushed to pull out the trapped
rear-gunner by smashing a hole in the perspex and breaking off the steel
supports.

Then another bomb exploded, throwing the rescuers to the tarmac again.
Ross's right hand was shattered by debris and his arm between the wrist

and elbow was virtually severed. He calmly walked over to the ambulance and got in. At the hospital later that night his hand was amputated. For his leadership and heroism Ross was awarded the GC.

Following the war Ross remained with the RCAF holding many senior posts, the last being AOC 5 Air Division Vancouver, B.C. He retired in 1961 after thirty-three years of service.

GC OBE CD   A/C   Born Mar 18 1907
RefScs: CA 239   CCMA 71   DHist bf   RAW 324   RCTFY f15 f30
205–206   RS&A 25 209 214   VM 217

This incident may seem out of line and somewhat irrelevant as it was not an act of heroism in the air. It was, however, air-related. There is another factor: three of the ground crew stationed at Tholthorpe shared in the deed that night, all of whom were decorated for bravery.

My particular purpose for including his valiant exploit is to highlight the role of the men behind the machines without whose unsung efforts the success of Canadian aircrews would not have been possible. These individuals, familiarly known as "Erks," shared none of the glory but often, as in this case, took a lot of the danger. Another risk was the bombing and strafing of their airfields by the enemy. These men were a dedicated band who worked tirelessly to keep the aircraft flying and fighting. A well-earned salute to them all!

RUSSEL Blair Dalzell

"Laid-Back Wing Leader Dropped Rank to Return to Operations"

As a wing commander Dal Russel always gave the impression of being totally relaxed. But behind that easy manner lay a brilliant leader, a gifted tactician and a rugged aerial duellist. One of the originals with No 1 Squadron RCAF during the Battle of Britain, Russel was so keen on combat that he later dropped his rank from Wing Commander to Squadron Leader to get back on operations.

Born in Toronto, Ont., Russel learned to fly at the Montreal Light Aeroplane Club at Cartierville, P.Q., in 1938. When WW2 started he joined 115 Squadron, training as a pilot then going overseas with 1 Squadron in 1940; at age twenty-three he was the unit's youngest member.

Russel quickly made his mark when the unit went into action flying

PL 19373

Hurricanes from Northolt in England starting in August. On August 31 he damaged a German Dornier 215 bomber. On September 4 he was credited with probably destroying a Messerschmitt Bf 110 fighter and damaging a Junkers 88. On September 15 he scored a probable against a Heinkel 111 bomber. On the twenty-seventh of the month he destroyed an ME 110 and shared in the destruction of another as well as shooting down an ME 109 fighter and damaging a Dornier 215. By October 25 he was awarded the DFC, one of the first three in the RCAF to be so decorated.

By the time the squadron was taken out of the front line and moved to Scotland late in October Russel had destroyed 3½ aircraft, probably destroyed two and damaged four. And in sixty-one operational sorties his Hurricane had never even been scratched by an enemy bullet. By the time the squadron moved back south to Driffield, Yorkshire, in February Russel was repatriated to Canada to 118 Squadron at Rockcliffe in Ottawa, Ont. It later moved to Dartmouth, N.S., flying Kittyhawks. In January 1942 Russel was given command of 14 Squadron stationed at Sea Island in Vancouver, B.C.

In November his request for a transfer back to England was granted and, after serving as a supernumerary to gain operational experience on offensive sorties over France, in April 1943 he was given command of 411 Squadron RCAF based at Redhill in Surrey. When the unit became part of a wing of three squadrons, officially named 126 RCAF Airfield in 83 Group of the 2nd Tactical Air Force, Russel was appointed Wing Commander Flying. In this capacity he led fighter sweeps and bomber-escort sorties over the continent. By October 15, when his second tour ended, he had completed a total of 189 operational sorties and was awarded a Bar to his DFC.

Posted to 83 Group HQ in charge of tactics Russel became impatient with his ground job. So when a new wing was formed under Johnny Johnson, the top ace in Europe, Russel dropped his rank back to Squadron Leader and took over as CO of 442 Squadron RCAF in April 1944. On June 15, following the Normandy invasion, Russel's wing moved to St-Croix-sur-Mer in France. On July 8 he was given command of his old 126 Wing, where he served until January 26, 1945, after having completed a total of 286 operational sorties in three tours during a 4½-year period.

Retiring from the RCAF in 1945, he served with 401 Auxiliary Squadron in Montreal, P.Q. In the 1970s he gave up his business interests to retire to Maine.

DSO DFC & Bar CdeGwSS(Fr) OONK(Dch) CzWC   W/C
Born Dec 9 1917
RefScs: CA 213   CCMA 56   CWC 259–75   DHist bf   HBB f30 31 34 37
42 45   OMAP(2) 123   RAW 134 167–68 179 200 232   RCTFFY 15–16
19–20 22–23 25–26 RCTFY 100 107–109 f126 231 234 237 239 241–42
249–50 261–62 264–67 270   SY 51   TSBW 137–41 202–205 215

SALE Douglas Julian

"Dedicated Pathfinder Refused to Take Leave after Evading Capture"

W hen Julian Sale showed up at Gibraltar in August 1943, having eluded the Germans after his Halifax was shot down on the night of May 12/13, he spurned an offer of respite and recreation and opted instead to report back to his squadron — 35 Pathfinder RAF — and get on with the war. His gesture was typical of him.

Born in Penetanguishene, Ont., Sale, who became only one of four in the RCAF to win a Bar to the DSO, thrived on danger and excitement. Enlisting in the RCAF as a pilot in May 1941 he went overseas a year later, joining 10 Squadron RAF at Melbourne. He made his first operational flight November 8, 1942, in a four-engine Halifax bomber laying mines in the East Frisian chain of islands.

On January 23, 1943, he was transferred to 35 Squadron, based at Gravely. He flew his first raid with that outfit on February 1 in an attack on Hamburg. After returning to his unit in September, following his evader escapade, Sale was awarded the DSO, the tenth member of the RCAF to receive the medal. In October he was made a flight commander.

Then on the night of December 20/21 Sale performed a feat that earned him a Bar to his DSO. He was returning from a raid on Frankfurt, in which he had flown as Primary Visual Marker. While approaching Gravely one of the bombs detonated and set the rear turret and a wing on fire. Climbing to 2,000 feet Sale ordered the crew to bail out. However he then saw that his mid-upper gunner's parachute was burned to a crisp. So he brought the flaming bomber down onto the field as far from the hangars as possible. As the aircraft slowed down both he and the gunner jumped. From 200 yards away the aircraft exploded, throwing them both to the ground. But neither man was injured.

Sale made his last flight on the night of February 19/20, 1944. Over Leipzig, the Halifax was attacked by a Wurnstorf-based Junkers 88 night-fighter. All the crew were able to bail out but Sale, who was badly wounded when his parachute failed to open properly and died in captivity two months later. That September he was posthumously awarded the DFC.

DSO & Bar DFC S/L Born 1914 DOW March 20 1944
RefScs: BB 198–99 DHist bf RAW 449 RCTFY 335 347–48

SCHULTZ Rayne Dennis

"Most Outstanding Night Fight of WW2"

Flying over the English Channel on the night of December 10, 1943, Mosquito pilot Joe Schultz and his navigator destroyed three twin-engine German Dornier 217 bombers within fifteen minutes. Historians maintain that this was the outstanding night-fight of the war.

First, one of the three enemy planes opened fire. But Schultz set the marauder's engines aflame with a short burst. A further fussilade sent the aircraft plunging into the sea before the crew could release their bombs. While his victim still burned on the water, Schultz opened fire on a second Dornier from dead astern — at such close range that he had to fly through the exploding debris.

No real problem thus far, but a third bomber proved to be a tough counter-puncher. Although Schultz set both engines on fire the pilot skillfully maneuvered his aircraft, placing his gunner in perfect aiming position to riddle the Mosquito with his fire. Before Schultz forced the Do 217 into a steep dive into the sea, the enemy had inflicted severe damage to his aircraft. Shells had shattered the instrument panel and set fire to the starboard engine. Fortunately the flames eventually burned themselves out and Schultz was able to coax enough power from the ailing motor to make a safe landing at his base at Hunsdon, Herts. Both he and his navigator received immediate DFCs for the night's performance.

A native of Bashaw, Alta., Schultz joined the RCAF in 1941 and after graduating went overseas in 1942. After OTU training he was posted to 410 Squadron RCAF in December, flying Beaufighters and Mosquitos from Acklington, Northumberland.

Schultz's first victory came on August 15 when he shot a Do 217 down over the Channel off Beachy Head. Following his hat-trick in December he scored again on February 13, 1944, destroying a Junkers 88 bomber over the North Sea near Yarmouth, another flamer. Taken off operations in June 1944, Schultz served as an OTU instructor until December when he rejoined 410 Squadron, then stationed at Vendeville near Lille in France. Before his second tour ended he added two more aircraft destroyed to his score, both Ju 88s. He made his last kill near Berlin, an area over which he was one of the first Allied night-fighter pilots to patrol.

Following the war Schultz remained in the RCAF and held a variety of commands, including Chief Operations Officer of 4 Fighter Wing in Germany from 1962 to 1966, and that of Director of Flight Safety for the Canadian Forces, a field in which he became so expert he was inducted into the USAF Hall of Fame and awarded the McKee Trophy. Schultz retired in December of 1977 after thirty-six years of service to his country.

DFC & Bar MM(Am) CD   G/C   Col(CF)   Born Dec 17 1922   MKTw
RefScs: DHist bf   OMAP(2) 124   RAW 255–57 266 269–70   RCTFY
148 152 f159   RS&A 96   SY 141 199 216 280 334–35 344 357–58

SCHWAB Lloyd Gilbert

"Biplane Ace in a Monoplane War"

L loyd Schwab of Niagara Falls, Ont., collected all six of his victories over enemy planes destroyed in a Gladiator at a time when the biplane had already given way to the new monoplane fighters.

Schwab joined the RAF as a pilot in 1936 and two years later was posted to North Africa. In 1938, after serving with 80 Squadron, he joined 112 Squadron RAF at Helwan as part of the defences of Cairo and the Nile Delta. When Italy entered the war in 1940 the unit formed part of a front-line wing of three squadrons that took the offensive at the start of the Mediterranean campaign.

Schwab's first victim was a Savoia Marchetti tri-motor bomber, which he shot down in flames on August 17. On October 31 he destroyed two Cant Z bombers and on November 18 brought down another SM. In January 1941, with the Italian invasion of Greece, his squadron was sent to an airfield near Athens, as were RAF bomber squadrons. In the following three months 112 Squadron was reduced to three Gladiators and Schwab, who had taken over as CO, added three more aircraft destroyed and a probable to his score. When the Germans entered the Balkans campaign the RAF withdrew. Late in June Schwab was posted back to England and later to Canada, where he served as an instructor. In 1943 he returned to England to take charge of an Advanced Flying Unit. Decorated with the DFC and the Greek Flying Cross he continued to serve with the RAF after WW2, retiring in March 1958.

DFC GFC   W/C   Born Jan 22 1915
RefScs: DHist bf   OMAP(2) 124   RAW 368   TTS 237–40

SHARP Frederick Ralph

"RCAF Bomber Commander Became Chief of Defence Staff"

Born in Moosomin, Sask., Fred Sharp, who commanded an RCAF bomber squadron during WW2, eventually became Chief of the Defence Staff of the Canadian Armed Forces. Sharp joined the RCAF in July 1938 after graduating from RMC. When WW2 broke out he was made an instructor and by 1943 was a member of the staff of No 2 Flying Instruction School. In January 1944 he attended the War Staff College then went overseas in March where he joined 408 Squadron RCAF flying Lancasters from Linton-on-Ouse in Yorkshire. On November 26 he took over as CO, a post he held until September 1945. Following the war he held a successive number of senior positions, including Vice-Chief of the Defence Staff and Deputy C-in-C of NORAD, until being appointed Chief of the Defence Staff on September 15, 1969.

DFC CD A/M G(CF) Born 1915
RefScs: DHist bf CCMA 163 RAW 94 SY 355

SHULEMSON Sydney Simon

"Rocket-Firing, Ship-Busting Expert"

On January 28, 1944, Syd Shulemson led a strike force of ten rocket-carrying and cannon-bearing Beaufighters from Wick in Scotland to Standlandt, off the coast of Norway. Their mission: to attack a German convoy of three 2,000- to 3,000-ton merchant ships, which included a three flak ship escort and a mine sweeper. Shulemson set one ship on fire, left the minesweeper burning and damaged two other vessels. Then four Messerschmitt 109 fighters bounced the Beaufighters, sending one crashing into the sea and damaging another. To allow the lame duck to escape Shulemson turned and flew into the enemy fighters; he hassled them for twenty minutes until the crippled Beaufighter was out of sight. That action, which earned Shulemson an immediate DSO, was typical of his expertise in ship-busting and bravery under fire.

He had devised almost flawless tactics that took into account angle of attack — from out of the sun whenever possible — wind direction, vessel speed, airspeed, as well as distance from the target. He became such an expert that, near the end of the war, he was called upon to

PL 29809

work out the kinks in the rocket-firing Mosquitos whose missiles kept falling short of their targets.

A native of Montreal, P.Q., Shulemson first made application to join the RCAF in 193ᴜ but, lacking the necessary educational qualifications, was turned down. When WW2 broke out he joined the army; then in August 1941 he enlisted in the air force. Graduating as a pilot he went overseas in 1942 and joined 404 Squadron RCAF in July 1943 at Wick; that unit was equipped with Beaufighters.

On July 28 Shulemson flew his first operation, escorting British warships off Norway, as wingman to his flight commander. During the flight a Junkers 88 bomber suddenly appeared out of the clouds. Shulemson opened fire and scared it off. Then he attacked a Blohm & Voss 138 tri-motor bomber, shooting it down in flames. By the time he made his DSO-winning sortie he was a flight commander.

His talent for attacking shipping continued to flourish. On July 8 he wrecked a merchant vessel using only eight rockets; he repeated the feat on October 9. Though he had become expert at his trade the danger never diminished. He always had to face fierce cannon fire and powerful anti-aircraft defenses from the flak ships. Many times his own aircraft was riddled but he survived them all, even his last operational flight on November 17.

He was then posted to Banff in Scotland to instruct on rocket-firing Mosquitos and to tackle the problem of why the rockets were failing to hit their targets. The answer, he discovered, was warping in the wooden wings, which occurred as the aircraft dived on the target. This he corrected by readjusting the angle of the rocket-carrier rails.

At the end of the war Shulemson retired from the RCAF and joined the family printing business. In 1947 he helped lay the foundations for Israel's air force, seeking volunteers and obtaining equipment. Among those he recruited was George Beurling of Malta fame.

DSO DFC S/L
RefScs: RAW 364–67   RCTFFY 254   RCTFY f318 319 321 325
RS&A 88   SY 154   TDS 11–15

SMALL Norville Everett

"Architect of Anti-U-boat Warfare Scored RCAF's First Kill"

F irst in the RCAF to sink a U-boat, "Molly" Small was instrumental in developing the methods employed by Eastern Air Command in the prosecution of anti-submarine warfare. Born in Vancouver, B.C., he joined the service in 1928 as a mechanic then in 1931 became a pilot. In 1937 he resigned to become a commercial flier but re-enlisted in 1939 shortly after the outbreak of WW2. Posted to 10 Bomber Reconnaissance Squadron at Halifax, N.S., because of his airline experience, he was given a variety of special jobs: instructing, surveying and, on five occasions, ferrying planes to England.

But on July 19 he was transferred to 116 BR Squadron, which was equipped with Cansos at Dartmouth, N.S. Frustrated with endless air searches for submarines, he devised a system whereby the crews went on stand-by while the Radio Directional Finding stations obtained a fix on a U-boat's position, then the aircrews were scrambled like fighter pilots. Small was also responsible for having EAC aircraft painted white to make them less conspicuous. For these efforts he was awarded the AFC.

On April 28, 1942, shortly before he was transferred to 162 Squadron at Yarmouth N.S., (also a Canso outfit) Small made the RCAF's first submarine sighting. Though he dropped two 250-pound depth charges the U-boat managed to submerge. In making his report he acknowledged that while the submarine and its crew got away he had at least "rattled their back teeth."

On June 26 Small was again transferred, this time to 113 Squadron as its CO, flying Hudsons. On July 31 he took off from Yarmouth in response to an RDF submarine fix and at 3,000 feet southeast of Cape Sable spotted a U-boat three miles ahead. Diving to attack, Small dropped four depth charges, bracketing the submarine forward of the conning tower just as it began to submerge. Remaining in the vicinity, when the vessel tried to resurface the Hudson's guns drove it under. Air bubbles appeared on the water followed by an explosion and an oil slick that spread over the surface. Small had scored EAC's first kill.

On January 1, 1943, he was awarded the DFC. Six days later Small and his crew were posted as missing when the Hudson in which he had been flying off Gander failed to return.

DFC AFC S/L KIA Jan 7 1943
RefScs: CA 225 CCMA 58 DHist bf RAW 106 TCNAF 435
TDS 87–89

SMITH Forgrave Marshall

"Four-Tour Fighter Pilot"

"Hiram" Smith's operational career as a Spitfire pilot began the day WW2 started and finished in the Far East after the Japanese surrender when he became the first to land a Spitfire in Malaya. Born in Edmonton, Alta., Smith joined the RAF in 1936 and after pilot training was posted to 1 Squadron RAF at Tangmere in Sussex. This flight formed the nucleus of 72 Squadron RAF, one of the first units to be equipped with Spitfires. By the outbreak of war in 1939 Smith was a flight commander with the new unit.

Originally assigned to convoy patrols the squadron saw little action until the evacuation of Dunkirk at the end of May and beginning of June 1940. Following that event the unit was stationed at Acklington in the north of England. On June 29 Smith scored his first victory, shooting down a twin-engine Dornier 17 bomber into the North Sea. On August 15, the day of the first and last raid by the Luftwaffe from Norway, Smith chalked up a hat-trick, destroying two Heinkel 111 bombers and a Messerschmitt 110. He nearly tallied a fourth, but his ammunition ran out. Later, in the Battle of Britain, the squadron moved south to Biggin Hill in Kent and there, three hours after arrival, Smith was shot down, wounded and hospitalized.

After recuperating, in April 1941 he was given command of 603 Squadron RAF, which moved from Scotland to Hornchurch in Essex flying offensive sweeps and bomber escort sorties over the continent. Smith scored his first and only victory with that unit on June 12 when he shot down an ME 109 in flames. On July 24 he ended his second tour, having logged eighty-six sorties. Smith was then posted to an OTU as Chief Flying Instructor.

In 1942 he was sent to the Middle East where he took over 145 Squadron RAF, the first unit to fly Spitfires in that theatre. After being posted about India, the Middle East and England, Smith became RAF Assault Force Commander in May 1945. His new unit was to prepare for the invasion of Rangoon, Malaysia. However by the time the unit landed at Kluang airfield near Port Swettenham the war had ended.

Smith remained with the RAF until 1957, when he retired to take up residence in Scotland.

DFC & Bar MID W/C
RefScs: CITR 52–55 191   CWC 277–84   OMAP(2) 125   RAW 160

SMITH Roderick Illingsworth Alpine

"Led in First Destruction of a Jet by Commonwealth Pilots"

On October 5, 1944, Rod Smith was leading his squadron of Spitfires — 401 RCAF — on a patrol over Holland when they spotted a German Messerschmitt 262 twin jet-engine fighter diving toward Nijmegen. Smith arced his formation into attacking position. Five pilots, including Smith himself, fired on the enemy aircraft and sent it crashing into the ground in flames. It marked the first time a jet aircraft had been destroyed by Commonwealth pilots. Although Smith shared in the victory with the others it was his tactical leadership that made the feat possible.

A native of Regina, Sask., Smith joined the RCAF in September 1940. After graduating as a pilot in March 1941 he went overseas where he joined 412 Squadron RCAF in June; this was a newly formed outfit flying Spitfires from Digby, Lincolnshire. After making several sorties over France Smith was posted to Malta in May to join 126 Squadron RAF. On July 18 he shared in the destruction of a Junkers 88 twin-engine bomber with another pilot — his own brother, Jerry Smith. In fact the brothers teamed up on several patrols. On July 24 each of them shot down a Ju 88. Four days later Smith destroyed a Ju 88 in flames.

PL 29398

That was their last victory together. On August 10 Jerry was posted missing, presumed killed in action.

On August 13 Smith shot down an Italian Savoia Marchetti tri-motor bomber. Then for the next month he was out of action, laid low with sinusitis. But in October, when a new German Blitzkrieg against Malta began, he was back in the thick of it. On the eleventh he sent a Ju 88 down in flames into the sea, the first enemy aircraft destroyed in the new assault on the island. Five days later he shot down a Messerschmitt 109 fighter, bringing his total to five destroyed. Two days later Smith became a target for enemy fighters himself; on October 15 his aircraft was so badly shot up he was forced to bail out. Smith scored his sixth and final victory over Malta on October 28 when he brought down another ME 109; at this time he was awarded the DFC.

Then a case of jaundice hospitalized him and he was posted back to England. After a stint as an OTU instructor he returned to Canada for leave. Then in December 1943 Smith joined 401 Squadron RCAF at Biggin Hill in Kent flying fighter sweeps and bomber-escort sorties over the continent.

In March 1944 Smith was appointed a flight commander with his old unit, 412 Squadron. At this time the Canadian fighter squadrons were engaged in dive-bombing missions in preparation for the Normandy invasion. Following D-Day the unit moved to an airstrip at Beny-sur-Mer in France, where on July 7 Smith shot down a Focke-Wulf 190, an experience he never forgot (see below). In early September the squadron moved to Brussels. When the Arnhem airborne landing began his unit covered the vital Nijmegen bridge. Between September 24 and 27 Smith shot down six enemy planes, a feat that earned him a Bar to his DFC. At this time he became CO of 401 Squadron. Following the victory over the ME 262 jet, Smith completed his second tour, having flown a total of 225 sorties and tallying 13 1/5 victories.

In 1945 he retired from the RCAF. From 1946 to 1953 he served with the Air Force Auxiliary then took up a law practice in Vancouver, B.C.

DFC & Bar S/L W/C(Aux) Born March 11 1922
RefScs: CA 240 DHist bf HBB 159–60 OMAP(2) 240 RAW 181
375 RCTFFY f239 358 TTS 241–45

That night in the mess tent Smitty described the incident to me over a drink. His tracers had set the FW 190's cockpit on fire and as he pulled up beside the other aircraft the enemy pilot jettisoned the hood and tried to bail out. For a few seconds he was half-way in and half-way out. Then flames engulfed and charred him like he had been barbequed. Finally he fell free, probably burned beyond recognition. "I don't mind telling you, it shook me rigid," Smitty admitted.

SOMERVILLE James Dean

"Destroyed Enemy Plane on First Night Sortie"

On his very first sortie as a Mosquito pilot with 410 Squadron RCAF stationed at Castle Camps, Cambs., "Red" Somerville of Exshaw, Alta., destroyed a German Junkers 88 twin-engine night-fighter. On February 13, 1944, he succeeded in bringing down a Ju 88 and damaging a Ju 188. On August 2, 1944, northwest of Pontorson, he shot down another Ju 188. Despite a faltering engine Somerville scored once more against a Ju 88 on August 6.

In October 1944 he was appointed CO of 409 Squadron RCAF, another Mosquito outfit based at Le Culot in Belgium. He flew with this unit through the Battle of the Bulge and in December he destroyed a Ju 88. By the end of WW2 his tally stood at seven enemy aircraft destroyed and one damaged.

After the war Somerville stayed in the RCAF and at one point was head of No 1 Wing of No 1 Air Division in Europe.

DSO DFC G/C
RefScs: OMAP(2) 125   RAW 239 260   RCTFY 151–52 f159 283–84 f303

SPROULE John Alexander

"Led First Overseas RCAF Transport Squadron into Battle"

John Sproule commanded 437 Squadron, the first RCAF transport squadron formed overseas, leading it in the Arnhem and Rhine crossing airborne operations. A native of Brandon, Man., Sproule joined the RAF in 1937 and at the outbreak of WW2 served with 58 Bomber Squadron RAF. This unit flew twin-engine Whitleys and took part in the first British night raid. Sproule flew with No 58 until December 1939, when he became a specialist navigation instructor.

In 1944 he transferred to the RCAF and on September 14 arrived at Blakehill Farm, Wiltshire, to form 437 Squadron equipped with Dakotas. Three days later the unit airlifted part of the British airborne force to Arnhem in conjunction with Operation Market Garden, the attempt to seize key bridges across the Maas, Waal and lower Rhine rivers. On September 21 the unit suffered its first casualties when four of ten aircraft, dispatched on a resupply mission to the same area, failed to return. Six months later the squadron was actively engaged in the Rhine crossing. On March 24, 1944, Sproule took off, followed at one minute intervals by twenty-three of his crews. They towed behind them Horsa gliders, carrying 230 officers and men, together with thirteen jeeps and trailers, six-pound guns, motorcycles and machine guns. The gliders were successfully released but four of the Dakotas were hit by flak. With the troops safely on the ground, the squadron dropped thousands of pounds of cargo to sustain them.

In September 1945 Sproule finished his tour but remained with the RCAF postwar. Among the senior posts he held were Director of Postings and Careers at AFHQ and Director of Studies at the Air Force College in Toronto, Ont.

DFC BL(N) G/C
RefScs: DHist bf   RS&A 134–35   TDS 178–81

SWETMAN William Herbert

"At Twenty-Three, Youngest RCAF Wing Commander"

On August 18, 1943, Bill Swetman took over as CO of 426 Squadron RCAF, a Lancaster outfit based at Linton-on-Ouse in Yorkshire. At 23 years old he became the youngest Wing Commander in the Canadian air force; in two years he had risen meteorically to that rank from Sergeant-Pilot. Born in Ottawa, Ont., Swetman joined the service in 1940, received his pilot's wings and went overseas in May of 1941. After OTU he was posted to 405 Squadron at Pocklington, the first Canadian bomber unit formed. With this unit he flew the initial part of his tour, using twin-engine Wellingtons, much preferring them to the four-engine Halifaxes on which he completed his tour.

During his two-year rise not only had he been appointed flight commander but he was also awarded the DFC. Swetman then joined 4 Group HQ, did some instructing and for a time was attached to the newly formed Canadian 6 Group.

Eventually, in May 1943, Swetman was appointed flight commander and reported to 426 Squadron RCAF at Dishforth, Yorkshire. On the night of August 17/18 Swetman arrived over the target — Peenemünde German rocket base — thirty minutes too soon and had to stooge about until the rest of the formation showed up. That night the squadron's CO was lost and next morning Swetman found himself in command. Throughout that winter the squadron participated in the bombing campaign against Berlin as well as other major targets.

In April 1944, when Swetman was taken off operations, a DSO had been added to his DFC. He returned to Canada, took leave and participated in a War Bond drive before being made Station Commander of No 4 Bombing and Gunnery School at Fingal, Ont. He thus became the first BCATP graduate to take command of a station. Postwar, Swetman served in various capacities, including that of CO of 412 Squadron and a stint at NORAD before retiring from the RCAF in 1967.

DSO DFC G/C Born 1920
RefScs: DHist bf RAW 291–94 RCTFFY 350 RCTFY 81 88 f223
RS&A 33 122 167

TIMMERMAN Nelles Woods

"Bomber Pilot Shot Down Two Enemy Planes"

On two missions Hampden bomber pilot Nelles Timmerman briefly turned fighter pilot to account for the destruction of two German aircraft. Born in Kingston, Ont., Timmerman learned to fly at the local flying club. Then in 1936 he worked his way to England aboard a cattle-boat and joined the RAF. In 1937 he was posted to 49 Squadron at Worthy Down, the first to be equipped with the twin-engine Hampdens. When the Germans invaded Norway in April 1940 the unit engaged in mine-laying and shipping strikes. On the twenty-third Timmerman sank a flak ship near Sylt. Returning from a mine-laying operation on the night of May 1, he spotted a flare path in the water near Norderney in the Frisian Islands, a sure sign an aircraft was about to land. He waited until he saw an Arado 196 seaplane turn on its lights and slipped deftly in behind to shoot it down with his 303 fixed machine gun.

By May 1940 the British policy included attacks on German cities and Timmerman and his squadron mates bombed such centres as Kiel, Cologne and Hamburg. On May 27 Timmerman received the DFC. Then on June 17 he shot down his second German plane as it came in to land at Schipol airport in Holland.

In July Timmerman was taken off operations and instructed at an OTU. Then in March 1941 he joined 83 Squadron RAF with which he started a second tour on Hampdens. In August he was given command of 408 Squadron RCAF being formed at Syerston, Nottinghamshire, also equipped with Hampdens. Timmerman led the unit on both night and daylight raids and in September was awarded the DSO.

In March 1942 he turned over his command and returned to Canada, where he was made Chief Flying Instructor at Pennfield Ridge, N.B.

The following year he was back in England where he served in several instructional posts, finishing the war as Station Commander at Skipton and Odiham.

Following WW2 he became one of the judges of the War Crimes Court in Germany. Later he served with the RCAF in Northwest Air Command and attended the National Defence College. He retired from the RCAF in 1962 after being made NORAD Deputy Commander.

DSO DFC   G/C
RefScs: CITR 179   DHist bf   RAW 380–81   RCTFFY 155   RS&A 94

TRAINOR Hugh Charles

"Ace Went the Full Distance"

During his six years with the RCAF Charlie Trainor flew the whole gamut — instructor, fighter ace, flight commander, squadron leader, evader, prisoner of war. Born in Charlottetown, P.E.I., Trainor joined the air force in February 1940, graduating as a pilot in October. For two years he served as an instructor until going overseas in 1942. Following OTU training he was posted to 402 Squadron RCAF in March 1943 flying Spitfires from Kenley to Surrey. In May he transferred to 411 Squadron RCAF, stationed at Redhill then Staplehurst, completing his first tour in September. After a period of OTU instructional duty Trainor rejoined 411 Squadron, then based at Biggin Hill, where he became a flight commander.

But it was not until his squadron moved to France in June 1944 that Trainor began his rapid series of victories, all within a month — four of them within three days. On June 28, flying from Beny-sur-Mer in Normandy, he shot down a Focke-Wulf 190 and a Messerschmitt 109. Next day he destroyed another Me 109. The day after that he repeated the feat. By July 31 he had brought down 8½ planes and probably destroyed another.

Meanwhile he had taken over as CO of 401 Squadron RCAF and was awarded the DFC. Then on August 18, by which time the squadron had moved to Cristot, Trainor's aircraft was hit by flak while attacking enemy transports and he was forced to crash-land behind enemy lines. However within a week he was back at his airfield, having successfully eluded capture, to take up his old post. Trainor continued to lead the squadron, mainly against ground targets, as the Canadian Army advanced into Belgium and Holland.

By September the unit had again moved, this time to Evere airfield

PL 28271

outside Brussels. On the nineteenth, while leading a patrol near Eindhoven at 23,000 feet, his engine seized as he switched over from the jettison tank to the main tanks. Gliding down to 4,000 feet covered by his wingman, glycol coolant began streaming from the radiators and Trainor, knowing his aircraft could catch fire at any minute, bailed out. A week later it was learned through the Belgian underground that he had been taken prisoner by the Germans. Repatriated at the end of the war he was discharged from the RCAF in 1945.

DSO DFC & Bar　S/L　Born July 17 1916
RefScs: DHist bf　HBB 153 155–58　OMAP(2) 126　RCTFY 239–41 251
267　RCTSY 184　RS&A 82

TURNBULL John Howard

"Second Leading RCAF Night-Fighter Ace Downed Three in One Fight"

On the night of July 15, 1943, flying a Beaufighter over Sicily, John Turnbull of St. Thomas, Ont., shot down three twin-engine Junkers 88s in succession, one of them in a death-defying head-on attack. Turnbull joined the RCAF in 1940 and after completing his pilot's training joined 125 Squadron RAF in November 1941. The squadron was based at Fairwood Common in Wales. As part of this squadron Turnbull had his closest brush with death.

On May 25, 1942, his Beaufighter developed a glycol leak in one engine while Turnbull was flying 10,000 feet over the Bristol Channel. Turnbull had to feather the motor and head for home while still rapidly losing height. Suddenly a row of houses faced him and his observer. Too late and too low to bail out, Turnbull bounced the aircraft off a house and landed — wheels-up — on the downward slope of wooded ravine. Trees tore a wing away and Turnbull's seat broke off as the aircraft came to rest. All the while the pair could hear gasoline dripping out. But they managed to get free.

On November 4 Turnbull scored his first and last kill with the squadron when he destroyed a Ju 88 over the North Sea.

In March 1943 he was posted to 600 Squadron RAF in Algeria and for the next eleven months the unit followed the Allied Armies from North Africa through Sicily to Italy. Turnbull's first night action took place on April 23 when he shot down an Italian tri-motor Cant bomber over Bone on the Tunisian coast. His most successful period occurred during the Sicilian campaign when, between July 11 and August 9, he and his observer downed eight German bombers, all but one of them multiple victories. On January 24, 1944, he gained his final score, a Ju 88 that he shot down over Anzio in Italy to bring his total to 12½ destroyed and earn him the DFC and Bar.

On returning to Canada in April he applied for a posting to the Pacific Theatre and was on his way to the West Coast when Japan surrendered. In October 1945 he retired from the RCAF and was recruited for service in China by "Moose" Fumerton to assist the Nationalists in forming Mosquito squadrons. With the evacuation of Hankow Turnbull returned to Canada and became a photographic equipment salesman, making his home in King City, Ont.

DFC & Bar   F/L   Born Dec 30 1915
RefScs: AIC 212   CA 229   OMAP(2) 126   RAW 244   RCTFFY 358
RCTFY 349   SY 141   TTS 249–55

TURNBULL Robert Steele

"Stellar Rise from Sergeant-Pilot to Wing Commander in Eleven Months"

Bob Turnbull of Winnipeg, Man. joined the RCAF in 1940 and graduated as a Sergeant-Pilot in January 1941. Posted overseas he flew seventeen missions on twin-engine Whitley bombers, which earned him the DFM. In November he was commissioned as a Pilot Officer. In August 1942, hurdling the rank of Flying Officer, he was promoted to Flight Lieutenant and that same month was made a Squadron Leader. In November he was promoted again, this time to Wing Commander. From September 1943 to June 1944 he commanded 427 Squadron RCAF flying four-engine Halifaxes and Lancasters from Leeming in Yorkshire. Before WW2 ended Turnbull was again promoted — to Group Captain rank — and given command of RCAF Station Middleton St. George in No 6 Group of Bomber Command.

Following the war he held senior positions in Training, Air Transport, Air Defence and Maritime Commands, RCAF HQ, the Air Division in Europe, and NORAD at McChord, Wash. Turnbull retired from the service in 1970 and died in Victoria, B.C., in 1977 at 58 years of age.

DFC & Bar AFC DFM CD MID CdeGwSS(Fr)   G/C   Col(CF)
Born 1918   Died Feb 8 1977
RefScs: DHist bf   RAW 308   RCTFFY 361   RCTFY 26 f78 94
RCTSY 8   RS&A 124

TURNER Percival Stanley

"Logged Most Combat Hours of Any Canadian"

In more than 500 operational sorties during WW2 Stan Turner posted a total of 1,125 hours and 35 minutes combat time, setting a Canadian record. Known as "The Bull" because of his combativeness, Turner also flew without rest from the beginning of the war to the end, was shot down, became wounded when his car struck a land-mine and survived the sinking of a navy cruiser. His score of victories — fourteen destroyed, two probables and six damaged — accumulated in such notable battles as France, Dunkirk, Britain, Malta, Sicily, Italy and Europe made him one of the country's top aces.

Born in Ivybridge, Devon, Turner and his parents eventually emigrated

Stan Turner (r.) with the Allies' top ace, Johnnie Johnson. PL 43239

to Toronto, Ont. At university he studied engineering and became a member of the RCAF Auxiliary. In 1938 he joined the RAF. Completing his pilot's training by the outbreak of hostilities he was posted to 242 Squadron, a unit made up of Canadians flying Hurricanes.

He first scored against the enemy while covering the British withdrawal from Dunkirk when he destroyed two Messerschmitt 109 fighters. By the time that epic ended he had run up a tally of four planes shot down and two probably destroyed. He added two more victories while in France during the British retreat through Le Havre. During the Battle of Britain Turner shot down two more German planes, damaged another, was appointed a flight commander and awarded the DFC.

In March 1941, by which time RAF Fighter Command had gone on the offensive with fighter sweeps and bomber-escort sorties over the continent, Turner was given command of 145 Squadron RAF. One of his more unique missions was escorting a bomber to drop an artificial limb on St Omer airfield for his former wing leader, the downed legless ace Douglas Bader, who had been taken prisoner. Before the year ended Turner damaged two more enemy aircraft, destroyed another and was awarded a Bar to his DFC.

After a brief two-month stint as CO of 411 Squadron RCAF, he was posted to the besieged island of Malta as CO of 249 Squadron RAF in February 1942. At that time the unit was flying Hurricanes at Ta Kali and later converted to Spitfires. During a fight with four ME 109s on February 23 Turner's goggles were blasted from his face, and his Hurricane momentarily set on fire and the hood sealed shut so that he was unable to bail out. Miraculously he brought the aircraft down for a perfect landing.

In April he was promoted to wing commander rank and attached to the Royal Navy to observe an air raid on Tobruk. However during that raid the cruiser on which he was sailing was bombed and sunk. In January 1943 Turner took command of 134 Squadron RAF, flying Hurricanes on ground attack missions, then became CO of 417 Squadron RCAF, flying missions over Sicily and Italy. In November he took charge of 244 RAF Wing, then attached to the Desert Air Force. In May he was awarded the DSO. At the beginning of 1945 he took command of 127 RCAF Wing based at Evere in Belgium.

Following the war Turner transferred to the RCAF and held various posts, including that of Canadian Air Attache in Moscow, Russia. On retirement he became an executive with the planning staff of Expo 67 in Montreal, P.Q.

DSO DFC & Bar G/C Born Sept 3 1913 Ind CAHF 1973
RefScs: CAHF 74 CWC 287–309 DHist bf OMAP(2) 126 RAW 176
381 406–407 RCTFFY 8 RCTFY 171 173–74 RS&A 98 109 222
TDS 20–24 TSBW 143 199–200 216 TTS 257–65

WADDELL Robert Charles Arthur

"Led Reconnaissance Wing in Rhine Crossing"

On March 24, 1945, during Operation Varsity, one of Canada's foremost aerial reconnaissance commanders, "Bunt" Waddell, led his wing on 100 sorties in support of the Allied Rhine crossing airborne assault. Six days later when the squadrons laded at Damme it became the first Allied air unit to occupy a German airfield.

A native of Peterborough, Ont., Waddell graduated from RMC and served with the Royal Canadian Artillery. Then in 1938 he joined 110 RCAF Auxiliary Squadron in Toronto, Ont. When WW2 started Waddell was called to active service with the unit that in 1940 was reformed as an Army Co-operation squadron and became the first RCAF outfit to go overseas. In England it was equipped with Lysanders and later Tomahawks but it was not until February 1942 — by then the squadron had been renumbered 400 Squadron RCAF and based at Odiham,

Hampshire — that it became operational.

Waddell, at the time second-in-command, flew his first sortie on the tenth of the month. Shortly afterward the squadron was refitted with Mustangs and on August 9 Waddell became its CO. Its assignment was photography and strafing missions, the latter carried out at night as well as in daylight. On August 19 Waddell led the squadron on ground support sorties during the Canadian attack on Dieppe. He finished his first tour in June 1943 and was awarded the DFC.

Next Waddell served as CO of 39 Reconnaissance Wing HQ, in charge of operations with three Canadian squadrons, 400, 414 and 430, under his command. Following the Normandy invasion the wing moved to France then, as the British and Canadian armies advanced, into Belgium and Holland. Waddell became Group Captain in charge on May 16, 1945, and continued to lead the unit on low-level missions. Following the Rhine crossing one of his squadrons, 400, moved to Lunenburg, the farthest point of advance of any Canadian flying unit before war's end.

Following the cessation of hostilities Waddell retired from the RCAF and went into the investment business in Toronto. He also served as Commander of 14 Auxiliary Wing RCAF from July 1957 to September 1961. In addition he was ADC to Governor General Georges Vanier. He died in 1975.

DSO DFC CD   G/C   Born 1915   Died Apr 5 1975
RefScs: DHist bf   RCTFFY 304–309 311–14 316 358   TDS 152–56

WALKER James Elmslie

"From Snow to Sand to Summer"

Jimmy Walker was the only Canadian airman to serve in Russia and North Africa as well as in Great Britain. Born in Claresholm, Alta., Walker joined the RCAF in May 1940. On arrival overseas in August 1941 he was posted to 81 Squadron RAF. Walker was now part of 151 Wing being sent to Murmask, Russia, both to demonstrate Allied unity and to teach the Soviets to fly Hurricanes with which Britain had agreed to supply the Red air force. During its three month sojourn in the Arctic the wing shot down sixteen German aircraft, Walker contributing one twin-engine Junkers 88 bomber destroyed and another probably destroyed. In November, 81 squadron returned to England, where it converted to Spitfires. On June 2, 1942, Walker chalked up his second confirmed victory over Le Touquet, France: a Focke-Wulf 190 fighter, which brought him his first decoration, the DFC.

PL 28933

In October the unit was transferred to Gibraltar to take part in Operation Torch, the Allied invasion of North Africa. Shortly after arriving Walker shot down a Ju 88. On New Year's Day 1943, during a Luftwaffe raid on Bone, Tunisia, Walker shot down one FW 190 and probably destroyed another. On February 13 he was made CO of 243 Squadron RAF with which in March he damaged two Messerschmitt 109s and was awarded a Bar to his DFC. In April he destroyed four more enemy aircraft, probably destroyed one and damaged seven. That month he was also shot down and forced to bail out. In June 1943 he was taken off operations and returned to England, where he learned he had been awarded a second Bar to his DFC. The following month he took over as Station Commander of 126 RCAF Wing, stationed at Staplehurst, Kent. In August he took leave in Canada then in March 1944 was appointed wing leader of the newly formed 144 RCAF Wing. Ironically the man who had had the unique experience of flying from snow in Russia, off sand in the desert and out of the green fields of England, was killed on April 25 when the wingtip of the light Auster touring plane he was piloting struck a tree top coming in to land at West Hampnett in Sussex and crashed into the ground.

DFC & 2 Bars   W/C   Born Apr 4 1919   KA Apr 25 1944
RefScs: RAW 179   RCTFFY f33 353   RCTFY 123 129   RS&A 221
224   TTS 267–71

WILLIAMS David John

"Shot Down Two Dorniers While Missing One Engine"

On July 21, 1944, flying a Mosquito, "Blackie" Williams was on convoy patrol off the Breton coast when he spotted a pair of twin-engine Dornier torpedo planes on the deck getting ready to attack the four British navy destroyers he had been assigned to protect. As he closed in the German bombers opened fire. But Williams' bullets found the mark and the rearmost Dornier exploded in flames. Just as the wreck struck the sea Williams' starboard engine began to sputter, forcing him to feather it. Nevertheless he attacked the second bomber and sent it crashing into the water, bringing his total number of enemy planes destroyed to five and adding a share in another.

Williams, who was born in Vancouver, B.C., joined the RCAF late in 1940 and went overseas at the end of the next year. After operational training in February 1942 he reported to 408 Squadron RCAF, based at Leeming in Yorkshire, flying twin-engine Hampden bombers. That August he scored his first victory. While en route to Kassel in Germany his aircraft was attacked by a Junkers 88 twin-engine night-fighter. Williams skillfully maneuvered his machine so the Junkers pilot overshot his mark, placing itself ahead of the Hampden and providing Williams with a perfect target for his Browning machine-gun. He instantly sent the enemy aircraft spiralling down in flames. Then, after having dropped his bombs on the target, Williams found himself coned by sixty searchlights in the middle of a balloon barrage. Heavy, accurate flak pitched the bomber over on its back and damaged one of the engines. Williams managed to right it, only to be attacked by a Messerschmitt 109, which he and the crew finally drove off. His troubles were far from over however.

While coming in to land, the damaged engine packed up, forcing him to make a single-motor landing. For his night's work Williams was awarded the DFC.

When his first tour ended in October he spent some time at RCAF HQ in London. Williams then was attached to 410 Squadron RCAF, a Mosquito unit based in Lincolnshire, to organize an intruder flight. From there he was sent to an OTU as an instructor until August 1943, when he joined 406 Squadron RCAF as a flight commander. This was a night-fighter unit in Devon, then equipped with Beaufighters but which soon converted to Mosquitos. In July 1944 he was made CO and in November he completed his second tour.

Following the end of WW2 Williams remained in the RCAF and served as Commander of No 1 Wing No 1 Air Division in NATO and also as a staff officer with the Northern NORAD Region HQ at North Bay, Ont.

DSO DFC CD   G/C   Col(CF)   Born Jan 6 1919
RefScs: DHist bf   OMAP(2) 127   RAW 257–58 284   RCTFFY 170–71
173–74 358   RCTFY 150 152–53 f159 278 281–82   RS&A 91   SY 141
161 228 242 255   TSBW 223

WONNACOTT Gordon

"Engaged Enemy Aircraft Attacking His Field"

On the morning of January 1, 1945, the day the Luftwaffe launched Operation *Bodenplatte* — the low-level fighter-bomber attack against RAF and USAAF tactical fighter airfields in France and the Low Countries — Gordie Wonnacott was returning to base from a patrol. When he reached Eindhoven he saw his own field being ravaged by Messerschmitts and Focke-Wulfs. Wading in he destroyed two ME 109s and damaged an FW 190, for which he was awarded a Bar to the DFC.

Wonnacott, who hailed from Edmonton, Alta., joined the RCAF in June 1940. After graduating as a pilot in January 1941 he was sent to the Central Flying School at Trenton, Ont., to train as instructor. After serving in that role for two years he was finally posted overseas early in 1943. After operational training in July Wonnacott joined 414 Fighter-

PL 22755

Reconnaissance Squadron RCAF, based at Dunsfold, Surrey, flying Mustangs.

Wonnacott quickly established himself as one of the squadron's most aggressive pilots. On November 2 he destroyed four trains and shared in shooting down an FW 190 south of Cambrai. On January 28, 1944, he was credited with an Me 109 destroyed and shared in shooting down an Arado 96B near Chartres. Shortly afterward he was appointed flight commander. For his work in directing naval bombardments during the Normandy invasion and low-level photographic work prior to D-Day he received the DFC.

Wonnacott took over as CO of 414 Squadron on October 1944; by this time his unit had been converted to Spitfires. His tour ended in March 1945. He returned to Canada and received his discharge from the service in October.

DFC & Bar   S/L   Born Oct 14 1914
RefScs: DHist bf   OMAP(2) 128   RAW 143   RCTFY 142 144 271
RS&A 104   SY 143   TSBW 213

WOODS Eric Norman

"Flew One of Longest Fighter Tours"

With 375 hours and 20 minutes operational time in his log book, "Timber" Woods of Vancouver, B.C., flew one of the longest fighter tours of any Canadian, flying most of it out of Malta. Woods joined the RAF in 1940 and after pilot training joined 124 Squadron in May of 1941 flying Spitfires from Castletown in Scotland. After a series of uneventful convoy patrols the unit moved south to Biggin Hill in Kent in mid-November. It conducted fighter sweeps and bomber-escort sorties over the German-occupied continent. Woods scored his first victory on March 13, 1942, against a Focke-Wulf 190 over St Omer; ten days later he damaged another. By the time he was posted to Malta at the beginning of August he had destroyed two enemy aircraft, probably destroyed another, damaged 2½ more and had been awarded the DFC.

Upon his arrival at the besieged Mediterranean island Woods was given command of 249 Squadron RAF, flying Spitfires from Ta Kali. There the battle see-sawed between defence and offence until the Allied North African landings in Africa in November. At that point the RAF seized the initiative and paved the way for the invasion of Sicily.

Before he went off operations temporarily in February 1943 Woods had flown 276 sorties and his score stood at 10 ⅔ enemy planes destroyed, four probables and 9½ damaged. For the next five months he served as an instructor at an OTU in Egypt. Woods then returned to operations, taking over his old squadron at Malta in July. By October the squadron had moved to Brindisi, Italy, where it engaged in armed reconnaissance and fighter-bomber sorties over Albania and Yugoslavia.

In November Woods was given command of 286 RAAF Wing (Australian). With this unit he scored his last victory: on December 4 he brought down a Junkers 87 Stuka bomber over Podgorica airfield. On December 16 Woods took off on his three hundredth and final sortie.

But Woods failed to return from it. He was never heard of again and was presumed killed in action.

DFC & Bar   W/C   Born May 8 1910   KIA Dec 16 1943
RefScs: CWC 311–21

WOODWARD Vernon Crompton

"Top Canadian Desert Air War Ace"

With twenty enemy aircraft shot down, five probably destroyed, eleven damaged and two destroyed on the ground to his credit, the "Imperturbable Woody," so called for his coolness under fire, ranked as the top Canadian desert ace and the second highest scorer among his countrymen.

Born in Victoria, B.C., Woodward enlisted in the RAF in 1938 and by the outbreak of WW2 was stationed at Amriya in Egypt with 33 Squadron flying Audet and Gladiator biplane fighters.

Woodward's first taste of action came on June 14, 1949. It was the beginning of the first British offensive against the Italians in Libya and his flight intercepted a bomber escort of Fiat CR 32s over Fort Capuzzo. In the ensuing fracas Woodward shot down one of the Cant bombers and damaged a Fiat, earning him the distinction of being the first to score against the Italian Air Force. Two weeks later he posted a double-kill by destroying two Fiats.

On July 25 he displayed the coolheadedness that earned him his nickname when — after shooting down one Fiat and sharing in the destruction of another — he found himself alone with seven Italian fighters. Knowing that to dive away meant certain suicide he calmly turned to face them in a head-on attack. Incredibly his machine received only three bullet holes from the encounter.

During December Woodward destroyed six more Fiats, probably destroyed one and damaged four others. Early in 1941 the squadron converted to Hurricanes and moved to Greece to meet the German invasion. On April 5 Woodward downed a Fiat, his first victory since the unit's arrival. The following day he scored a triple-kill by downing a trio of CantZ.1007 bombers from the Greenmice Squadron, commanded by Mussolini's son. Then a week later he shot down his first German plane, a Messerschmitt 109, and damaged another. Woodward added two Junkers 87 Stuka dive-bombers to his tally on the following day. On April 19

PL 19348

Woodward shot down a Henschel 126 in the morning and later in the day destroyed his second ME 109. Next day the squadron encountered a gaggle of over 100 German bombers and fighters headed for their own airfield. In the ensuing melee Woodward accounted for one twin-engine ME 110 down in flames, three probables and one twin-engine Ju 88 damaged before he ran out of ammunition. With only four Hurricanes left the squadron flew to Crete. Even those last remnants were eventually destroyed by strafing attacks.

The seven remaining pilots were evacuated to Egypt, where they became attached to 274 Squadron RAF at Geralwa. On June 17 Woodward got back in stride by bringing down a Fiat G 50 fighter and damaging another. Then on July 12 he scored his final victory in the air by shooting down a Ju 88 in flames near Amriya.

After completing his tour in September and a stint as an instructor in Rhodesia Woodward returned to operations in January 1943 with 213 Squadron RAF guarding convoys off North Africa with Hurricanes. In September he was attached to the Headquarters Staff of the Middle East Air Force.

Following the war Woodward remained in the RAF, commanding a wing with NATO. After retiring in 1963 he took up commercial flying in Australia until 1972, when he joined the Corps of Commissionaires in the Security Section of Canadian Forces Base Esquimalt in his native Victoria.

DFC & Bar   W/C   Born Dec 22 1916
RefScs: DHist bf   OMAP(2) 128   RAW 368   TDS 45–47
TFAOR 182–87   TTS app

WRAY Lawrence

"Senior RCAF Prisoner of War Saved Fellow Captives' Lives"

On March 18, 1944, when the Lancaster in which he was a passenger was shot down over Germany, Larry Wray became and remained the most senior RCAF officer to fall into enemy hands. A native of Toronto, Ont., Wray joined the RCAF in 1930 and during the prewar years served as a fighter pilot and an exhibition pilot, took part in photo survey operations, and later commanded the Test and Development Organization.

At the outbreak of WW2 he was posted to No 6 Torpedo Squadron at Jericho Bay, B.C. Subsequently he became commander of RCAF Station Patricia Bay, B.C. In 1941 he was transferred to Air Force HQ as Director of Operations then was made CO of RCAF Station Gander, Nfld. In late 1943 Wray was posted overseas, where he became CO of RCAF Station Skipton, Yorkshire, in 6 Group Bomber Command.

On the night he was shot down — during a raid on Frankfurt — he and the crew were forced to bail out. Wray was taken prisoner and sent to Stalag Luft 111 at Sagan, where he became SBO (Senior British Officer). As the most senior officer Wray risked the wrath of the Camp Commandant, the Gestapo and the SS by adamantly insisting that the 1945 forced marches of the evacuating POWs be slowed. The result was that many prisoner, who might otherwise have died of exhaustion from the gruelling pace the Germans had ordered were saved. Wray also demanded — and got — improved accommodation and food once the destinations were reached. For his efforts he was awarded the OBE.

Following the war Wray continued his career with the RCAF. Among the senior posts he held was AOC Air Defence Command with headquarters at St-Hubert, P.Q.

OBE AFC A/V/M   Born 1908
RefScs: DHist bf   RS&A 6 7 28 208 211   SY 180

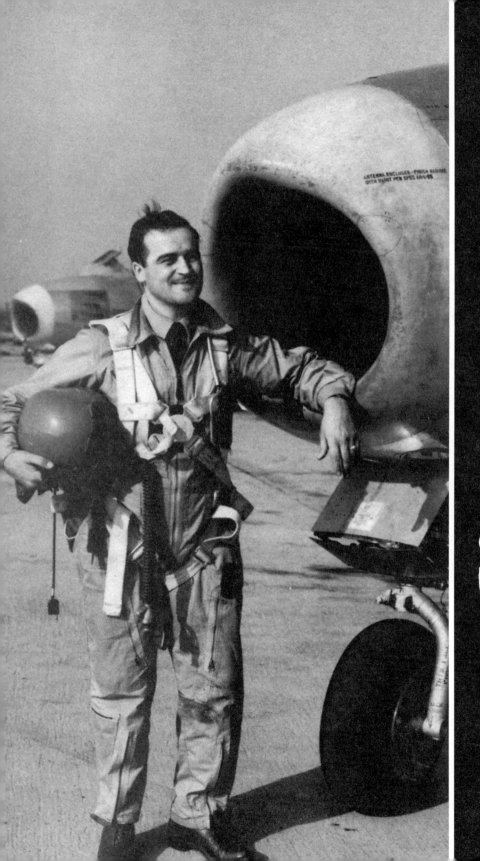

KOREA

During the Korean War, which began in 1950, the RCAF's contributions consisted of ferrying troops, mail and freight by North Stars from McChord Field at Tacoma, Washington, to Tokyo and Misawa in Japan, with refuelling stops at Alaska and the Aleutians en route. In all, a round trip of twenty hours flying time. During the nearly four years that the war lasted, Canadians flew seven million pounds of freight and 13,000 passengers, and chalked up 34,000 flying hours without a single loss of life or cargo.

Canada had no combat units for service in Korea but many RCAF fighter pilots — twenty-two officers — flew F86 Sabres with the U.S. Air Force. They destroyed nine communist aircraft, probably destroyed two others and damaged eight for the loss of only one of their own.

The RCAF established that any pilot applying for combat duty in Korea had to have fifty hours flying experience on jets and that a tour consisted of fifty missions or six months duration, whichever was completed first.

GLOVER Ernest Arthur

"Top Canadian Ace in Korea"

E rnie Glover emerged as the top Canadian scorer of the Korean War by destroying three MiG-15 jet fighters. He was also the first Canadian ever to receive the DFC when, technically, the nation was at peace.

Born in Niagara Falls, Ont., Glover joined the RCAF in October 1941 and flew Hurricanes and Typhoons with 1 Squadron RAF until he was shot down in May 1943.

After WW2 he stayed in the RCAF and in June 1952 was posted to the American 334 Fighter Interceptor Squadron at Kimpo Airfield near Seoul in Korea flying Sabres on patrols south of the Yalu River. He made his first score in August when he damaged two MiGs. On September 8 he chalked up his first MiG destroyed and sent another one high-tailing it across the Yalu. Next day, during an attack on the North Korea Military Academy at Sakchu, Glover set a MiG on fire. Then on September 16, while leading a flight, he shot another one down in flames, his third confirmed victory. Glover completed his tour on October 18 after having flown fifty missions.

DFC DFC(Am) F/L
RefScs: CA 271   CCMA 120   DHist bf   SY 470   TSBW 241

LEVESQUE Omer

"First Commonwealth Pilot to Engage in Jet-to-Jet Aerial Combat"

F lying F86 Sabres with the USAF in Korea, Omer Levesque of Mont Joli, P.Q., was the first Commonwealth pilot to engage in jet-to-jet air combat and the first member of the RCAF to score a victory in that war. Levesque joined the RCAF in 1940 and went overseas in 1941, joining 401 Squadron RCAF at Biggin Hill in Kent. On November 22 he was one of the first pilots to shoot down a German Focke-Wulf 190 and his sketch of the new fighter was circulated throughout Fighter Command.

After shooting down three more aircraft Levesque himself was shot down during the German battleship dash through the English Channel by the *Gneisenau*, *Prinz Eugen* and *Scharnhorst* on February 12, 1942.

PL 51164

He was picked out of the water by the Germans and taken prisoner.

Following WW2 he stayed in the RCAF and in December 1950, as an exchange officer, was posted to the USAF 334 First Interceptor Squadron at Kimpo in Korea. On March 31, while escorting B29 bombers at 40,000 feet to attack one of the Yalu River bridges, his wing was bounced by North Korean MiG fighters. Turning into the attack Levesque got into a corkscrewing dogfight down to 17,000 feet. Once firmly on the enemy's tail he opened fire from 500 yards and sent the MiG spiralling into the ground. Before his tour ended Levesque had flown seventy-one missions and was awarded the American DFC and Air Medal. Levesque remained in the RCAF until 1965, serving with the International Control Mission in Vietnam as well as doing a stint at NORAD.

DFC DFC(Am) AM(Am) W/C
RefScs: CA 265   CCMA 117   DHist bf   OMAP(2) 117   RAW 190 208
430–31 444–45   RCTFFY 48 50   SY 180 216 259–61 356–58 365

LINDSAY James Douglas

"Outstanding Flight Leader in Korean Air Battles"

Doug Lindsay so distinguished himself in the skies over Korea that the United States awarded him the American DFC. A native of Arnprior, Ont., Lindsay joined the RCAF in February 1941 and after graduating as a pilot spent fifteen months as an instructor before going overseas in 1943. In October he joined 403 Squadron RCAF, flying Spitfires from Kenley in Surrey.

Lindsay scored his first victory on May 7, 1944, when he destroyed a Messerschmitt 109 and damaged a Focke-Wulf 190. On July 2 he shot down three Me 109s within one minute. Before his tour ended he was credited with 6½ aircraft destroyed and five damaged, and was awarded the DFC.

Remaining with the RCAF following WW2 he served in Korea as an exchange officer between July 15 and November 28 with the USAF 51st Interceptor Wing flying F86 Sabres. During this time he destroyed two MiG fighters and damaged two others. When his tour ended he returned to his post as CO of 416 Squadron based at Bagotville, P.Q.

DFC CD DFC(Am) S/L
RefScs: DHist bf   OMAP(2) 117   RAW 193–94 219   RCTFY 130–32
240 245 f254 261   RS&A 87 169 232   SY 259

PL 26643

MacKENZIE Andrew Robert

*"Only Canadian to Become Korean Air Casualty
Prisoner of Chinese"*

Andy Mackenzie was the only Canadian pilot shot down in Korea. He was captured by the Chinese and spent two years less three days as a prisoner. He spent 465 days of his captivity in solitary confinement, surviving endless interrogations and attempts to brainwash him.

A native of Montreal, P.Q., Mackenzie emerged from WW2 as an ace with 8½ German aircraft destroyed and one damaged to his credit after having served with 421 and 403 Squadrons RCAF and 133 and 135 Squadrons RAF. For his exploits he was awarded the DFC.

On December 20, 1943, he shot down three aircraft in one combat: two Focke-Wulf 190s and a Messerschmitt 109. At the end of the war he left the RCAF but rejoined in October 1945.

In November 1952 he was posted to Korea on an exchange basis with the USAF. Mackenzie joined 139 Squadron of the 51st Wing of the U.S. Fifth Air Force based at Suwŏn, twenty miles south of Seoul, flying F86 Sabres. On December 8, in a fight with North Korean MiG fighters, he was accidentally shot down by an American pilot and forced to bail out. Landing on a hillside he was immediately captured by Chinese soldiers and taken across the Yalu River to Manchuria to be imprisoned. During his confinement he was cruelly treated by the Chinese and was given food that was so bad and in such little amounts that he lost seventy pounds. On December 5, 1954, approximately eighteen months after the Korean Armistice, Mackenzie was released by his captors at the Hong Kong border.

On repatriation he was able to provide USAF authorities with information about American airmen still being held prisoner by the Chinese Communists.

Following his ordeal Mackenzie continued to serve with the RCAF. After his retirement he made his home in Kemptville, Ont., breeding dogs. At one time he served a stint as president of the Canadian Fighter Pilots Association.

DFC   S/L
RefScs: AIC 217   CCMA 123   DHist bf   OMAP(2) 118   RAW 178 180 194 445   RCTFY 110 115 132 238 245   SY 132–33 245 259 261 174 356 365

Only the dead have seen the end of war.

Plato

GLOSSARY

PROP-WASH

In the wake of this work the reader may wonder, and is entitled to know, about certain factors relating to military aviation that have little or no place, either factually or technically, in the process of providing personal profiles. They nevertheless need to be said. The following "gen"[1] may prove helpful.

ARMAMENT

In 1914 and the early part of 1915 airmen armed themselves with pistols and rifles, and later with machine guns. Machine guns were mounted in two ways: fixed firing forward, and on swivel frames for front and rear gunners. Introduction of the interrupter and synchronized firing gears allowed forward firing through the gaps in the revolutions of the propeller.

In WW2 many fighters had machine guns and cannons mounted in the wings; these were synchronized to fire at various ranges, usually in the vicinity of 400 yards. The most lethal armament consisted of rockets, which were used principally against ground targets.

SCORES

Ancestrally sensitive on the subject? No way. The controversy over numbers of victories lies a lot deeper than that. It affected many people who have been subjected to the most scurrilous and unfair scrutiny. The fact is that all Canadian claims — whether they be planes shot down, or aircraft probably destroyed or damaged — had to be corroborated by any one or all of such witnesses as fellow aircrews, observer corps and, in WW2, cine-gun camera film confirmation. Some historians (in most cases those of pseudo-calibre) and a great many writers — most of whom have never seen a bullet fired in anger — have made capital out of challenging individual scores. It is unfortunate they have been given the coverage and notoriety they enjoyed because they sully our heritage and our history. Instead they should be condemned. My own sources, where applicable, are the London *Gazette*, official combat reports, some cine-gun footage and the Directorate of History biographical files. I have also relied heavily on the published records of two of Canada's most eminent and authoritative military aviation historians, both veterans of the Canadian War Museum: Ron Dodds (WW1) and Hugh Halliday (WW2).

[1]Meaning information — abbreviated from Intelli"gen"ce.

SPEEDS

During both world wars aircraft speeds increased steadily, yet at any given time stayed comparatively competitive. Between 1914 and 1918 fighter planes averaged 80 to 140 mph, with bomber and reconnaissance machines flying relatively slower. By the outbreak of WW2 the speed of fighters had advanced dramatically to — give or take — some 300 mph.

Bomber speeds were a mixed bag. At the outset the British had long-range aircraft with speeds as low as 140 mph while twin-engine bombers on both sides rivalled that of their fighters. By the end of WW2 piston-propelled aircraft bordered around the 450 mph mark; then, with the advent of the jet fighters, speeds zoomed to between 500 and 600 mph.

PARACHUTES

These were used sparingly in WW1 due to their unreliability. German airmen wore them in combat while the Allies employed them for dropping spies and supplies. Though it was never confirmed, a rumour persisted that the British refused to allow their pilots to carry them for fear they would jump to avoid battle. But their value from a safety standpoint could not be denied. In WW2 fatalities in the air would have been manifoldly greater had it not been for the parachute.

OXYGEN

One of the first uses of oxygen in aerial warfare was made by German Gotha bomber crews in 1917. Flying at altitudes over 17,000 feet, they were equipped with two compressed oxygen bottles from which they fed through a mouthpiece to ward off the cold. The measure was not entirely popular. Airmen complained it gave them a dry throat. "A gulp of brandy would have served the same purpose," one of them argued. But by the beginning of WW2 oxygen had become an established fact with aircraft climbing upwards to 30,000 feet. Bottles were installed in all aircraft and the oxygen was fed through masks. One of the first pressurized aircraft was the high-altitude Spitfire V-1, which saw limited use due to its unreliability.

WEAPONRY

First attempts at bombing took the form of tossing hand-grenades out of the cockpit. But this soon graduated to bombs that began at 50 pounds and, by the end of WW2, graduated to the 20,000-pound Blockbusters.

MAKE-UP

group   Consisting of a number of squadrons.
wing   Made up of two or more squadrons.
squadron   A basic unit made up of twelve or more aircraft.
flight   Subdivision of a squadron; two or three flights.

section Subdivision of a flight, consisting of two aircraft.
jagdstaffel German term for a fighting unit, basically a squadron.

OPERATIONS

balboa A large formation.
circus Fighter-escorted daylight bombing attack on short-range target. Main objective: to lure up enemy fighters.
no-balls V-1 (Flying Bomb) launching sites.
ramrod Fighter sweep similar to a circus, but with destruction of the target as the main objective.
rodeo Fighter sweep over enemy territory.
scramble Signal for fighter pilots on readiness to take-off instantly for an interception.

ABBREVIATIONS

DECORATIONS

AFC Air Force Cross
AFM Air Force Medal
AM(Am) Air Medal (American)
BL(N) Bronze Lion (Netherlands)
CdeG Croix de Guerre–(Bel) Belgian (Fr) French (wGC) With Clasp (wSS) with Silver Star
CdeG(It) Italian Vroc de Guerra
CB Commander of the Order of the Bath
CBE Commander of the Order of the British Empire
GC George Cross
CD Canadian Decoration
CGM Conspicuous Gallantry Medal
CLM(Am) American Commander of the Legion of Merit
COON Dutch Command Order of Orange Nassau
COSMSL(It) Italian Cavaliere Order of St Maurice & St Lazarus
CzWC Czech War Cross
DC(Am) American Degree of Cavaliere
DFC Distinguished Flying Cross (Am) American
DFM Distinguished Flying Medal
DSC Distinguished Service Cross
DSO Distinguished Service Order
ED Efficiency Decoration
GFC Greek Flying Cross
GOOC(Bel) Belgian Grand Office of the Order of Crown
KHCOL(Nor) King Haakon VII's Cross of Liberation
Ld'H Legion d'Honeur (Bel) Belgian (Fr) French
LoM(Am) American Legion of Merit

MBE   Member of the Order of the British Empire
MC   Military Cross (Bel) Belgian (Cz) Czechoslovakian
MID   Mentioned in Dispatches
MM(Am)   American Medal of Merit
MM(Fr)   French Medaille Militaire
MV(It)   Italian Medaglio Valori
NFC   Netherland Flying Cross
OBE   Order of the British Empire
OdeC(Bel)   Belgian L'Ordre de Couronne
OOON(Dch)   Dutch Order of the Orange-Nassau, Officer
OL(Bel)   Belgian Order of Leopold
OONK(Dch)   Dutch Order of the Orange-Nassau, Knight Officer (WS) With
                 Swords
OPR(Pol)   Polish Order of Polonia Restituta
OSA(Rus)   Russian Order of St Anne
OSS(Rus)   Russian Order of St Stanislas
OWL(Cz)   Czech Order of the White Lion
SM(Am)   American Silver Medal
SS(Am)   American Silver Star
VC   Victoria Cross
VM   Polish Virtuti Militari
Bar   Consecutive award of a decoration

DESIGNATIONS

ADC   Aide-de-Camp
AFHQ   Air Force Headquarters
AFU   Advanced Flying Training Unit
AOC   Air Officer Commanding
BAASF   British Advanced Air Striking Unit
BCATP   British Commonwealth Air Training Plan
BR   Bomber Reconnaissance
CAS   Chief of the Air Staff
CFI   Chief Flying Instructor
CFS   Central Flying School
C-i-C   Commander-in-Chief
CGS   Chief of General Staff
CO   Commanding Officer
DND   Department of National Defence
EFTS   Elementary Flying Training School
HQ   Headquarters
ITS   Initial Training School
MD   Military District
NATO   North Atlantic Treaty Organization
NCO   Non-commissioned Officer
NORAD   North Atlantic Air Defence Command
NWAC   North West Air Command

OC Officer Commanding
OTU Operational Training Unit
POW Prisoner of War
RDF Radio Direction Finding
RMC Royal Military College
SASO Senior Administrative Staff Officer
SBO Senior British Officer
SFTS Service Flying Training School
SHAEF Supreme Headquarters Allied Expeditionary Forces
TAF Tactical Air Force
TCA Trans Canada Air Lines
VLR Very Long Range
WW1 World War One
WW2 World War Two

GENERAL

CF Canadian Forces
DOT Department of Transport
DOW Died of Wounds
Ind CAHF Inducted into Canada's Aviation Hall of Fame
KA Killed Accidentally
KFA Killed in a Flying Accident
KIA Killed in Action
MKTw McKee Trophy Winner
OdCWM On display at the Canadian War Museum, Ottawa
☉ Personal Annotation
WTw Webster Trophy Winner

RANKS

A/C Air Commodore
A/C/M Air Chief Marshal
A/M Air Marshal
A/V/M Air Vice-Marshal
B/G Brigadier General
Capt Captain
Col Colonel
Cpl Corporal
F/L Flight Lieutenant
F/O Flying Officer
F/S/L Flight Sub-Lieutenant
Gen General
G/C Group Captain
Lt Lieutenant
Lt/Col Lieutenant-Colonel
Lt/Gen Lieutenant-General

Maj Major
M/G Major General
M/Gen Major General
W/C Wing Commander
Sgt Sergeant
S/L Squadron Leader
(Aux) Auxiliary
(Hon) Honorary
(Res) Reserve

SERVICES

CAF Canadian Air Force
CEF Canadian Expeditionary Force
IF RAF Independent Force Royal Air Force
RAAF Royal Australian Air Force
RAF Royal Air Force
RCAF Royal Canadian Air Force
RCNAS Royal Canadian Naval Air Service
RCNVR Royal Canadian Volunteer Service
RFC Royal Flying Corps
RNAS Royal Naval Air Service
USAAF United States Army Air Forces
USAF United States Air Force

TRANSITION

RFC & RNAS formed	April 13, 1912
Canadian Aviation Corps formed	September 18, 1914
RFC & RNAS merged into RAF	April 1, 1918
RCNAS formed	September 18, 1918
CAF formed	February 18, 1920
RCAF inaugurated	April 1, 1925
Independent status granted RCAF	November 19, 1938
Tri-Services enacted	February 1, 1968
Canadian Forces established	1975

TIMETABLE

WW1 Aug 1, 1914–Nov 11, 1918
WW2 Sept 1, 1939–Aug 14, 1945
Korea Jan 25, 1950–July 27, 1953

R*EFSCS: REFERENCE SOURCES*

AH *Aces High*. Chris Shores. The Garden City Press.
AIC *Aviation in Canada*. Larry Milberry. McGraw-Hill Ryerson Ltd.
AIF *And I Shall Fly*. Periodical.

AMCI   *A Man Called Intrepid*. William Stevenson. Ballantine Books.

BB   *Bomber Barons*. Chaz Bower. William Kimber & Co.

BS   *Blue Skies*. Bill Olmsted. Stoddard.

CA   *125 Years of Canadian Aeronautics*. A. Fuller, A. Griffin, K. Molson. Canadian Aviation Historical Society.

CA&FWW   *Canadian Aviation & the First World War*. Syd Wise. University of Toronto Press.

CAHF   *Canada's Aviation Hall of Fame*. Brochure.

CCMA   *Chronology of Canadian Military Aviation*. Hugh Halliday. National Museum of Man.

CFA   *Canada's Fighting Airmen*. George Drew. MacLean Publishing Limited.

CFH   *Canada's Flying Heritage*. Frank H. Ellis. University of Toronto Press.

CFP   *Canada's Fighting Pilots*. Edmund Cosgrove. Clarke, Irwin & Company Limited.

CITR   *Canadians in the Royal Air Force*. Less Allison (Also Publisher).

CSA   *Canadian Flying Operation in South East Asia*. T.W. Melnyk. DND DHist.

CWC   *Canadian Wing Commanders of Fighter Command in World War II*. G.A. Brown, J.P.A.M. Lavigne. Battleline Books.

CWM   *Canadian War Museum*. Ken Molson. Canadian War Museum.

DHist   Directorate History, National Defence, bf–biographical files.

H   *Hero: The Buzz Beurling Story*. Brian Nolan. Lester & Orpen Dennys.

HBB   *High Blue Battle*. Dave McIntosh. Stoddard Publishing Co. Limited.

KHP   *Kittyhawk Pilot*. J.P.A. Michael Lavigne & J. Edwards. Turner-Warwick Publications.

MS   *Malta Spitfire*. George F. Beurling & Leslie Roberts. Arms and Armour Press.

NM   *National Aviation War Museum*. Ken Molson. NAWM.

OMAP   *Of Men and Planes (1) & (2)*. John Gordon. Love Printing Services.

OTF   *One of the Few*. J. A. Kent. Corgi Books.

P   *Pilots*. John Melady. McClelland & Stewart Inc.

RBH   *RAF Biggin*. Graham Wallace. Putnam & Co. Ltd.

RAW   *The Royal Canadian Air Force at War, 1939–1947*. Hugh Halliday, Larry Milberry. CANAV Books.

RCTFFY   *The RCAF The First Four Years*. Oxford University Press.

RCTFY   *The RCAF The Fifth Year*. Oxford University Press.

RCTSY   *The RCAF The Sixth Year*. Oxford University Press.

RFTS   *Reach For the Sky*. Paul Brickhill. Collins.

RS&A   *RCAF Squadrons & Aircraft*. Samuel Kostenuk, John Griffin, Samuel Stevens. Hakkert & Company.

SORAF   *Squadrons of the Royal Air Force*. James T. Halley. Air-Britain Limited.

ST   Stewart K. Taylor (1) & (2). Personal Correspondence.

SY   *Sixty Years*. Larry Milberry. CANAV Books.

TDS   *The Dangerous Sky*. Tom Coughlin. The Ryerson Press.

TBYW   *The Brave Young Wings*. Ron Dodds. Canada's Wings Inc.

TCNAF *The Creation of a National Air Force.* W.A.B. Douglas. University of Toronto Press

TCOTEM *The Courage of the Early Morning.* William Arthur Bishop. McClelland & Stewart Limited

TCY *242 Squadron: The Canadian Years.* Hugh Halliday. Canada's Wings Inc.

TFAOR *The Fighter Aces of the RAF.* E.C.R. Baker. New English Library.

TGE *The Great Escape.* Paul Brickhill. Faber and Faber Limited.

TISS *Terror in the Starboard Seat.* Dave McIntosh. General Publishing Co. Limited.

TNM *The Narrow Margin.* Derek Wood and Derek Dempster. Arrow Books Limited.

TR50Y *Trenton: 50 Years.* Brochure.

TRAFOTR *The Rise and Fall of the Third Reich.* William Schirer. Simon and Schuster.

TRKG *The Red Knight of Germany.* Floyd Gibbons. Garden City Publishing Co. Inc.

TSBW *There Shall be Wings.* Leslie Roberts. Clarke Irwin & Company Limited.

TTS *The Tumbling Sky.* Hugh Halliday. Canada's Wings Inc.

VM *Valient Men.* John Swettenham. Hakkert & Company.

WIS *Wings in Space.* Periodical.

WL *Winged Leader.* J.E. Johnson. Chatto & Windus, Ltd.

WWIC *Who's Who in Canada (1984–85).* Global Press.

app appendix

f facing page

NAME INDEX